T0221092

The Simulation of Human Intelligence

JB

Wolfson College Lectures

The Simulation
of
Human Intelligence

Edited by
Donald Broadbent

BLACKWELL
Oxford UK & Cambridge USA

Copyright © Basil Blackwell Ltd. 1993

First published 1993

Blackwell Publishers
108 Cowley Road
Oxford OX4 1JF
UK

238 Main Street, Suite 501
Cambridge, Massachusetts 02142
USA

All rights reserved. Except for the quotation of short
passages for the purposes of criticism and review, no
part of this publication may be reproduced, stored in a
retrieval system, or transmitted, in any form or by any
means, electronic, mechanical, photocopying, recording or
otherwise, without the prior permission of the publisher.

Except in the United States of America, this book is
sold subject to the condition that it shall not, by way
of trade or otherwise, be lent, resold, hired out, or
otherwise circulated without the publisher's prior
consent in any form of binding or cover other than that
in which it is published and without a similar condition
including this condition being imposed on the subsequent
purchaser.

British Library Cataloguing in Publication Data

A CIP catalogue record for this book is available from
the British Library.

Library of Congress Cataloging-in-Publication Data

The Simulation of human intelligence/edited by Donald Broadbent.
p. cm.
Includes bibliographical references and index.
ISBN 0–631–18587–9 (hard: alk. paper). – ISBN 0–631–18733–2
(pbk.: alk. paper)
1. Philosophy of mind. 2. Artificial intelligence. 3. Philosophy
and cognitive science. I. Broadbent, Donald E. (Donald Eric)
BD418.3.S56 1993
153 – dc20

Typeset in 11 on 13pt Bembo
by Graphicraft Typesetters Ltd, Hong Kong

This book is printed on acid-free paper

Contents

Preface

This volume is based on a series of eight Wolfson College Lectures given at Oxford in the spring of 1991. The aim of the series was, as usual in those series, to interest a general, non-specialist, audience; and the topic was clearly timely. During the past decade, developments in computing techniques have allowed machines to perform many functions that were previously the preserve of human beings. The ideas that underlie those techniques have stimulated new thinking among psychologists, physiologists and philosophers, about the nature of our minds and brains.

At the same time, doubts have been expressed about the limits of using machine analogies to understand human beings, by none more effectively than Professor Penrose. We were fortunate in securing him as the first lecturer, and equally in those who followed him. All those invited from outside Wolfson are authorities on different aspects of the problem and all went to great lengths to speak and to write. Illness, war and harsh weather did not prevent them, and I shall remain for ever grateful to them.

At a late stage in the production of the book, we were all saddened to hear of the death of Allen Newell. He has of course long earned a place of honour in scientific history; but his infectious enthusiasm and his contributions to the book continued to the end. We remember him not only with respect, but with affection.

The college also encouraged and supported the series; many of the Fellows and the staff contributed, but special mention should be made of the advice and help of the President, and that of the College Secretary, Janet Walker.

Any thoughtful person, regardless of their own training, must surely wish to survey the recent knowledge of this area, and to understand the issues. Our contributors have risen to this challenge, and it is a pleasure to have played a part in their efforts.

Wolfson College, Oxford
D.E.B

1

Setting the Scene: the Claim and the Issues

Roger Penrose

Artificial minds?

The advent of high-speed electronic computer technology has provided a new reality, and perhaps also even an urgency, to the arguments concerning some of the most basic and long-standing of philosophical issues. If computers can, before too long, achieve a genuine artificial intelligence, then may they not also have artificial minds? We are used to the idea of artificial hips, or legs or arms, or artificial kidneys or even hearts. Why not an artificial brain? Would an artificial brain have to have a mind? Somehow, we feel that it would not be much use to us if it did not!

The whole question hangs on the resolution of deep philosophical issues. What is a mind? Are minds merely features that inevitably arise in association with the physical actions of (say human) brains? Is the essential feature of such a physical action the carrying out of an immensely complicated computation, of the particular sort that one supposes is being performed by a human brain during the act of thinking? Or is there something else that the brain does that cannot be described in merely computational terms? Perhaps minds are not even things that can be considered in scientific terms at all. Perhaps minds do not really exist.

Electronic computers offer us the possibility of objects that might ultimately be able to calculate more effectively in every way than biological brains, being not limited by biological restrictions such as imprecise structuring and the need to grow from a single cell. Already computers can be programmed to play chess better than

all but a very small number of human experts. It seems not unreasonable to suppose that in many other areas where human
intelligence had seemed to reign supreme the computers will
overtake even the best of us. Are such 'artificially intelligent'
systems *really* intelligent? Does actual intelligence require a degree
of awareness and understanding of what one is doing?

In my own use of the word 'intelligence', I would take this last
to be the case. I would not use the word 'intelligence' unless some
actual understanding is involved; nor would I like to use the word
'understanding' unless I am prepared to believe that there is some
element of awareness present. This does not remove the problem,
of course. How will we be able to tell if an electronic system is
'actually' intelligent, rather than merely *simulating* intelligence, if
we need to know whether it is aware or not in order to be able
to tell the difference? How might we be able to tell if an electronic
system is aware or not? Indeed, how can we tell whether human
beings other than ourselves are aware or not? With human beings, we try to judge this from the way they talk or move, by
their actions, by their writings or other creations, and so on – all
external characteristics of their behaviour. Should we not apply
similar operational criteria to electronically controlled robots?
Would such a robot that *appears* to behave intelligently necessarily
'actually' possess awareness and understanding? Would it be
possible to tell? Does the question have genuine meaning? While
I shall certainly not be able to provide definitive answers to these
age-old conundrums, I shall outline, below, various possible alternative viewpoints; and I shall also give reasons for the beliefs
on this issue that I hold to myself.

The prospect of genuine artificial intelligence

While, on the whole, rather little has been achieved by artificial
intelligence to date – in any important area of intellectual expertise
where genuine human understanding and insight has seemed to
be important – there have been some very impressive developments in recent years, most particularly the development of
powerful chess computers. But for the most part, the very op-
timistic claims that had sometimes been made by proponents of

artificial intelligence and promoters of expert systems, etc., have not yet been fulfilled. But these are still very early days, if we are to consider what artificial intelligence might ultimately achieve. There would appear to be some enormous potential advantages over brains that electronic computers could eventually make use of. Electronic circuits are already about a million times faster that the firing of the neurons in the brain. Furthermore, they have an immense precision in timing and accuracy of action that is in no way shared by our own neurons. There is a great deal of randomness in the brain's 'wiring' that could apparently be vastly improved upon by the deliberate and precise organization of electronic printed circuits. Moreover, in those places where the brain now does have an advantage, it would seem that this advantage may be short-lived. In its total neuron number – some hundreds of thousands of millions – the brain is perhaps temporarily ahead (although this depends, to some extent, upon how one does that calculation, for example because different computer units can always be added together to form larger and larger ones). Also, there are, on the average, a good deal more connections between different neurons than there are connections between transistors in a computer. But it is clear, especially when one takes into account the rapid increase in computer technology over the years, that these few remaining *numerical* advantages that the brain may have will not last longer than a few decades at the very most. Moreover, there may well be technological revolutions waiting in the wings, such as the replacing of the wires and transistors of our present computers by appropriate optical (laser) devices, thereby achieving enormous increases in speed, power, and miniaturization. There seems to be little doubt that on any issue of merely computing power, if computers do not have the advantage over brains already, then they *will* certainly have it before too long.

But are the relevant issues merely those of computing power, or speed, or memory, or perhaps of the detailed way in which things are 'wired up'? Might we, on the other hand, be doing something with our brains that cannot be described in computational terms at all? How do our feelings of conscious awareness – of happiness, pain, love, aesthetic sensibility, will, understanding, etc. – fit into such a computational picture? Will the computers of the future indeed actually have *minds*? Does it make sense to talk about such things in scientific terms at all or is science in no way competent to address issues that relate to the human mind? It seems to me that there are at least four different viewpoints[1] (or extremes of viewpoint) that one may reasonably hold on the matter:

1 All thinking is computation, and the mere carrying out of appropriate computations will evoke feelings of conscious awareness.
2 It is the brain's physical action that evokes awareness and any physical action can in principle be simulated computationally, but computational simulation by itself cannot evoke awareness.
3 Appropriate physical action of the brain evokes awareness, but this physical action cannot even be properly simulated computationally.
4 Awareness cannot be explained in physical, computational, or any other scientific terms.

The point of view expressed in **4**, which negates the physicalist position altogether and regards the mind as something that is entirely inexplicable in scientific terms, is the viewpoint of the mystic; and at least some ingredient of **4** seems to be involved in the acceptance of religious doctrine. My own position is that questions of mind, though they lie uncomfortably with present-day scientific understanding, should not be regarded as being forever outside the realms of science. If science is as yet incapable of saying much that is of significance concerning matters of the mind, then science itself will have to change. While I reject mysticism in its negation of scientific criteria for the furtherance of knowledge, I believe that within an expanded science and mathematics there will be found sufficient scope to accommodate even what is needed for an understanding of mind. I shall expand on some of these ideas later on, but for the moment it will be sufficient to say that under my own viewpoint, I am rejecting **4**; and I am attempting to move forward along the path that science has set out for us. I believe that this route will eventually reveal enough mysteries of its own, so that it may not seem so strange if the mystery of mind may be ultimately explicable in terms of it.

Let us consider what seems to be the opposite extreme to **4**: the viewpoint **1**. This is what is referred to as *strong AI* (strong artificial intelligence) or *functionalism*.[2] It is regarded by some as the only viewpoint that an entirely scientific attitude allows. Others would take **1** to be an absurdity that is barely worth serious attention. It is the viewpoint that the arguments of my book, *The Emperor's New Mind* (Penrose, 1989) were most specifically directed against. The length of that book alone (466 pages in hardback) should make it clear that, while I do not myself believe that **1** is correct, I do regard it as a serious possibility that is worthy of considerable attention. It is an implication of a highly operational attitude to science, where, also, the physical world is taken to operate entirely computationally. In one extreme of this view, the universe itself is taken to be, in effect, a gigantic computer,[3] and appropriate sub-calculations that this computer performs will evoke the feelings of awareness that constitute our conscious minds. I suppose that this viewpoint – that physical systems are to be regarded as merely computational entities – stems partly from the belief that physical objects are themselves merely 'patterns of information', in some sense.

Even if we do not think that it is appropriate to regard the universe as simply being a computer, we may feel ourselves operationally driven to viewpoint **1**. Suppose that we have a robot that is controlled by a computer and which responds to questioning exactly as a human would. We ask it how it feels, and find that it answers in a way that is entirely consistent with its actually possessing feelings. It tells us that it is aware, that it is happy or sad, that it can perceive the colour red, and that it worries about questions of 'mind' and 'self'. It may even give expression to a puzzlement about whether or not it should accept that *other* beings (especially human beings) are to be regarded as possessing a consciousness similar to the one that it feels itself. Why should we disbelieve its mere *claims* to be aware, to wonder, to be joyful, or to feel pain, when it might seem that we have as little to go on with respect to other human beings whom we *do* accept as being conscious? The operational argument does, it seems to me, have some considerable force, even if it is not entirely conclusive. If all the *external* manifestations of a conscious brain can indeed be simulated entirely computationally then there would be a case for accepting that its *internal* manifestations – consciousness itself – are also present in association with such a simulation.

What about **2**? I think that it is the viewpoint that many would regard as the 'common-sense' one.[4] Like **1**, it affirms a view that all the physical objects of this world must behave according to a science that, in principle, allows that they can be computationally simulated. On the other hand, it strongly denies the operational claim that a thing that behaves externally as a conscious being must necessarily be conscious itself. As the philosopher John Searle has stressed, a computational simulation of a physical process is indeed different from that process itself.[5] (A computer simulation of a hurricane, for example, is certainly no hurricane!) On view **2**, the presence or absence of consciousness would depend very much on what actual physical object is carrying out a computation. Thus, the action of a biological brain might evoke consciousness, while its electronic simulation might not. It is not necessary, in viewpoint **2**, for this distinction to be between biology and physics. But the actual *physical* constitution of the object in question (say a brain), and not just its computational action, is regarded as all-important.

The viewpoint **3** is the one which I believe myself to be closest to the truth. It is more of an operational viewpoint than **2** since it asserts that there are external manifestations of conscious objects (say brains) that differ from the external manifestations of a computer: consciousness cannot even be properly *simulated* computationally. I shall be giving my reasons for this belief in due course. Since **3**, like **2**, maintains the physicalist standpoint that minds arise as manifestations of the behaviour of certain physical objects (brains – although not necessarily only brains), it follows that an implication of **3** is that *not* all physical action can be properly simulated computationally. It is not completely clear whether present-day physics allows for the possibility of an action that is in principle impossible to simulate on a computer. Rather little is known of a precise mathematical nature on this issue. My own opinion is that such non-computational action would have to be found in an area of physics that lies outside the presently known physical laws. Later on, I shall briefly indicate some of the reasons, coming from within physics itself, for believing that a new understanding is indeed needed, in an area that lies intermediate between the 'quantum level' of molecules, atoms and subatomic particles and the 'classical level' of everyday objects.

However, it is not by any means universally accepted, among physicists, that such a new physical theory is required.

What of the future?

What do the viewpoints **1**, **2**, **3**, **4** tell us to expect for the future of this planet? According to 1, there will come a stage when appropriately programmed supercomputers will reach – and then race beyond – all human mental capabilities. Of course different people who hold to **1** could have very different views as to the time-scales involved in this. Some might reasonably take the line that it will be many centuries before computers will reach our level, so little being presently understood about the calculations that the brain must indeed be performing (they would claim) in order to achieve the subtlety of action that we undoubtedly attain – a subtlety that would be necessary before appreciable 'awareness' would take place. Others argue for a much shorter time-scale. In particular, Hans Moravec, in his book *Mind Children* (1988), makes a reasoned case in support of his claim that 'human equivalence' will be reached in a mere forty years, basing his arguments on the rate at which computer technology has moved forward at an accelerating rate over the past half century, and on the proportion of the brain's activity that has already been successfully simulated. (Some have argued for a much shorter time-scale, sometimes, even, where the predicted date for human equivalence has already passed!) Lest the reader feel dismayed by the prospect of being overtaken by computers in (say) forty years' time, hope is offered – indeed promised – by the assured prospect of our being able to transfer our 'mind programs' into the shining metallic bodies of the robots of our choice, thereby obtaining for ourselves a form of immortality (Moravec, 1988).

Such optimism is not available to the holders of viewpoint **2**, however. Their standpoint does not differ from **1** with regard to what computers will ultimately be able to achieve. Whether it would take centuries or a mere forty years, computers would again be expected to reach human equivalence, and then race beyond whatever we are able to achieve with our relatively puny brains. Now the option is not open to us to 'join' the computer-

controlled robots, and it would seem that we must resign ourselves to the prospect of a planet ultimately controlled by insen-
tient machines! Of all the viewpoints **1**, **2**, **3**, **4** it seems to me that
it is **2** that offers the most pessimistic view of the future of our
planet – despite its apparently 'common-sense' nature!

According to **3** or **4**, on the other hand, it would be expected
that the computers, as we understand them today, would (or
should) always remain subservient to us, no matter how far they
advance with respect to speed, capacity and logical design. Viewpoint **3**, however, is open with regard to future scientific developments that might lead to the construction of devices – *not* based
on today's concept of computers – which could achieve *actual*
intelligence and awareness. Since we at present lack almost all the
scientific understanding that would be necessary, let alone any of
the technological know-how, little can be gained from such
speculation at the present time.

Irrespective of such digressions into futurology, we must ask:
what is it that we actually *do* with our brains? Is 'computing', in
one form or another, the only possibility? Might we, on the other
hand, sometimes be doing something *else* with our brains and
minds – something very different from computation, for which
our very awareness and (apparent?) free will may be playing an
essential role? Are these things that can be discussed at all in anything like scientific terms – as would be denied by viewpoint **4**?
I believe that they can be, and that viewpoint **3** is a genuine scientific possibility, although we must be prepared for the eventuality
that our scientific criteria and methods may undergo subtle but
important shifts. We must be prepared to examine clues that may
present themselves in unexpected ways, in areas of genuine understanding that may at first appear to be largely irrelevant.

The non-computability of mathematical thinking

In a moment, we shall need to turn to some mathematics. It is
there that our thinking processes have their purest form. If thinking is just carrying out a computation of some kind, then, we
ought to be able to see this most clearly in our mathematical
thinking. Yet, remarkably, the very reverse turns out to be the

case. It is within mathematics that we find the clearest evidence that there must actually be something in our conscious thought processes that eludes computation.

Nevertheless, one might reasonably ask why we shall need to turn to mathematics at all, in order to find a suitable area in which to demonstrate that there must be something non-computational in conscious thought processes. Indeed, mathematics is certainly very far from being the *only* animal activity requiring consciousness. It is a very specialized human activity, whereas the phenomenon of consciousness is commonplace, being likely to be present in much non-human as well as human mental activity. The reason for needing to address the question of consciousness here in a mathematical context is that it is only within mathematics that we can expect to find anything approaching a rigorous demonstration that some, at least, of conscious activity *must* be non-computational in nature. (The issue of computation, by its very nature, is after all a mathematical one.) If it can be demonstrated that whatever we do with our brains or minds when we consciously understand *mathematics* is different from anything that we can achieve by use of a computer, then the possibility of non-computational thinking generally has been established. Moreover, since understanding seems to be a conscious activity, it is *conscious* thinking that seems to have this non-computational character.

Of course consciousness has many other manifestations. The perception of the colour red, for example, is something that requires consciousness, as is the sensation of pain, the appreciation of a melody, the bringing to mind of an early memory, the willed action to get up from one's bed, and so on. Some might dispute an all-embracing role of some single concept of consciousness in all of these various manifestations. In my own view, there is indeed a unified concept of 'consciousness' that is central to all these separate aspects of mentality, but it will not be necessary to worry about this here. Let us just concentrate on 'understanding', and this will include 'mathematical understanding'.

In order to address this issue, we shall be concerned here with *calculations*. By a calculation I mean, in effect, the action of a general purpose computer operating according to some computer program. (Strictly speaking, the computer must be idealized in that it has an in principle unlimited storage capacity – which could be in the form of an unlimited supply of floppy discs, say. The appropriate idealized mathematical concept is that of a *Turing machine*, but it will not be necessary to go into the details of what this term means here.) Another word for a calculation is an *algorithm*. Operations that can be achieved (in principle) calculationally are referred to as *algorithmic*. It should be realized that calculations (algorithms) are not merely the performing of ordinary operations of arithmetic, such as just adding or multiplying numbers together, but can involve other things also. Well-defined *logical operations* can also be part of a calculation. For an example of a calculation, we might consider the following task:

Find a number that is not the sum of three square numbers.

(A)

By 'number', I mean here a 'natural number', i.e. one of

0, 1, 2, 3, 4, 5, 6, 7, 8, 9, 10, 11, 12, ...

A *square* number is the product of a natural number by itself, i.e. one of

$0 = 0^2$, $1 = 1^2$, $4 = 2^2$, $9 = 3^2$, $16 = 4^2$, $25 = 5^2$,
$36 = 6^2$, ...

The calculation (A) could then proceed as follows. We try each natural number in turn, starting with 0, to see whether or not it is the sum of three squares. We need only consider squares that are no larger than the number itself. Thus, for each natural number, there are only finitely many square numbers to try. As soon as three square numbers are found that do add to it, then our calculation moves on to the next natural number, and we try again to find a triplet of squares (less than the number) that sum to it. Our calculation stops only when a natural number is found for which each such triplet of squares fails to add to it. To see how this works, start with 0. This is $0^2 + 0^2 + 0^2$ so it is indeed the sum of three squares. Next we try 1 and we find that although it is not $0^2 + 0^2 + 0^2$ it is indeed $0^2 + 0^2 + 1^2$. Our calculation tells us now to move on to 2 and we ascertain that although it is not $0^2 + 0^2 +$

0^2 or $0^2 + 0^2 + 1^2$, it is indeed $0^2 + 1^2 + 1^2$; we then move on to 3 and find $3 = 1^2 + 1^2 + 1^2$; then to 4, finding $4 = 0^2 + 0^2 + 2^2$; then $5 = 0^2 + 1^2 + 2^2$; then after finding $6 = 1^2 + 1^2 + 2^2$ we move on to 7, but now all triplets of squares (each member no greater than 7)

$$0^2 + 0^2 + 0^2. \quad 0^2 + 0^2 + 1^2. \quad 0^2 + 0^2 + 2^2. \quad 0^2 + 1^2 + 1^2.$$
$$0^2 + 1^2 + 2^2. \quad 0^2 + 2^2 + 2^2. \quad 1^2 + 1^2 + 1^2. \quad 1^2 + 1^2 + 2^2.$$
$$1^2 + 2^2 + 2^2. \quad 2^2 + 2^2 + 2^2.$$

fail to sum to 7, so the calculation halts and we reach our conclusion: 7 is a number of the kind we seek, being *not* the sum of three squares.

However, with the calculation (A) we were fortunate. Suppose we had tried, instead, the calculation:

Find a number that is not the sum of four square numbers.

(B)

Now when we reach 7 we find that it *is* the sum of *four* squares: $7 = 1^2 + 1^2 + 1^2 + 2^2$, so we must move on to 8, finding $8 = 0^2 + 0^2 + 2^2 + 2^2$, etc. The calculation goes on and on: $23 = 1^2 + 2^2 + 3^2 + 3^2$, $24 = 0^2 + 2^2 + 2^2 + 4^2$, and it never seems to stop at all. In fact it never does. It is a famous theorem first proved by the great eighteenth-century mathematician Joseph L. Lagrange that *every* number is, indeed, the sum of four squares. It is not such an easy theorem (and even Lagrange's contemporary the great Swiss mathematician Leonhard Euler, a man of astounding mathematical insight, originality and productiveness, had tried but failed to find a proof). I am certainly not going to go into Lagrange's argument here, so let us instead try something very much simpler:

Find an odd number that is the sum of two even numbers.

(C)

I hope that it is obvious that *this* calculation will never come to an end!

I have given two examples ((B) and (C)) of calculations that never terminate. In the first case this fact, though true, is not at all easy to ascertain, while in the second, its non-termination is obvious. Calculations may or may not terminate and, moreover, in the cases when they do not terminate it may be hard to see that they do not, or it may be very easy. We may reasonably ask: by what procedures do mathematicians convince themselves and others that certain calculations do not in fact terminate? Are they themselves following some calculational (or algorithmic) procedure in order to ascertain things of this kind?

The answer appears to be 'No'. This is essentially one of the implications of Gödel's famous incompleteness theorem, and it is important that we try to understand it. This theorem tells us that no set of rules whatsoever will be sufficient to ascertain correctly, in all cases, that non-terminating calculations do not in fact terminate. Here, by a 'set of rules' I mean some system of formalized procedures for which it is possible to check entirely computationally whether or not the rules have been correctly applied. But Gödel's theorem appears to tell us more than this, namely that the insights that are available to human mathematicians – indeed, to anyone who can think logically with understanding and imagination – cannot be completely formalized as such a set of rules. Rules can sometimes be a partial substitute for understanding, but they can never replace it entirely.

In order to see how Gödel's theorem (in the simplified form that I shall give, which depends on some ideas due to Alan Turing) demonstrates this, we shall need a slight generalization of the kind of statement about calculations that I have been considering. Instead of asking whether or not a single calculation, such as (A), (B) or (C) ever terminates, we shall need to consider a calculation that depends on – or *acts* upon – a *natural number n*. Thus, if we call such a calculation $C(n)$, we can think of this as providing us with a *family* of calculations, where there is a separate calculation for each natural number 0, 1, 2, 3, 4, . . . , namely the calculation $C(0)$, $C(1)$, $C(2)$, $C(3)$, $C(4)$, . . . , respectively, and where the way in which the calculation depends upon n is itself entirely calculational. This means that $C(n)$ is the action of some algorithm applied to the number n. Think of an ordinary general purpose computer, and regard n as merely providing the 'data' for the action of some computer. What we are interested in is whether this computer action ever stops or not, for each choice of n.

In order to clarify what is meant here, let us consider two examples, slightly generalizing the ones given above:

Find a number that is not the sum of n square numbers (D)

and

Find an odd number that is the sum of n even numbers. (E)

It should be clear from what has been said above that the calculation (D) will stop *only* when $n = 0, 1, 2$ and 3 (finding the numbers 1, 2, 3 and 7, respectively, in these cases), and that (E) stops for no value of n whatever. If we are actually to ascertain that (D) does not stop when n is 4 or larger we require some formidable mathematics (Lagrange's proof); on the other hand, the fact that (E) does not stop for any n is obvious. What are the procedures that are available to mathematicians for ascertaining the non-stopping nature of such calculations generally? Are these very procedures things that can be put into a calculational form?

Suppose, then, that we have some calculational procedure A which, when it successfully terminates, provides us with a demonstration that a calculation such as $C(n)$ actually does *not* ever stop. I am certainly not requiring that A can *always* decide that $C(n)$ does not stop when in fact it does not, but I *do* insist that A does not ever give us wrong answers, i.e. that if it comes to the conclusion that $C(n)$ does not stop, then in fact it does not. (If A did give us wrong answers of this kind, then in principle we could check up on this fact because its error would be recognized as soon as $C(n)$ comes to a halt.) If A does not in fact give us wrong answers, we say that A is *sound*.

In order to understand how A could itself act as a calculation, we need to have a way of coding the different calculations $C(n)$ on which A acts. All possible different Cs can in fact be listed, say as

$$C_0(n), C_1(n), C_2(n), C_3(n), C_4(n), C_5(n), \ldots\ldots,$$

where we can take this ordering as being given, say, as some kind of numerical ordering of computer programs. (To be explicit, we could take this ordering as being provided by the Turing machine numbering given in *The Emperor's New Mind*, so that then the calculation $C_q(n)$ is the action of the qth Turing machine T_q acting on n.) One technical thing that is important here is that this listing is *computable*, i.e. there is a single calculation C that gives us C_q when it is presented with q, or, more precisely, the calculation C acts on the *pair* of numbers q, n (i.e. q followed by n) to give $C_q(n)$.

The procedure A can now be thought of as a particular calculation that, when presented with the pair of numbers q, n, tries to ascertain that the calculation $C_q(n)$ will never ultimately halt. We are going to try to imagine that A might be a formalization of *all* the procedures that are available to human mathematicians for validly deciding that calculations never will halt. But it is not necessary for us to think of A in this way just now. A is just *any* sound set of calculational rules for ascertaining that some calculations $C_q(n)$ do not ever halt. Being dependent upon the two numbers q and n, the calculation that A performs can be written $A(q,n)$, and we have:

If $A(q,n)$ stops, then $C_q(n)$ doesn't stop. (F)

Perhaps you are worrying that A might be able to decide that $C_q(n)$ actually *does* stop and would itself stop as soon as it had made that decision. But that is not what we are asking for A to do. If, in some way, our procedure comes to the conclusion that $C_q(n)$ actually does stop, then we must ensure that this conclusion makes A go into a 'loop', rather than output some finite conclusion, so that A does *not* in fact stop in the circumstance that $C_q(n)$ does stop. This is just a technical point, and it does not imply any restriction on what procedures we are considering for ascertaining that calculations do *not* stop.

Now let us consider the particular statements (F) for which q is put equal to n. This may seem an odd thing to do, but it is perfectly legitimate. With q equal to n, we now have:

If $A(n,n)$ stops, then $C_n(n)$ doesn't stop. (G)

We now notice that $A(n,n)$ depends upon just *one* number n, not two, so it must be one of the calculations $C_0, (n), C_1, (n), C_2, (n), C_3, (n), \ldots$ (as applied to a general value of n). Let us suppose that it is in fact $C_k(n)$:

$$A(n,n) = C_k(n). \qquad (H)$$

Now put $n = k$. We have, from (H),

$$A(k,k) = C_k(k) \tag{I}$$

and, from (G), with $n = k$,

If $A(k,k)$ stops, then $C_k(k)$ doesn't stop. $\tag{J}$

Let us try to see whether the calculation $A(k,k)$ actually stops or not. First, suppose that it does. Then (J) tells us that $C_k(k)$ does not stop. But by (I), $C_k(k)$ is the same as $A(k,k)$, so it follows that $A(k,k)$ does not stop after all. This must therefore be the right answer: $A(k,k)$ does not stop. Moreover $C_k(k)$, being the same as $A(k,k)$ does not stop either. We conclude that our procedure A is incapable of ascertaining that this particular calculation $C_k(k)$ does not stop even though it does not!

At this point it might be advisable to go over the whole argument again, just to make sure that I have not 'put one over' on the reader! Admittedly there is an air of the conjuring trick about the argument, but it is perfectly legitimate, and it only gains in strength the more minutely it is examined. We have found a calculation $C_k(k)$ that we know does not stop; yet the given calculational procedure A is not powerful enough to ascertain that fact. This is the Gödel(-Turing) theorem in the form that I require. It applies to any calculational procedure A whatever, that we know to be sound, for ascertaining that calculations do not stop. We deduce that no sound set of calculational rules (such as A) can ever suffice for ascertaining that calculations do not stop. Moreover, since from the knowledge of A and its soundness, we can actually construct a calculation $C_k(k)$ that we *know* to be sound, we deduce that A *cannot* be a formalization of the procedures available to mathematicians for ascertaining that calculations do not stop, no matter what A is. Hence:

Human mathematicians are not using a knowably sound algorithm in order to ascertain mathematical truth.

It seems to me that this conclusion is inescapable[6]. However, many people have trouble coming to terms with it, and certainly many have argued against the stronger deduction that there must be something essentially non-calculational in our thought processes. Indeed, there are various possible loopholes to consider. Let us try to go carefully through these in turn.

Some possible viewpoints

Let us accept, on the basis of the preceding argument, that human mathematicians, when they form their views of the truth or otherwise of mathematical statements, are not using any knowably sound algorithm. What procedures might they in fact be using? Let me list a number of possibilities. They might use:

1　A horrendously complicated *unknowable* algorithm X;
2　An *unsound* (but presumably approximately sound) algorithm Y;
3　An ever-changing algorithm;
4　The environment;
5　Random elements;
6　Mysticism;
7　Non-algorithmic physics.

Let us consider these possibilities in turn.

1　Do we use a horrendously complicated unknowable algorithm X?

An important thing to realize about the insights that allow mathematicians to come to their conclusions about the truth, or otherwise, of mathematical statements is that these insights are *communicable*. Thus, if a certain argument convinces one mathematician, then the same argument can also be used to convince any other mathematician – at least in principle, but with (admittedly) considerably varying amounts of difficulty. It should always be possible to break down a mathematical argument into steps that themselves represent things that are 'obvious' to all, rather than being things that are personal to particular individual mathematicians. The same comment would apply to the 'Gödelian insight' that allows one to deduce from a belief in the soundness of a procedure for ascertaining that certain calculations do not stop (such as A above) that a particular calculation (such as $C_k(k)$ above) does not in fact stop. It is not that we are talking about different possible horrendous algorithms that might happen to be running around in different mathematicians' heads, depending upon how each one's brain might happen to be 'wired up'. We are talking about *one* horrendously complicated unknowable algorithm X that applies universally to the mathematical community as a whole.

It is true that a good deal of mathematics is often carried out within what are called 'formal systems', and these are essentially algorithmic structures, but these cannot encompass the *entirety* of the insights that are available to mathematicians, as Gödel's procedure demonstrates. Such formal systems are never so complicated that they are actually 'unknowable', but some people might consider that, in certain cases, their meanings are so esoteric that their *soundness* is unknowable. However, any system whose soundness cannot be trusted cannot itself be used without qualification in a mathematical argument. An argument based on a questionable formal system F would have to run something like 'Assuming F, then it follows that . . .' if it is to be acceptable to the mathematical community as a whole. I do not see how any such F could possibly encompass precisely the insights that are available to the mathematical community. If F is accepted as sound, then the Gödel procedure yields a mathematical proposition G that must also be accepted as sound, yet which is inaccessible by the methods of F. (Here, F plays the role of A, and G is essentially the assertion that $C_k(k)$ does not terminate.) If F is not accepted as sound, then we cannot use it (without qualification) for ascertaining the truth of mathematical propositions. Either way, F cannot precisely encompass all the insights available to human mathematicians.

It seems to me that a similar kind of argument would apply to our putative *unknowable* algorithm X. Can it be that, unknown to all of us, when mathematicians come to their conclusions about the truth of mathematical statements they are just acting according to the horrendous X? This seems to be totally at variance with what mathematicians seem *actually* to be doing when they express their arguments in terms that can (at least in principle) be broken down into assertions that are 'obvious', and agreed by all. I would regard it as far-fetched in the extreme to believe that it is *really* the horrendous unknowable X, rather than these simple and obvious ingredients, that lies lurking behind all of our mathematical understanding.

There is another argument that, in my view, adds convincing support to the belief that mathematicians do not actually use X. For how is it that X could have arisen by natural selection? One need but glance at the contents of any respectable mathematical research journal to see how far removed from everyday experience are the subject-matter and lines of reasoning that are used by mathematicians. If X is needed for doing all this, and if X is shared among all mathematicians – and, in principle, among all thinking people – then somehow X would have to have arisen by natural selection, the process that, over thousands of centuries, has made Man what he is. Yet the selective value of a potential ability to do such sophisticated mathematics must have accounted for *nil* throughout Man's history! Even today, there is very little direct survival value related to an ability to reason accurately with obscurely defined infinite sets. If such an ability depended upon the possession, within the heads of at least a significant proportion of us, of the horrendously complicated unknowable X, then one is faced with the apparently insuperable problem of comprehending how anything like X could have arisen by natural selection.

In my own view, what underlies an ability to do mathematics, whether sophisticated or not, is something very different from the putative algorithm X; it is our general (non-algorithmic) ability to *understand*. What natural selection has provided is an ability to understand one's surroundings and to reason about the implications of one's actions. Accordingly, Man's superb ability to survive must, in large measure, have arisen from his ability to understand. This ability would have enabled him to achieve an effective superiority over his less comprehending adversaries. It would have had a profound value to him for his survival in many different ways, such as in the construction of mammoth traps and the like. The quality of understanding is, perhaps fortuitously, also the crucial quality that is needed for doing mathematics. It was not an *algorithm* X that was favoured, in Man (at least) by natural selection, but this wonderful ability to understand! The Gödel argument shows that *mathematical* understanding, at least, is not an algorithmic activity, and it seems to me that we must accept that a non-algorithmic quality, namely an ability to understand, can indeed arise by natural selection.

2 *Do we use an unsound (approximately sound) algorithm Y?*

What about the possibility that mathematicians might use an algorithm Y that is only approximately sound? Mathematicians, after all, do make mistakes – not infrequently, in fact (and I write from personal experience here). It would appear that Alan Turing himself may have believed that this was the loophole in the Gödelian argument, when it is applied to the algorithmic action that he himself apparently believed applied to the actual processes taking place in the human brain. For myself, I find this possibility to be unlikely as the real explanation. Many of the above objections to X, it seems to me, would apply also to Y. Moreover, although mathematicians do indeed not uncommonly make mistakes in their personal workings and in their guesses as to the truth, it is rare for these errors to survive significantly in their published writings. The essential point is that the errors are *recognizable* as errors. When a mistake has been pointed out, either by someone else or else by the same mathematician at a later time, it is *seen* to be an error – or at least if, for some reason a mental blockage persists, such a blockage could in principle be removed by further explanation and insight. The way that mathematics progresses is not at all like the blind following of an unsound algorithm Y.

Moreover, unsound algorithms are liable to land one in contradictions. In particular, in the arguments given above, if the algorithm A were unsound, then it would incorrectly assert that some calculation $C_q(n)$ does not stop when indeed it does. If the calculation $C_q(n)$ is actually stumbled upon and performed, and is seen to come to an end while $A(q,n)$ successfully terminates, then we would know that something is amiss. Of course things like this do occur with working mathematicians: errors in an argument may be spotted when a counter-example to the conclusion is found.

But that would seem to be something very different from what is being envisaged here. Actual errors in a mathematical argument could, *in principle*, have been spotted in any case. The counter-example merely provides a route to finding something that could also be found directly, namely by checking through all the details of the original argument. In the case of Y, this putative algorithm is supposed to represent the *totality* of all the means that are available to human mathematicians. Thus Y is in principle *not* correctable by human reasoning, since whatever means are available for achieving this should already have been included in the procedures of Y. (I shall return to the issue of possible self-improving algorithms under the next heading.)

There is a type of procedure that is sometimes referred to, in the context of AI, as 'heuristics', which should be included under the present heading. Heuristics refer to 'judgements' or 'rules of thumb' that may be included in a computer program, but that do not provide definitive mathematical solutions to the problem at hand. For example, in a chess-playing computer program, the computer may be instructed to analyse positions by calculating the results of all possible alternative successions of moves by each player, a good many moves deep. It would not be possible to take this analysis as far as checkmate (or as far as some accepted winning position) in most cases, there being far too many alternatives to work through before an adequate depth of move can be achieved for this. Instead, the various strands of computation would be terminated as soon as some appropriate 'heuristic' criterion is satisfied. The resulting program would not play perfect chess, but nevertheless it could be made to play chess extremely well, and some such programs – most particularly 'Deep Thought' constructed by a group at Carnegie Mellon headed by Hsiung Hsu – can defeat all but a very small minority of human players.

Computers that act according to such procedures are still acting algorithmically, of course, even though their action is not given by some algorithm that is *guaranteed* to provide the desired result (e.g. to play perfect chess). If such procedures were applied to the solving of mathematical problems as a whole, then they could be thought of as giving an algorithm such as Y, and it might be imagined that this is indeed how mathematicians actually operate. However, a *known* procedure of this type would certainly not be accepted by the mathematical community as providing an adequate criterion of mathematical proof. Mathematicians require a degree of rigour that makes such heuristic arguments unacceptable – so no such known procedure of this kind can be the way that mathematicians actually operate. We are left with the possibility that Y might be a horrendously complicated unknowable algorithm, and we are really back with the situation that we had before, with the unknowable algorithm X (but with Y as actually an inferior inaccurate version of X), and the same objections will apply as before. Most particularly, the arguments from natural selection are at least as damning as they were before.

3 Do we use an ever-changing algorithm?

There is, however, the possibility that we might be using an algorithm, perhaps like X or Y, but that is continually changing with time by being improved with experience. But now we must ask, as we did briefly before: by what procedures is our putative algorithm supposed to improve itself. If these very procedures are things that could be programmed on a computer, then they are themselves algorithmic. All the arguments that we have been considering before should really be applied to the *entire* algorithm controlling the computer's action, including that part which governs its mode of change. This algorithm includes all the 'learning procedures' that have been laid down at the beginning. If the only ways in which the algorithm can change is by such pre-assigned algorithmic means, then we do not, strictly speaking, have a changing algorithm at all but just a single algorithm, say X or Y, as before and all the objections raised above will still apply.

There is a particular type of learning system that has gained considerable popularity in recent years, referred to as a *neural network*. This type of system is based initially on certain ideas about how brains actually work – most particularly, the idea of *brain plasticity*, according to which the strengths of the various connections between neurons in the brain are continually being modified in order to improve performance – but in a 'neural network' the system is implemented entirely electronically. At the present time, such systems are normally run on ordinary general-purpose electronic computers, but the intention is that, eventually, special-purpose electronic hardware would be constructed, so that a much greater speed and efficiency can be achieved. (It should be mentioned that the biological mechanisms whereby the strengths of connections between neurons in the brain are *actually* modified are largely unknown. Neural networks use their own procedures, and these probably differ in important ways from what happens in the brain plasticity of actual brains.) Neural networks have been applied to many varieties of different task, such as the recognizing of faces, or distinguishing the quality of different sounds, or prospecting for mineral deposits, or controlling a robot arm. They can be effective for tasks where understanding seems not to be playing a crucial role – so it is hard to see that they could be of much use in forming mathematical judgements.

A basic feature of a neural network, distinguishing it from the normal type of algorithmic programming, is that rather than having a previously given algorithm that is specifically provided in order to solve some particular problem or class of problems (which would sometimes be referred to as the normal 'top-down' organization) we are, instead, initially provided with merely a loosely connected family of units (the electronic 'neurons') where the strengths of the various connections are continually being modified in order to maximize the quality of the output. In this way the system continually 'learns', so that the output improves all the time. The action of such a system is still algorithmic, since it can be implemented on an ordinary general-purpose electronic computer, but there is a crucial difference in the intentionality underlying the algorithm. Now, the algorithm according to which the system acts at any one time is not one that has been fed in initially in order to provide a specific solution to a pre-assigned problem, but it is one that has gradually evolved on the basis of improving the quality of its output ('bottom-up' organization).

Nevertheless, the procedure taken as a whole still constitutes an algorithm, provided that the judgement as to the quality of the output at any given stage is made according to some (possibly 'heuristic') algorithmic criterion. This would indeed normally be the case if one is thinking of using the neural network to solve some clearly specified problem. Certainly, if one attempted to use a neural network to solve problems in pure mathematics, then its action would be entirely algorithmic. Thus, we would again have a situation of the type already considered under the previous heading: an approximate algorithm Y; and the various objections to this being *actually* the procedure that mathematicians use would apply as before.

4 Is the role of the environment essential?

Of course, it might be the case that it is the continual input that we get from the environment that gives our mathematical understanding its (apparently?) non-algorithmic character. It is undoubtedly the case that mathematicians are indeed being continuously influenced by their environment. Even the very idea of what we mean by a natural number could hardly have formed in our minds were it not for our experiences with various different manifestations of such numbers – at least of the smaller ones: 'three oranges', 'two socks', 'ten pennies', etc. Moreover, although advanced mathematics need not have any very precise correspondence with our immediate experiences, and mathematical reasoning is wholly abstract, mathematicians frequently do gain their inspirations from everyday things in the world around them.

But is this input from the environment something that has an essentially non-algorithmic character? To put the question another way, might it be that it is in principle impossible to simulate the environment computationally? The question is not whether or not the actual environment of a particular individual could be precisely simulated, but whether or not everything that might be relevant to the building up of an individual's mathematical understanding could be computationally simulated. I find it hard to see where there can be any essentially non-algorithmic input coming in here. In any case, if one takes refuge in the possibility that it is the environment that supplies the needed non-algorithmic ingredient in our mathematical thinking, then one is left with the problem of explaining how the physical environment can behave non-algorithmically. If one is prepared to believe that the physically governed external world could behave in a way that cannot be simulated computationally, then one must surely also accept that a (physically controlled) human brain might behave non-computationally. This after all, is what the thrust of my argument is intended to show.

5 Do random ingredients change the discussion?

In the discussions so far I have been considering 'algorithmic action'
to be essentially that which could be carried out in principle by a
modern general-purpose electronic computer (with an unlimited
store) – which, technically, means by a Turing machine. The
action of a Turing machine is always completely determined
in advance, even though the ultimate behaviour of the machine
might be hard to predict. One might expect that some essential differences could arise when we relax this condition, and
allow the presence of random ingredients to be introduced into
the calculations. In modelling the environment, in particular,
one would normally expect that there would be many uncon-
trollable parameters, and these would have to be modelled in
some way in terms of a random input. Moreover, in the action
of the brain itself, it is to be expected that there would be
a great deal of random activity, and one could imagine that
this could have important implications with regard to its overall
performance.

However, in computational simulations of physical systems,
the presence of random ingredients poses no problem, provided
that one is not asking for a prediction of the actual detailed way
in which a particular physical system is going to behave, but is
merely asking for a typical example of the way in which such a
physical system *might* behave. The latter, after all, is all that we
would be asking of an artificially intelligent system. There are
many algorithmic means of producing an *effectively* random input. In place of a 'genuinely' random sequence of digits, the
computer produces a sequence of what are called 'pseudo-random'
digits which, for all intents and purposes, behaves as a random
sequence would, despite the fact that the sequence is generated
entirely algorithmically. Thus, in practice, it does not seem to be
any significant restriction to limit one's attention to entirely algorithmic computation.

In present-day physics, there are two distinct ways in which
(apparently) random behaviour can result in a seemingly well-
specified physical system. In the first place, there is the phenomenon known as *chaos*, whereby a completely deterministic
classical system can, in practice, behave as though it were not

deterministic at all. This is because the accuracy according to which the initial state needs to be known, for a deterministic prediction of its future behaviour, can be totally beyond anything that is conceivably measurable. An example that is often quoted in this connection is the detailed long-range prediction of the weather. The laws governing the motion of air molecules, and also the other physical quantities that might be relevant, are all perfectly well known; however the weather patterns that may actually emerge, after only a few days, depend so subtly on the precise initial conditions that there is no possibility of knowing these conditions accurately enough for reliable prediction. Of course the number of parameters that would have to enter into such a calculation would be enormous, so it is perhaps not surprising that prediction, in this case, might prove to be virtually imposs- ible in practice. However, such so-called chaotic behaviour can occur also with very simple systems consisting of only a small number of particles. Imagine, for example, that one is to pocket the fifth snooker ball E in a chain A, B, C, D, E by hitting A with the cue so that A hits B, causing B to hit C, then C to hit D, and finally D to hit E into the pocket. So long as no two successive balls are initially close up against one another, the accuracy needed for this is far in excess of the abilities of any expert snooker player. If there were ten in the chain, then even if the balls were perfectly elastic perfect spheres, the task of potting the final ball would be far beyond the most accurate machinery of modern technology. In effect, the behaviour of the later balls in the chain would be random, despite the fact that the Newtonian laws gov- erning the behaviour of the balls is mathematically completely deterministic.

From time to time, it has been suggested that this phenomenon of chaos, if it occurs in the internal action of a physical brain, might be what enables our brains to behave in ways that appear to differ from the computably deterministic activity of a Turing machine. However, if all that we can get from chaos is random- ness, then this will be no use to us. For randomness itself does not give us anything usefully beyond ordinary algorithmic com- putation. Does chaos give us anything that is usefully non- computable, rather than just randomness? In fact the behaviour of chaotic systems can sometimes be highly structured and much more interesting-looking than purely random behaviour. It remains to be seen, however, whether this kind of structure contains anything approximating genuinely non-algorithmic behaviour. It would be very interesting to see if this is possible, but so far no one appears to have argued any kind of case that it is.

The other place where modern physics asserts that randomness arises in the precise behaviour of a physical system is in *quantum mechanics*. Many people are familiar with the fact that quantum theory does not give us a deterministic picture of the time-evolution of the world and that it merely provides probability values for the various alternative outcomes of experiments that may be performed on a system. What is not so commonly appreciated is that this probabilistic – i.e. random – behaviour does *not* occur at the submicroscopic *quantum level* of molecules, atoms and subatomic particles. For at that level, things are described as evolving according to the precise deterministic Schrödinger equation, and the behaviour is just as deterministic as it is at the *classical level* of everyday experiences, where the laws of Newton and Maxwell (and also Einstein) hold sway. Instead, the quantum randomness is effectively taken to occur at some mysterious middle-ground level, intermediate between the quantum and classical levels. A feature of the quantum level is that all the various alternative things that a system *might* do have also to be allowed to happen *together* in some mysterious kind of quantum superposition. But when the effects of some of these superposed alternatives become magnified to the classical level, in accordance with a *measurement* being performed on the system, one alternative or the other becomes realized as actuality. At this stage, Nature's choice of alternative is governed merely by probability. According to theory, what one must do – and this is all that quantum mechanics tells us about what happens during measurements – is to adopt the strange procedure referred to as *state-vector reduction* (or *wavefunction collapse*). According to this, the quantum description (the state-vector, or wavefunction) undergoes a discontinuous random change, where what happens is restricted only by the probability laws that the theory tells us how to calculate. It is here, and only here, that the deterministic character of the underlying theory is changed to a probabilistic one. At both the quantum level (Schrödinger's equation) and the classical level (Newton-Maxwell laws) the behaviour is basically deterministic (considerations of chaos notwithstanding), and the randomness comes in only when one tries to bridge the gap between the two. In this connection it should be pointed out that the difference between the quantum and classical levels is not really one of size. (Quantum effects have been observed to take place over a separation of many metres.) It would be somewhat more accurate to say that the quantum level refers to phenomena for which the differences in energy between the states under consideration are small. In fact the whole issue of what *actually* happens when the alternative effects of differing quantum possibilities are magnified to the classical level whenever such a 'measurement' takes place is fraught with controversy. But whatever one believes quantum theory is telling us about the actuality of the world, some procedure akin to the one just described must be adopted in order that the necessary probability calculations can be made.

What might be the relevance of this to the activity of a human brain? As was the case with chaos, all that we appear to obtain, when the procedures of quantum theory are adjoined to the mechanistic determinism of classical theory, is a random element that would seem to be of little use to us if we are expecting to find something usefully non-computable coming out of it all. (In fact, there are certain profoundly intriguing features of the behaviour of quantum systems that differ significantly from what can be achieved by classical systems – such as non-locality[7], and the possibility that certain calculations can, in principle, be performed more rapidly – but these do not change the class of problems that can or cannot be solved from what they were for a Turing machine.) As our understanding rests at the moment, the incorporation of conventional quantum mechanics into our discussion does not significantly help us in our search for a non-algorithmic ingredient that could be relevant to our thought processes.

Thus, as things stand, chaos and quantum mechanics both leave us with only randomness and not with something usefully non-algorithmic. There remains a hope, in each case, that future developments in theory might improve the situation. With chaos, this hope rests on the possibility that something more useful than mere randomness might arise in suitable circumstances; with quantum mechanics, it rests on the finding of a new physical theory with a more satisfactory way of handling the transition between the quantum and the classical level. Both hopes represent highly unconventional viewpoints at the present time. I shall return briefly to these possibilities under the final heading.

6   Must we resort to mysticism?

Since we seem, so far, to have been led into an impasse by following the methods of conventional scientific theory, is it not perhaps reasonable that we should abandon the physicalist view of the mind altogether and turn, instead, to a viewpoint more in line with some form of mysticism? Even Kurt Gödel appears to have found himself driven to a rather mystical standpoint. In commenting on Alan Turing's computational view of the mind[8], Gödel suggested that the mind need not be limited by the brain's finiteness. He seemed to have believed, along with Turing, that the objects of the physical world should behave 'mechanically' – by which he meant, in effect, 'algorithmically' – but unlike Turing, he appeared to believe that the human mind was something beyond the physical brain. In this way, the mind would be able to perceive the Platonic truth of mathematical statements in some way not totally dependent on the physical action of the brain.

As I have stated in my introductory remarks, I intend to stay within the framework of scientific possibilities in addressing the issues of mind. The evidence that mental attributes result from activity in the physical brain seems to me to be overwhelming. While it is certainly true that we do not understand how mental phenomena can arise from the activity of a physical object, the case is surely powerful that somehow they can, at least when the 'physical object' is a living human brain. To my own way of thinking, the resolution of the profoundly puzzling issues raised by the evident fact that certain types of physical object can indeed give rise to conscious minds must ultimately lie in our finding a deeper understanding of what physical objects actually are. As science has progressed, our descriptions have become more and more accurate and complete; but at the same time, they have become more and more abstract and mathematical. Our very picture of concrete reality has changed to something almost totally abstract and, in many ways, mysterious. It seems that we need to turn to the abstract Platonic world of mathematical forms if we are to find where ultimately concrete reality is to find its home. The mystery of mind can ultimately be understood only in terms of the mystery of matter itself, and in the undoubted mystery of the mathematics that so precisely seems to control its every action. This is not mysticism; it is the ultimate purpose of science itself.

7   Are there non-algorithmic physical laws?

If we are to stay within the laws of physics in our search for a non-algorithmic action that might underlie our conscious thought processes (such as those that give rise to the mental quality of mathematical understanding), then we must find something usefully non-algorithmic in those laws. As I asserted earlier, mere randomness will not do. We need something a good deal more sophisticated than randomness if we are ever to find a possible physical basis for our conscious understanding.

What kind of physical laws could exhibit non-algorithmic behaviour? It is certainly possible to provide various different kinds of 'toy model universe' that are non-algorithmic. Such a model can even be completely deterministic, as the following (admittedly totally unrealistic) example illustrates: Let the state of our 'universe' be given by a pair of natural numbers n, q, where the (discrete) time is also given by a natural number t. The rule for the evolution of this universe is that, if the state at time t is (n,q), the state at time $t + 1$ is to be $(n+1,q)$ if the calculation $C_n(n)$ stops and it is $(q+1,n)$ if $C_n(n)$ doesn't stop. Since there is no general algorithm for deciding whether a calculation $C_n(n)$ stops or not, the future behaviour of our model universe is not computable, even though it is completely deterministic. Although this particular model is not to be taken seriously as a picture of reality, of course, it is not at all impossible that the *actual* physical laws could exhibit a non-algorithmic behaviour of this general kind. There are many classes of mathematical problem that are non-computable and that could take the place of the non-stopping of $C_n(n)$ in the example just cited (the solubility of families of polynomial equations in terms of natural numbers, the topological equivalence problem for four-dimensional manifolds, the problem of deciding which finite sets of polygonal tiles will cover the Euclidean plane without overlaps or gaps, etc.). There could also be other kinds of example of a much more subtle, and possibly more realistic, nature.

There is, as yet, no indication that the phenomenon of chaos can exhibit anything usefully non-random that approximates a non-algorithmic action of this general kind. In this connection it should be pointed out that chaotic behaviour can certainly be simulated computationally, and I think that the arguments that I have given earlier argue strongly against such a computational model of conscious understanding. For reasons such as these, I think that it is unlikely that chaos can supply our needed answer.

On the other hand, there are numerous reasons, coming from physical theory itself, for believing that present-day quantum theory must someday be profoundly modified, the procedure of state-vector reduction being distinctly unsatisfactory physically. It is my own opinion that such a necessary modification will someday be discovered, and that it is here that we shall find our needed non-algorithmic behaviour – to replace or amend the probabilistic procedures that present-day quantum theory seems to require. Such a theory would need to have an even deeper, more profoundly subtle, and universal nature than the theories that science has provided to date, and its unity with the Platonic world of mathematics should also be more secure. Perhaps, then, we shall be better able to find a basis for mental phenomena within scientific explanation than has been remotely possible hitherto.

Notes

Opening lecture, Wolfson Lecture series on Artificial Intelligence; 15 January, 1991; Wolfson College, Oxford. This account is partially based on a draft of part of the opening chapter of a new book by the author, to be published, in due course, by the Oxford University Press.

1   These four alternatives are explicitly described in, for example, Johnson-Laird (1987), p. 252. (It should be noted, however, that what he refers to as the 'Church-Turing thesis' is not given altogether appropriately, and its relevance to 'viewpoint 3' requires further

discussion.) For a spectrum of opinions on the mind-brain-computer issue, see also various other articles in Blakemore and Greenfield (1987).

2 Johnson-Laird (1987) attributes this viewpoint originally to Craik (1943). Other proponents appear to include Alan Turing(?), Allen Newell, Herbert Simon, John McCarthy, Marvin Minsky, Douglas Hofstadter and Hans Moravec.

3 See the discussion in Moravec (1988), chapter 6.

4 From his explicit writings, I take this to be the originally stated viewpoint of Searle (1980).

5 See, for example, Searle (1980).

6 For earlier arguments in support of the thesis that Gödel's theorem shows that (mathematical) thinking cannot be computational, see Nagel and Newman (1958), Lucas (1961). There have been numerous counter-arguments to these; see, for example, Benacerraf (1967), Lewis (1969, 1989), Hofstadter (1979).

7 See Bell (1987).

8 See his collected works: Gödel (1990).

References

Bell, J. S. 1987: *Speakable and Unspeakable in Quantum Mechanics.* Cambridge, Cambridge University Press.

Benacerraf, P. 1967: God, the Devil and Gödel. *The Monist*, **51**, 9–32.

Blakemore, C. and Greenfield, S., eds 1987: *Mindwaves: Thoughts on Intelligence, Identity and Consciousness.* Oxford: Basil Blackwell.

Craik, K. 1943: *The Nature of Explanation.* Cambridge: Cambridge University Press.

Gödel, K. 1990: *Kurt Gödel, Collected Works, Vol. II (publications 1938–1974).* (Edited by S. Feferman, J. W. Dawson, Jr., S. C. Kleene, G. H. Moore, R. M. Solovay, J. van Heijenoort) New York: Oxford University Press.

Hofstadter, D. R. 1979: *Gödel, Escher, Bach: an Eternal Golden Braid.* Hassocks, Sussex: Harvester Press.

Johnson-Laird, P. 1987: How could consciousness arise from the computations of the brain? In Blakemore, C. and Greenfield, S. (eds), *Mindwaves: Thoughts on Intelligence, Identity and Consciousness.* Oxford: Basil Blackwell.

Lewis, D. 1969: Lucas against mechanism. *Philosophy*, **44**, 231–3.

Lewis, D. 1989: Lucas against mechanism II. *Can. J. Philos.*, **9**, 373–6.

Lucas, J. R. 1961: Minds, Machines and Gödel. *Philosophy*, **36**, 120–4;

reprinted in Alan Ross Anderson 1964: *Minds and Machines*, Englewoods Cliffs: Prentice Hall.

Moravec, H. 1988: *Mind Children: The Future of Robot and Human Intelligence*. Cambridge, Mass./London: Harvard University Press.

Nagel, E. and Newman, J. R. 1958: *Gödel's Proof*. London: Routledge & Kegan Paul Ltd.

Penrose, R. 1989: *The Emperor's New Mind: Concerning Computers, Minds, and the Laws of Physics*. Oxford: Oxford University Press; see also summary, commentaries and author's response in *Behavioral and Brain Sci.*, **13** (1990) 643–705.

Searle, J. R. 1980: Minds, Brains and Programs. In *Behavioral and Brain Sci.*, **3**, reprinted: *The Mind's I*, D. R. Hofstadter and D. C. Dennett (eds) 1981: Hassocks, Sussex: Harvester Press.

2

The Approach Through Symbols

Allen Newell, Richard Young and Thad Polk

The nature of intelligence, being a great mystery, generates a multitude of diverse approaches. Ours is that of science. This hardly gets rid of the mystery, which will dissolve only with deep discoveries about the nature of man. However, science does tell us how to approach a mystery. One discovers (it matters not how) some phenomena in the universe, here, that reflect intelligence. One proceeds by careful observation and controlled experimental investigation to accumulate their properties. One attempts to explain these properties by constructing a theory. To the extent possible, one grounds the theory in the vast network of other science. Throughout, one challenges the theory by additional observation and experimentation. The picture is a familiar one, surrounded as we are by successful science. The details vary with the nature of the phenomena and the domain – chemistry does not feel quite the same as astronomy, which does not feel quite the same as ethology. But the central way remains.

Given our starting point, we need to look again at the series title, *The Simulation of Human Intelligence*. This title reflects the emergence of the field of artificial intelligence (AI) over the last thirty years, as the effort to get computers to perform functions that, if performed by humans, would require intelligence. *Simulation* occurs in the series title, because AI programs are often talked about as *simulating* human problem solving and learning. Such a description injects a certain conceptual distance between what is happening in the AI program and what is happening in the human – it may be getting the same result but it is *merely* simulating it. Thereby, we are warned that it may bear no resemblance to what really goes on in the analogous exercise of human intelligence. If our approach is that of science, we cannot be happy with accepting *simulation* as the defining term for what we are after. We are after a *scientific theory* of human intelligence that lets us understand the nature of that capability, not merely simulate it.

The situation can be illuminated by reference to, say, chemistry and the familiar valence theory of chemical molecules (H_2O and all that). One can produce simulations of chemical reactions, which are computer programs that produce behaviour and results in accordance with the theory. These simulations do not inject any conceptual distance, because they simply model according to what the theory says. When the results of the simulation fail to agree with experiment – which can happen easily because valence theory provides an imperfect approximation – this is taken to show the approximate nature of the theory, not something about the simulation 'not doing it the same way nature does'.

This difference in attitude appears to arise because in AI there is often only the simulating system, not the separately stated theory. What can be stated separately is only a high-level description of the AI system, so that system itself – the simulation system – seems to embody the hypotheses about the nature of the intelligence. In fact, our goal is a theory of human intelligence, just like a theory of chemistry. We may make general statements about the processes of human intelligence, but we may also put together an operational system that embodies such statements. The latter has advantages in being able to demonstrate whether the theory really explains intelligence. It has disadvantages in not separating out so clearly the general principles of its operation from a number of less important (but still necessary) details. There will be no difficulty in all of this, just as long as we remain clear that the ultimate goal is to understand the nature of human intelligence, not just to simulate it in the pejorative sense of the term.

Our goal in this paper, then, is to present a picture of how an approach to human intelligence through science proceeds, and to convey its yield. We will start by accumulating some phenomena that attend intelligent behaviour in humans. These show up primarily as intellectual functions that have to be performed in order to accomplish some task. A theory of human intelligence should explain these phenomena. Of course it should explain other phenomena of intelligence as well, but selecting out some limited phenomena for attention is the way of science. The starting point is often adventitious and indeed different scientists start at different points. Since we are all ultimately explaining the same thing, all must converge together in the long run.

We will develop a theory of these accumulated phenomena by constructing an operational embodiment of the theory, that is, by constructing a system that exhibits the phenomena we identified and, in so doing, exhibits intelligent behaviour in performing the tasks. *Symbol systems* will turn out to play a central role in this development, thus justifying our own title of *The Approach Through Symbols*. We will then gradually refine our notion of how human intelligence operates and what phenomena it exhibits. Correspondingly, we will extend the theory so that it covers not only a wider class of tasks, but also exhibits other characteristics of human intelligence. In the end, we will have revealed a substantial theory that lets us understand something about the nature of human intelligence. This will provide the basis for reflections on the ingredients that have made this possible.

Some phenomena of intelligence

We start by considering a simple example of the exercise of human intelligence. Figure 2.1 shows a man viewing a simple scene in which there is a barber, a chef and a doctor. The man is asked a simple question (we imagine an interlocutor off to the side), 'What is the relation between the barber and the doctor?' He answers straightaway, 'The barber is to the left of the doctor.'

The whole situation seems simple enough, but only because the natural standpoint to take is that of an intelligent human being. But let us change the standpoint, by putting something else in place of the man – say a puppet head, a sack of potatoes, or a kitten. It is inconceivable that these substitutes would give the answer that the man does. Human capacities are at work here, however mundane they seem when considered from a human standpoint. These capacities add up to being able to successfully perform a task (to view the situation and answer the question). Such performances seem of the essence of behaving intelligently.

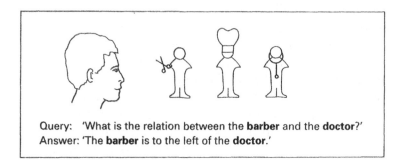

Query: 'What is the relation between the **barber** and the **doctor**?'
Answer: 'The **barber** is to the left of the **doctor**.'

Figure 2.1 A simple example of human intelligence.

Working our way through the task from beginning to end, it
is easy to identify some required capacities:

- *Perception*. Must recognize and make sense of the scene.
- *Language comprehension*. Must understand the sentence and the
  demand that it makes.
- *Intelligent selection*. Must construct a correct response from the
  perceived situation and the demands of the question.
- *Language production*. Must form a sentence that is both com-
  prehensible and carries the meaning of the selected response.

In each case it is obvious that such an intellectual function is
required if the task is to be successfully completed. Less clear is
exactly what are the phenomena of being able to perceive, comprehend, select intelligently or produce an utterance. But this is
again the way of science. The initial identification of a phenomenon
is based on superficial observation. The characterization of its
nature arrives along with its scientific understanding in terms of
a theory that explains it. As long as we can point with reasonable
reliability to an occasion where a phenomenon is exhibited, we
can get started. In our situation, we have available a reliable test
for the occurrence of our four phenomena, namely, that the task
as a whole is accomplished successfully.

Let us modify the task of figure 2.1 slightly, as shown in figure
2.2. The man sees the same scene. However, before the question
is asked he is blindfolded, so he can no longer see the scene.

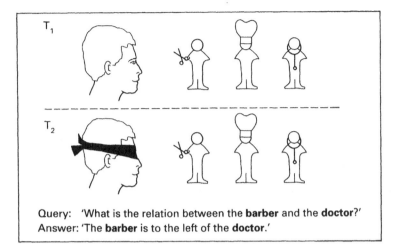

Figure 2.2   A simple example of human intelligence, extended.

Now, to answer the questions successfully (and the same answer will do) requires an additional capability:

- *Remember the situation.* Must be able to represent the situation internally.

That is, there must be some configuration of matter and energy inside him that embodies somehow the aspects of the external situation, so the man can do an intelligent selection and produce the correspondingly appropriate response.

Yet another slight modification, as shown in figure 2.3, provides another phenomenon to be added to our list. We forget the blindfold, but we also take away the scene. Instead we describe the scene in language. We have already listed the requirement for comprehending language. However, it was required to comprehend the question to be answered. What might be involved in that is somewhat obscure. But in figure 2.3 we are describing a scene that we have depicted in earlier figures. So we can add a more specific capability:

- *Extract knowledge from a description.* Must be able to construct an internal representation of a scene from a linguistic description.

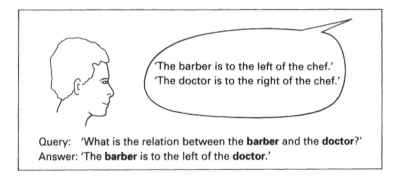

Figure 2.3   A simple example of human intelligence, extended again.

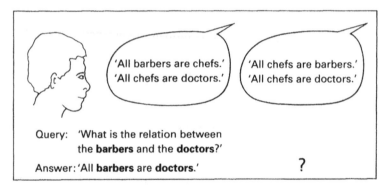

Figure 2.4   A simple example of human intelligence, extended one more time.

One final modification is shown in figure 2.4. We have now shifted to making general statements that cover many situations (*All barbers are chefs*) and asking what holds in general between people of different types. We have actually shown two such questions. In the first, at the left, it is pretty evident that *All barbers are doctors*. But in the second, at the right, matters are not so clear (and we have conveniently failed to provide the answer, so that readers may themselves ponder the question). What has been added here to all the other demands for processing capabilities is the need to deal with difficult tasks, where the information is in the situation in some implicit way and must be ferreted out and combined to produce a successful answer. We may capture this as one more requirement:

- *Extract implicit knowledge.* Must be able to do difficult tasks that require discovering relevant knowledge that is not immediately available.

We have now accumulated seven phenomena of intelligence. Intelligence is a characteristic of the way humans perform tasks. We usually recognize an occasion of intelligent behaviour if performance is successful. Sometimes this recognition reflects that a capability is necessary to perform the task, where all humans normally have the capability. The contrast is with other systems – animals, puppet heads or whatever – that don't have the capability at all and hence can't exhibit intelligent behaviour. Most of our phenomena are of this kind. Sometimes the recognition reflects degrees of an ability, so that humans have more or less difficulty in doing a task and can exhibit more or less intelligence. Our last phenomenon is of this kind – only a few people do well on all syllogisms.

In any event, we now have our list of phenomena – seven of them. They are diverse enough that a theory that explained how a human could exhibit them all in the course of succeeding on the various tasks we have described would seem to provide a good start on a theory of human intelligence. But of course, there is an indefinite variety of tasks, and many will reveal additional phenomena of intelligence quite distinct from the ones here. No guarantee exists that a theory to explain our seven will extend to the others. Indeed, in science, we may confidently expect an unending series of surprises, which will require us to extend and elaborate our theory, and occasionally revise it, perhaps right down to the roots. But that, again, is the way of science. It proceeds iteratively, not being overly concerned about dealing with phenomena and data it does not yet have, confidently expecting revisions (though of course not necessarily welcoming every twist!). For instance, nothing in our list, either tasks or phenomena, touches on human creativity – whatever that might turn out to be. There is no requirement to do so, or to believe that we are not usefully on our way with a theory of our seven phenomena, even without a clue to the phenomenon of creativity or a theory of it.

A system that does these tasks

We are ready for the next step – to develop a theory to explain how humans succeed on these tasks, thereby exhibiting these phenomena. Explaining all seven is too ambitious for a single paper, and we will focus on the last task, in figure 2.4. We thereby give up perception of a scene, but retain the element of differential difficulty. Even within this task, we will not be able to get to language production.

What form should a theory take? A good theory specifies a set of principles or propositions or equations, such that a scientist skilled in the art, can use these to make the predictions of the theory. Suppose such a theory has been specified. How does it deal with our task? It is easy enough for the scientist, himself, to read the situation description, read the query and give the answer. Indeed, the scientist might predict that the answer he just gave is exactly what a human would give. But this is the *scientist* making the prediction, not the *theory*. What could be written down in this theory so the scientist could crank out the prediction from the theory, rather than his own personal knowledge of what humans can do? It would have to tell the scientist what goes on with language comprehension and the rest. Indeed, it would have to be a specification of how intelligence operates, and the scientist's use of this theory would, in fact, be a specification for how to behave intelligently.

We have backed into a curious, but important, proposition. The only satisfactory way to know whether a theory explains intelligence is whether a system built according to the tenets of the theory actually exhibits the requisite intelligence. Any theory that is able to predict the results of intelligence, permits anyone, just by following the theory, to act intelligently.[1] What is curious is that this same condition does not necessarily apply to theories for other aspects of mind. Intelligence is a *functional capability* of the human mind. Emotions, pains and qualia are not. To predict a functional capability is to be able to produce the function – by other means than the original, perhaps – but nevertheless to produce the function.

Our theory to explain how humans perform our task will be a

system for performing intelligently. The phenomena we enumerated are themselves functional capabilities, from perceiving to extracting implicit knowledge. So the system will predict that humans exhibit these phenomena by itself exhibiting them, e.g. comprehending and extracting implicit knowledge.

There may be lots of different ways of perceiving, comprehending language, and on to extracting implicit knowledge. These different ways may exhibit many diverse phenomena that make it possible to distinguish how humans accomplish these functions from how other systems accomplish them. The advent of AI has made familiar diverse ways of being intelligent. But we will not be happy with a theory that merely exhibits our functional capabilities. We want it also to exhibit its intelligence in human ways, and definitely not in ways that are far from how humans exercise their intelligence. Such a demand is well justified. But it does not thereby bypass the need to start with a system that exhibits the capabilities.

We might begin designing our system by top-down decomposition into a number of subsystems, such as encode input, and produce result. However this approach cannot be carried very far – the original functional requirements provide too little guidance for further decomposition. Rather, we need a *hypothesis* about the mechanisms to be used in accomplishing the functions. This will be a genuine psychological hypothesis. This is where we adopt the *approach through symbols*, in the words of our title. The human mind exercises its powers through a specific type of system, called a *symbol system*.[2] This is the hypothesis at the heart of all cognitive science – that mind, in its functional aspects, is computational.[3]

Symbol systems form a large general class of systems, which pervade all of computer science and which can be described abstractly and formally. However, we will focus on our example and describe just the version of a symbol system that suits our needs. Figure 2.5 lays out the essentials. Starting at the top, labelled **1**, it posits a *medium* for representation, some physical material out of which specific representations will be fashioned. It posits that the situations that the human sees or thinks about (e.g. those in figure 2.4) will be represented by *models* of them. That is, as shown at **2**, there will be a specific part of the representation for an individual and aspects of that part will indicate whether

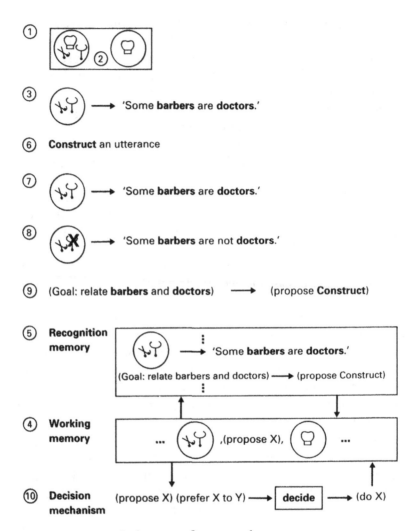

Figure 2.5 A symbol system for our tasks.

it is a barber, chef and doctor (on the left) or just a chef (on the right). This is a model representation just because parts of the actual representation (the internal medium) correspond to the parts of what is being represented. Other kinds of representations are possible, namely *propositional* representations; the linguistic expressions that populate our figures are prime examples. Here, no direct correspondence need exist between the parts of the representation (the words and phrases) and the parts of what is being referred to. For example, the situation at the top of figure 2.5 could be described by 'There are two individuals. Both are chefs. But the one on the left is also a barber and a doctor.' No simple correspondence exists here between the words and the situation. The power of language lies precisely in the freedoms it has about how to describe situations. But correspondingly it can be difficult to ferret out the knowledge it conveys. Models, on the other hand, are simple to process, but are correspondingly limited in what they can represent.

What makes the little box with circles and icons, **1** and **2**, a *representation*, rather than simply some inked lines? The answer for you is easy – we told you what it stood for and thereafter it is a representation, rather than just lines on paper. But, what makes it a representation for the system? The system has *patterns* that can *match* features in the medium. The pattern shown at **3** will match any individual that has the features for a barber and a doctor. The patterns lead to other representations, which the system then also knows. In this case it is a text, 'Some barbers are doctors.' So our system represents situations by models, but it can also represent linguistic utterances.

We now need to distinguish in our system a *working memory*, **4** towards the bottom of the figure, which holds the momentary task situation, from a memory that holds the permanent knowledge that the system can bring to bear to behave intelligently, **5**. This knowledge is encoded in these patterns with their associated representations, which they put into working memory. This permanent memory is called *recognition memory*, because its activity consists of patterns recognizing whether the current situation, as encoded in working memory, has something that corresponds to it, hence that the working memory should be augmented by what that pattern knows.

It may seem that a pattern-with-association hardly constitutes what the objects mean to you, once told what they represent. That is because a single pattern is a mere sliver of meaning. There need to be thousands, even millions, of patterns-with-associations to cover all the meanings for all the possible objects with their features. These myriad patterns seem to cover only meanings that immediately spring to mind, for the patterns respond immediately whenever something they recognize shows up in working memory. More considered meanings arise, not through some different mechanism, but through associations from some patterns combining with other codes in working memory to trigger yet other patterns, causing a flow of recognitions with their associated codes that correspond to a flow of meanings, ending with a resultant meaning far from the initial situation.

The patterns-with-associations are the tiniest fragments out of which the system operates. They need to be organized together into *operators* – larger units that form functionally coherent actions. At **6**, the figure shows part of an operator to *construct an utterance*. All the patterns include a part that indicates the operator; only if an object in working memory is a code for *construct an utterance* will any of these patterns match. This is how multiple patterns are bound together into a single operator. The operator contains many patterns, only a couple of which are shown, **7** and **8**, each one translating a different situation of objects into an utterance. For simplicity, we show the association to be the entire utterance. In fact the utterance is composed word by phrase out of other patterns-with-associations that deal with words, phrases and how to combine them.

Beyond the organization into operators, there needs to be additional organization for doing whole tasks. For instance, to do arithmetic requires a number of operators – add, subtract, multiply, divide, and housekeeping operations, such as copy. It also requires knowledge about when to apply certain operators in relation to others, **9**. Such a collection of operators and patterns packaged together to deal with an entire task can be termed a *space* for that task (though no space is shown in the figure). Tasks, such as figure 2.4, consist of a hierarchy of many smaller tasks. Correspondingly, a system will be organized with many spaces, which can be evoked as spaces and subspaces to accomplish tasks and subtasks. The final ingredient, **10** at the very bottom, is a *decision mechanism*, which will take the assembled coded knowledge in the working memory and determine what should be done next (by putting yet another code back into working memory).

Figure 2.6 lays out the picture of a specific symbol system – a computational system – to do the task of figure 2.4. The basic

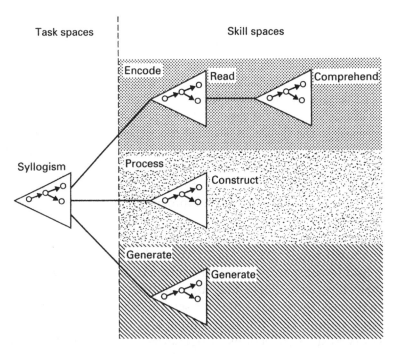

Figure 2.6 Expanded version of the system using symbol system of figure 2.5

operational structure is built around spaces, which respond to the various major tasks that have to be performed. There is a space to *comprehend* language input. There is also a space to *read*, which governs the deployment of comprehend to particular tasks – read a sequence of items, read this item again, etc. These two spaces comprise what is needed of the processes that constitute the human ability to take in knowledge from the external world. At the bottom of the figure there is a space to *generate* the language expression which is to be uttered. In the middle, in the region of the system called *process* in figure 2.5, there is a single space, called *construct*. This constructs the essential specification of an external utterance. But it is not *generate*, since there is much to be done to go from the intent to say a certain content to the vocal utterance.

All the above spaces are labelled *skill spaces* at the top of the figure. They represent things that a person can do before ever committing to performing our task – indeed, before ever hearing about the task. At the point just before the experiment, the person has all these skills, represented in all these spaces, and yet can't perform our task at all, because the person simply does not know what the task is. Of course, the person will be instructed about the task and, in understanding it, will add knowledge about how to behave in the task. That knowledge will be embodied in some space, since that is how knowledge about how to behave is embodied. In the figure, it is called the *syllogism space*. At the top it is classified as a *task space*, to indicate that it is different from the skill spaces, being built up by the person right in the experimental situation, just after being asked to do the task. In contrast, the skill spaces have been under development for the entire lifetime of the person.

We should remember several things about figure 2.6. First, we have shown single spaces (just five of them), but each of these may lead to subspaces to perform subparts of the task, and on to further subspaces. There may be hundreds of spaces involved. Even the task space may implicate several other spaces, depending on how complicated the instructions and the task are. Second, spaces consist of collections of operators, along with the knowledge to control when they are used, individually or relative to each other. We have indicated this, conventionally, by the little circles and arrows in each space, where the circles are the situation being attended to and the arrows indicate that an operator changes the situation to some new one. There is a tree of operators, because often an operator is applied but does not lead where desired, so a back-up occurs. Thus, these spaces can often turn out to be search spaces. Third, all of the spaces with their operators are built up on the architecture of a recognition memory, with patterns-with-associations matching against a working memory, and with a decision mechanism controlling what spaces and operators occur. There is a lot of structure here in our little system, but there is a lot of structure in the human mind.

The entire structure of figures 2.5 and 2.6 should seem vaguely familiar to anyone with any contact with computers. The organization of a computer in terms of its hardware (its architecture) and its software corresponds directly to the architecture of our system and all the patterns-with-associations. Indeed, we described our major hypothesis, not only as 'the human is a symbol system', but as 'the computational view of mind' – the ground assumption of cognitive science. But there are good reasons why the architecture of our system is quite different from that of standard computers. Ours is fashioned to be the architecture of human cognition, as far as there is current evidence for it. There is no particular reason why current commercially driven computer technology should be the same at all.

However, these two types of computers are alike in deeper ways. They are both built to compute many different functions – many different relations between their inputs and their outputs. To say it in different words, they are both built to provide *flexible, contingent response.* Humans need a mind capable of extreme flexibility so they can shape their action to whatever is demanded by their goals in whatever environment they find themselves in. Commercial computers need to be capable of extreme flexibility so that users can program them to do whatever the users intend. This deep identity of function – extreme flexibility – leads both systems to have the same essential structure at an abstract level. It is this abstract structure that identifies the class of symbol systems.

One thing missing from our picture in figures 2.5 and 2.6 is how new information gets into recognition memory. We did not discuss any way of modifying the permanent knowledge. The tasks are very short and do not require operations in other than working memory. However, acquisition of new permanent knowledge is an essential feature of any symbolic system and we will come back to fill this void. First, we return to our specific symbol system and follow its story. It will soon enough lead back to the acquisition of knowledge.

How humans do these tasks

We emphasized early in the prior section that it was important to obtain an organization that had the functional capabilities to be intelligent, at least up to the demands of our task. The organization of figures 2.5 and 2.6 is still sketchy. They can plausibly be completed to perform our syllogism task – indeed, there are many ways to do so. Humans, of course, exhibit characteristic regularities when they perform syllogisms in the typical experimental situation, which our figure 2.4 approximates. A theory of human intelligence should perform syllogisms in just these ways. Here are some of the more important:

1 *Difficulty effect.* Syllogisms are difficult for people, even college students. For example, 20 collegiates did all 64 possible two-premise syllogisms, and only got 42 per cent correct over all. This is the basic effect that has seemed surprising to many – if humans are capable of reason, they should be able to perform syllogisms correctly, which are simple to state and simple to understand what is desired.
   (a) Syllogisms vary strongly in their difficulty for people. In the group of 20, some syllogisms were answered correctly by 100 per cent of the students, while others were answered correctly by none of the students.
   (b) People vary strongly in their ability to do syllogisms. In the group of 20, the worst person got 19 per cent correct and the best person got 59 per cent correct.
2 *Validity effect.* On the other hand, people do respond to the syllogistic task in an adaptive way. The 42 per cent average correct is to be compared with only 15 per cent correct that would have been obtained by chance (there are nine possible responses, with an average of 1.4 correct).
3 *Consistency effect.* The conclusions drawn from syllogisms are always (99 per cent) consistent with the premises.
4 *Atmosphere effect.* A famous effect is that somehow the *atmosphere* created by the premises influences the results that are obtained, even if not warranted. For instance, when an error occurs, if *some* and *not* occur in the premises, they show up preferentially in the conclusion.
5 *Figural effect.* The syllogism, *Some A are B* and *All B are C*, has two valid conclusions, *Some A are C* and *Some C are A* (indeed, whenever one of these two is valid so is the other). People mostly produce the first one (*Some A are C*) rather than the second.
6 *Premise elaboration effect.* If the premises are elaborated, then people will do better in syllogisms involving these premises. For example, fewer errors occur when *No A are B* is elaborated to *No A are B and no B are A*.

7 *Concreteness effect.* If syllogisms are expressed in concrete terms, such as *All barbers are doctors*, rather than in abstract terms, such as *All A are B*, then the syllogisms are easier.

8 *Belief bias effect.* If the conclusion of the syllogism is believed, it is more likely to be accepted as valid than if it is not believed. Since syllogisms are true only by virtue of their form (the way *all*, *not* and *some* occur), a conclusion can vary arbitrarily from what is empirically true or what a human might believe.

If our theory of intelligence is a theory of human intelligence, it should show these regularities, and indeed it does. We cannot go into the full story of how the theory fills out figures 2.5 and 2.6. Many details can be found in (Newell, 1990; Polk and Newell, 1988; Polk, Newell and Lewis, 1989), with the definitive treatment still coming up (Polk and Newell, 1992). We can describe some additional elements of the theory to make plausible how it conforms to human behaviour on syllogisms.

Task uses existing language skills. As figure 2.6 makes clear, the basic organization for doing the task is to deploy the human's existing skills. Because of the nature of the task (figure 2.4), these are language skills, namely, comprehending, reading (i.e., well-learned strategies for deploying comprehension), and constructing utterances. These serve the subject well. Without them the task would not even be approachable. But these skills are not attuned perfectly to the demands of doing syllogisms. Furthermore, they can be evoked by the subject, but they cannot be dynamically reshaped to the demands of the task within the confines of the experiment, which is very short. Skills do things their own way, so to speak, and it is up to the subject to try to accomplish the task as best possible with what these skills provide.

Comprehend produces a model, but guarantees neither necessity nor completeness. The process of comprehension produces models of particular possible situations. Once it is seen that the premises refer to people with various properties, then the models are like the pictures in our figures.[4] This view only admits expressing certain kinds of situations. In particular, it cannot represent what a premise implies that speaks of *all* barbers being doctors. Certainly all the barbers *in the situation* can be doctors, but these are only some of the barbers and doctors that might exist, even in this situation, for new things may be said later, e.g., in another premise.

Another feature of comprehension is that it provides information only about the topic of the sentence. *Some A are B* is comprehended as providing some knowledge about As. But it is not seen as providing knowledge about Bs, which it also does, namely, that *Some B are A*. Reading a premise delivers only part of the knowledge that the premise contains. Of course, the subject can obtain additional knowledge, but this requires encoding other premises (perhaps recalled from memory).

Construct utterance *inspects the model with respect to a topic, but takes what it gets.* For a selected topic, the construct space generates an utterance about that topic according to the knowledge in the model that is available to immediate inspection (i.e., can be matched by available patterns). The conclusions are generated from the available topics.

The task space generates conclusions and tests for acceptability, but only superficially. The task space is responsive to the demands of the task, having been constructed by the subject in response to the instructions for the task. The strategy of first reading (hence, comprehending) both premises, and then generating a conclusion (using construct) is knowledge in the task space. A condition of the task is that the conclusion should be between the two terms that are unique to each premise (A and C), and not the one common to both (B). This can be tested on candidate conclusions, and the task space does this, making the overall organization a form of generate and test. But there is no way to test for the condition that the conclusion *necessarily follows* from the premises. The subject simply does not do this, accepting whatever conclusion passes the unique-terms test.

The details of the above considerations are embodied in the operators of the spaces in figure 2.6 plus the knowledge about when to use these operators. These are all realized in the pattern-with-association architecture of figure 2.5. In short, there is an operational system that corresponds to this theory. This lets us test directly whether all the regularities that characterize human behaviour on the syllogism task are also characteristic of this theory, by running the system on all 64 possible syllogisms. And indeed, they are. It is too tedious to trace through why all of them hold. But some can be seen easily. Consider the consistency effect. Comprehension always creates models that are possible situations, hence, these situations are always consistent with the premises. Since the inspection process of construct utterance doesn't change anything, any conclusion built by this process remains consistent with the premises. Consider the premise-elaboration effect. Providing a premise of *No A are B and no B are A* instead of just *No A are B* compensates for the fact that comprehension only delivers knowledge about the topic by explicitly providing both topics, *A* and *B*, in the premise, rather than just one, *A*.

The most important effect, that of difficulty, is more complex. The model representation is inadequate to represent universally quantified situations (premises with *all* and *no*). Therefore, there is no way a system that simply uses this model representation can get all the syllogisms correct (although it can get about 75 per cent). This has led Johnson-Laird (1983) to posit that the fundamental reason for the difficulty of syllogisms is the model-based representation, and to posit further that humans build multiple models of alternative situations, which is one way to overcome the limitations of the representation. In fact, as with most complex processes, there are many places where errors can occur, not only the representation, which forces the encoding into particular possible situations, but also the default assumptions in **comprehend** that produce unwarranted models, and the failure to get all the knowledge in a premise because of the one-topic aspect of comprehension. Errors can also be caused in constructing conclusions through the selection of the topic. And, although subjects rarely do it (a few per cent), there can be a failure to apply the test for the unique terms, so subjects produce conclusions involving the common term *B*. The total difficulty effect is made up by contributions from all of these factors.

These general regularities capture much that is important about syllogistic reasoning. They provide a signature of human behaviour to certify that a theory of cognition that was both operational and operates in *this* particular way would be a theory of human cognition. But more is possible in the way of assessing how good a theory of human cognition is. A theory can be asked to predict the responses of individuals doing syllogistic reasoning, not just capture the general regularities. Individuals differ from each other

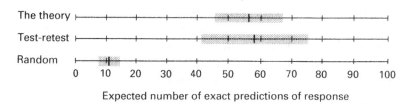

Figure 2.7 Evidence for predictions of individual differences by the theory.

on almost any task they are given. Predicting *individual differences* is a stringent test.

To predict individuals it is necessary to describe them in ways relevant to the task. As described, the theory seems to provide a single description of how humans reason about syllogisms, so it would predict all humans would behave the same. In fact, there are many dimensions along which the theory admits possible differences in syllogistic reasoning. These stem from the places where error can creep into the reasoning process – how the premises are encoded, how conservative the person is about making unwarranted assumptions, whether all the knowledge in the premises is extracted, whether there is persistence in seeking valid conclusions. The possibility of variability on these characteristics arises from the structure of our system – they are ways in which people *could* be different that would make a difference for how they did syllogistic reasoning. It is an empirical question whether individuals behave consistently in such ways, so that these become dimensions of individual differences.

Figure 2.7 shows that not only do individuals show consistency, but that our theory predicts it. The data is from 40 individuals, each of whom did all 64 syllogisms.[5] Each syllogism has nine possible responses: eight conclusions, *All A are C*, *Some A are C*, *No A are C* and *Some A are not C*, along with the same four with *A* and *C* reversed, and finally *no valid conclusion*. The figure shows the expected number of exact predictions made by each model. The top line shows our theory, with the expected number of hits (56 per cent) for the 40 subjects and the standard deviation of the prediction over this collection of subjects (10 per cent).[6]

The theory can be compared with various null models. At the

bottom of figure 2.7 is the *random model*, which simply guesses at random from the nine possible responses. This gives 11 per cent exact predictions on average (with a standard deviation of 3 per cent). The random model is a standard base line. In this case, its level of prediction is so low compared with the theory that it tells very little. A more useful null model is the *test-retest model*, where a subject is used to predict his or her own responses at a different time. One group of 20 subjects did the same experiment (all 64 syllogisms) twice, a week apart. The prediction accuracy of this null model is 58 per cent, with a standard deviation of 15 per cent. This number provides a rough upper bound for what can be predicted by any model that assumes subjects behave consistently over time, for it indicates the variability that exists within an individual. It is only an approximation, since the ideal (but un-attainable) test-retest situation would be the same subject doing the tasks twice at essentially the same time. The test-retest null model shows that the theory is close to being as good as it can be. In absolute terms, coming close to 60 per cent accuracy in a 1-in-9 situation represents impressive predictive power. We may take it as ample confirmation that our theory is a theory of human intelligent behaviour for this task.

Extending the theory to learning

A theory of human intelligence is not just a theory of syllogisms. What we have established is the core of such a theory – not, of course, because it is syllogisms, which after all is simply one task, but because the functions we laid out at the beginning are charac-teristic of human intelligence. The first priority in broadening the theory is to extend it to learning, since figures 2.5 and 2.6 dealt just with performance.

Humans learn continuously from experience without deliber-ation. There is an integrated arrangement of *when* to learn, *what* to learn and *how* to store it away for later retrieval. Our theory too has such an integrated arrangement. Doing syllogisms is not the best place to examine it, because syllogism experiments discourage learning by providing no feedback. A better exam-ple, closely associated with performing syllogisms, is how the

Recognition memory

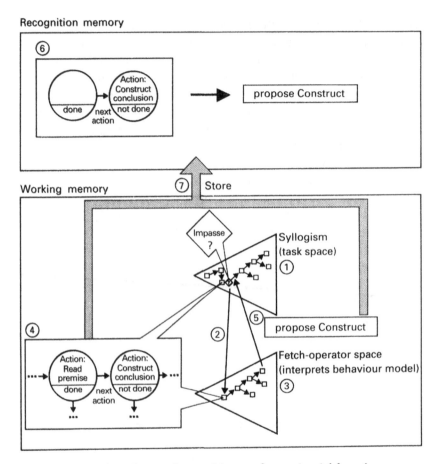

Figure 2.8   The when, what and how of experiential learning.

subject becomes organized to perform the task. How does the subject come to have the task space? It wasn't there, just before the experiment started. But immediately after being instructed, the subject performs according to our theory, although it is apparent the subject would not have performed the task before. Learning clearly occurs in the minute or two between receiving the instructions and attempting the first syllogism task. In terms of the architecture of figure 2.5, patterns-with-associations get created and added to the recognition memory. What needs to be shown is the when, what and how that lies behind these creations.

Figure 2.8 shows what happens in our theory (and system). It is a complex figure, but we will take it piece by piece. Right in the middle of the figure, labelled **1**, is something familiar, namely, the task space for syllogisms. The situation being described occurs after the subject has read the instructions and just as the first syllogism is engaged. The subject knows there is a task to do, so has constructed (learned) a task space. At the moment of the figure, however, the subject does not know how to proceed. Although he has read the instructions he has not assimilated (learned) what they mean. So the subject is at an *impasse* **2**, which is to say he cannot continue in the task space. What happens then is that a subgoal is created to be able to continue and a new problem space is selected in which to attain this task, called the *fetch-operator space* **3**. In this space, the working memory is searched for relevant information from the instructions. The subject has read and comprehended the instructions, in the sense of creating an internal model of their meaning – that the subject should take some action under certain circumstances, and take some other action under others, etc. At **4** there is one fragment of such a model of the subject's behaviour, namely, that if the actions of reading the premises are done, then the action should be taken of constructing the conclusion. To have comprehended the instructions – in terms of decoding the language – is not to have assimilated this information into the subject's own behaviour. This latter is what is going on in the figure. The search operator in the fetch-operator space finds this fragment as the one that fits into the situation where the impasse has occurred. Other operators of the fetch-operator space now interpret this behaviour model and propose (in the task space) that the construct-utterance operator **5** be applied. This resolves the impasse in the task space, so that the subject can now continue working in the task space.

So far, what has been described is simply a bit of performance – how the subject in the task space **1** doesn't know what to do, hence impasses **2**, sets a subgoal to resolve the impasse **3**, finds a relevant action in the comprehended instructions in working memory **4**, interprets that action as an internal operator it does know how to do **5** and thus proceeds.

This performance becomes the occasion for an act of learning. This entire episode establishes that, if the instructions say **4**, then the operator to construct-the-conclusion should be proposed. That is, a pattern-with-association can be formed, with the pattern being what will detect the bit of instructions in the behaviour model, and the association being to propose the construct operator. Building that pattern-with-association **6** and storing it away in recognition memory **7**, to be like all other patterns-with-associations, activating itself whenever it detects the appropriate situation, finally completes the act of learning. The system has converted a bit of experience into an augmentation of its permanent memory. This learning act is accomplished by the architecture itself, not by the subject deliberately executing some operator.

Figure 2.8 has exhibited the integrated arrangement for the elemental act of learning in our system. *When* learning occurs is whenever there is an impasse, that is, a lack of knowledge about how to proceed. *What* is learned is the knowledge that the problem solving produces to fill that lack, i.e. resolve that impasse and proceed. *How* it is learned is by building a new pattern-with-associations whose association is the new knowledge and whose pattern is the conditions under which that knowledge is appropriate to retrieve. The structure of the recognition memory, with its pattern-recognition powers, takes care of actually getting this knowledge retrieved when the appropriate circumstances arise. At the centre of learning sits an act of storing a new element in memory, namely a pattern-with-association. It is surrounded by an arrangement of when, what and how, that permits the learning to automatically capture each little fragment of functional experience – functional because the experience captured is how to behave appropriately in future circumstances based on current experience.

Figure 2.8 is the *elemental* act of learning. It is happening throughout behaviour. Impasses are occurring all the time, every second or two for humans, according to the theory. They occur whenever something is not immediately known, however tiny such a thing might be. Thus, the entire process of acquiring the instructions for the syllogism task occurs by a multitude of not-knowings, hence findings-out, hence addings of appropriate patterns-with-associations to memory. It may take doing several syllogisms and several rereadings of the instructions or parts of them before the appropriate ensemble of experiences occurs that leads the system (and the human) to assimilate the task of syllogisms completely.

This same learning occurs in all other behaviour of the system, the performance on syllogisms, as well as learning the instructions, and in any other tasks that the system might do. Thus, we have extended our theory from one that simply accounts for performance in a specific task to one that exhibits learning quite generally.

Extending the theory to comprehension

The extension that we just saw helps account for part of the structure of the system, namely the task space, which gets defined at experiment time in response to the instructions. We have left untouched the skill spaces, not just how they might arise, but the prior question of how they operate. A theory of human cognition must account for comprehension as much as it accounts for syllogistic reasoning.

The theory we have been gradually delineating can indeed cover language comprehension. The basic situation is that the words of the utterance arrive sequentially, one by one. As each word arrives, it conveys additional knowledge about what the utterance means. The knowledge that it conveys is conditional on the partial utterance heard so far. The knowledge it delivers is about all the possibilities for the rest of the utterance yet to come. Any language comprehension system must cope with this situation.

The structure of our theory is simply to apply an operator to each word as it arrives – a *comprehension operator*. Each operator comprises a set of patterns-with-associations that constitute exactly the knowledge required – the patterns being conditional on what has already arrived and leaving associated structures in working memory to be utilized by the comprehension operators of subsequent words, whatever they are. But this seems too easy – to have comprehension operators constructed in such a way that nothing more than recognition is required. That is indeed correct. Comprehension operators will not always know what to do. Then an impasse will occur, just as in figure 2.8, subgoals will be set up and subspaces entered to find the missing knowledge.

Figure 2.9 gives the set of problem spaces used in comprehending. At the top is the *comprehension space*, which contains the

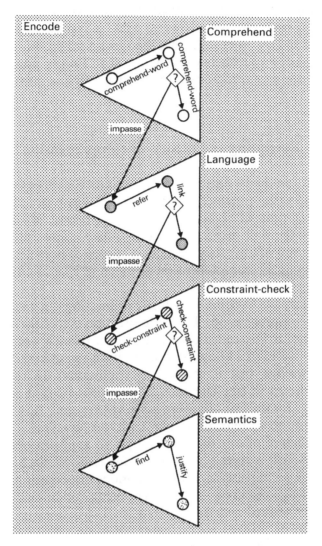

Figure 2.9 The process of language comprehension.

comprehension operators just discussed. If a comprehension operator does not immediately have the knowledge, then the system goes into a *language space*, in which a deliberate search can be made for the knowledge of language structure to comprehend the current situation. The operators of this space seek to link up the newly arrived word with the structure that has been built so far, where each word can be seen as playing a specific linguistic role.[7] Before the link operator can accept a way of linking in the current word to structure the incoming utterance, many constraints must be satisfied – grammatical, semantic and pragmatic. The link operator may simply know whether these constraints are satisfied or not, but again it may not. Then another impasse occurs, a subgoal is set up to find this knowledge, and the *constraint-check space* is entered. The operators of this space deliberately examine the knowledge built up so far, both the utterance structure and model of the situation. The information already explicit in working memory may be sufficient for the constraint-check operators to obtain an answer, but additional knowledge may be required (for instance, whether 'John' is the proper name of a man or a woman may be needed for pronoun gender agreement). Again there is an impasse, a subgoal is set to obtain the missing knowledge, and the *semantics space* is entered to find that knowledge. This space attempts to retrieve new knowledge from recognition memory. Other information gathering activities are possible, leading to other spaces, but this is essentially the end of the line.

Figure 2.9 shows an effective processing organization for comprehending language – for bringing the knowledge to bear to create a situation model of what the utterance is saying. Its structure reflects three main influences. First, the task structure of utterances is a sequence of words that arrive one at a time. Second, the nature of the language encoding, which must be unravelled. Third, the knowledge for decoding is not all immediately evocable by the surface characteristics of the utterance and must be ferreted out of permanent memory by problem solving. Thus, we have extended the theory of cognition one more step, to provide the same sort of organization for language comprehension that we did for syllogisms.

Figure 2.9 is analogous to figure 2.6. It describes a functionally adequate processing system.[8] Also, analogous to the situation for syllogisms, humans comprehend language in characteristic ways. A theory that explains human intelligence must predict not only that language can be comprehended (the functional question) but also that it happens in the way it does with humans. Again, our theory predicts aspects of human comprehension, although the number of such aspects that are known is legion – far more than for syllogisms. The theory currently deals only with a few major aspects.

Humans comprehend language in real time

This is a striking characteristic of human comprehension, when taken against the background of our understanding of computational schemes for parsing language.[9] Humans comprehend a sentence within a second of having heard the final word, often less. The time complexity of most parsing systems precludes this, and this fact has been used to draw strong conclusions for the kinds of comprehension schemes that can and cannot be used by humans.

The scheme of figure 2.9 comprehends language in real time. The organization of comprehension operators yields real-time operation by its design. If each comprehension operator has all the knowledge it needs, then to comprehend a sentence of N words would take N comprehension operators – which is the essence of real-time processing. The glitch is that comprehension operators aren't perfect and, when they impasse, they throw the system in an open problem-solving mode of behaviour involving all the lower spaces. However, learning operates to make comprehension operators ever more perfect – ever more purely recognitional, with all the knowledge encoded in directly available patterns-with-associations. As discussed in the previous section, learning occurs whenever there is an impasse. Whenever a comprehension operator doesn't have the knowledge, there will be a bit of learning. That learning creates patterns-with-associations to provide by immediate recognition the same knowledge that the problem solving provided. The problem solving in the lower spaces of figure 2.9 gets captured by the act of learning. The learning moves the comprehension operator that impassed one step closer to being complete. But learning occurs on every impasse, so that the process of using language is also a process of moving the language toward real-time comprehension.

Some stray ends need attention. First, language is capable of indefinite novelty. Comprehension operators are never actually complete. Comprehension develops an equilibrium in which some

fraction of the comprehension operators impasse on any particular occasion, the rest being able to operate recognitionally. What
counts for real-time comprehension is whether this fraction stays
small enough most of the time. Second, although our presentation of learning didn't discuss it, patterns-with-associations, once
created, can apply in situations other than those in which they
were created – there is transfer of learning to other situations. The
learning that occurs for comprehension operators covers more
than just the exact case in which it was created. This doesn't
change the fact that there will always be some comprehension
operators which run into an impasse, but it does influence the size
of the fraction, which is the important thing. Third, learning
occurs everywhere as a function of all experience. It occurs for all
the lower spaces in figure 2.9, not just the comprehension operators. These lower problem-solving parts of the comprehension
process get faster as well. This does not change the fraction of
impasses that occur, but it does diminish the fraction of time
problem solving takes.

In sum, the theory provides a major hypothesis for how humans
attain real-time comprehension. Further, this hypothesis arises
naturally from the total structure of the theory.

Humans comprehend ambiguous utterances in real time

This is a more focused statement about human language comprehension than just real-time comprehension. Sentences, such as
the following, are ambiguous: 'I saw the man on the hill with the
telescope.' The question is whether 'with' refers to the man or the
hill or the seeing. Utterances contain a lot of ambiguity, and to
consider all possibilities would require combinatorial time. Humans do not take appreciable additional time. Neither does our
theory (and system). The theory does this by committing to a
single path, whenever there is an ambiguous choice point. In terms
of figure 2.9 if there are two possible ways in the language space
to link the new word into the existing structure, after all available
knowledge has been brought to bear from the constraint-check
and semantic spaces, then an arbitrary choice is made and only
one link is put in place. Many detailed studies confirm that humans also solve the ambiguous-utterance problem by committing

to likely paths, so that the theory is positing the same internal processes as the human is using.

Humans sometimes recover from committing to the wrong path

Commitment, of course, opens the way for error, even while salvaging the processing of utterances in real time. Humans sometimes are able to recover. Consider the sentence: 'I saw the man on the hill with the telescope at its top.' Humans usually take the man as having the telescope, so at the point of ambiguity ('with') it is assigned to man. The trailing 'at its top' shows that 'with the telescope' actually refers to the hill. Humans are able to comprehend this sentence without difficulty, permitting the inference that they must somehow have recovered from taking the wrong path and reassigned 'with' to modify 'hill'.

But humans cannot always recover (if they could they would have found a way to beat the combinatorial explosion). A classical case is: 'The horse raced past the barn fell.' This is called a *garden path* sentence, because it leads the hearer down a garden path. Humans almost always stumble when they arrive at 'fell'. Sometimes they cannot see that the sentence is perfectly grammatical, meaning the same thing as: 'The horse that was raced past the barn fell down.'

The theory (and system) exhibits the same behaviour, both successful recovery and unsuccessful recovery. It has a mechanism for recovery, in which a link, which gets set wrong, can be repaired and relinked in a different way. This repair works only in some circumstances, basically where the knowledge that reveals the error arrives while the right structures are still around. When this fails to happen, as in the horse and barn above, then no recovery is possible. The limitations on the repair mechanisms are related to its having to happen, like its counterpart in humans, in real time, i.e. so that, when successful, comprehension continues to flow smoothly along with the utterance.

We have now described the comprehension skill space and shown it to be basically the same general shape as human language comprehension. There are many other aspects in which human comprehension shows itself. The theory itself is not developed to the place where we know it exhibits these other aspects or, contrariwise, that the theory has gone off course. Moreover, we have not shown how knowledge of language is acquired – the analogue of building up the task space from the instructions. For skill spaces, such as comprehension, this starts very early in life and builds up over years of varied experience. All we have shown is how, once the knowledge is acquired, the mechanism of real-time comprehension gets built up.

The broader view

It is time to reflect. We sought to approach human intelligence through science – through starting with some phenomena of human intelligence, formulating a theory and showing how that theory explained them. Our starting point was adventitious – despite Aristotle, no good argument can be made for syllogistic reasoning as an especially fundamental arena of human intellectual endeavour. On the other hand, it was quite apparent that the functions required for humans to do syllogisms were very general, and a good theory for this form of human intellectual activity would already penetrate significantly into the nature of human intelligence in general.

The Soar theory and system

We told the story mostly as a reconstruction of how one approaches the task of obtaining a scientific theory. In fact, we were describing an existing theory, the Soar theory (Newell, 1990; Lewis et al., 1990), but doing so in a way that not only its structure emerged, but also the relation of this structure to human intelligence. Soar is an effort to put together a unified theory of cognition – a single set of mechanisms to explain all of cognition.[10] The story we told is true to the actual Soar theory. Just as in our story, the Soar theory is centrally a theory of the architecture of human cognition. It asserts that human memory is composed of an immense number of patterns-with-associations, that subgoals are formed automatically from impasses, that learning is a continuous process of packaging experience in functionally useful new patterns-with-associations, etc. Just as in our story, the Soar theory is realized as an operational (simulation) system. In part, this is because (as in the story) only an operational system can demonstrate intelligence, hence predict it of humans. Just as in our story, the Soar theory not only exhibits the appropriate intelligent functions, it also does so in the same way that humans do – it is indeed a theory of *human* intelligence.

In terms of the Soar theory, our story stops short in one crucial way, namely, the breadth of the theory. The ambition of a unified theory is to cover all of cognition. We attempted to indicate this by showing how the theory applied to the syllogism task, to taking instructions, and to language comprehension. This hints at breadth – one does not often find three such disparate tasks all within a single theory. Cognition today is populated almost entirely by theories of single domains, such as a theory of syllogisms or a theory of language comprehension. But the Soar theory has been applied to many domains: problem solving, immediate responses to presented stimuli (so called chronometric experiments), the effects of long practice, strategy change in problem solving, the development of number conservation, the performance of routine cognitive skills, the acquisition of names and rapid interaction with a changing environment (such as a video game). Describing the extension of Soar to these tasks would, in many ways, have been like what we described for language comprehension. There are a collection of spaces for each task, which hold the knowledge (i.e. the competence) that the system has about the task, continuous learning from experience causes a flow of knowledge between these spaces that changes the way the task is performed in characteristic ways; and the existence of these spaces raises additional issues of how they came into being.

The contribution of cognitive science

That the story of the scientific approach to intelligence has been told through a single theory, Soar, does not imply that Soar stands alone. Soar should be seen as representing the efforts of *cognitive science*. This is an interdisciplinary field, whose main contributory fields are AI, cognitive psychology and linguistics.[11] Each of these fields is characterized by its own approach to the nature of intelligence. They are bound together by two things. First, they all subscribe to a scientific approach to intelligence. Their diversity can easily be traced to the aspects of the total phenomena they have chosen to tackle, which place different demands and offer different opportunities. Second, they all subscribe to the view that the functional mind is computational in nature. The parts of psychology and linguistics that remain outside of cognitive science are largely those areas for which the assumptions about the computational nature of mind are irrelevant or alternative views exist that reject this assumption. In terms of Soar, cognitive science has provided the ingredients out of which Soar is built, and these are everywhere evident throughout our story.

AI has explored the mechanisms for intelligent action. It established the point of view, evident throughout the paper, that functional capability is an essential characteristic of intelligence, which can only be demonstrated by having operational systems that exhibit the requisite intelligence. Most of the mechanisms that make up Soar came out of AI – for problem solving and planning, for language processing, for the role of large bodies of knowledge coded in pattern-association form, for learning and induction.

Cognitive psychology has accumulated an amazing array of regularities about human cognition. We have listed a number of these for syllogisms, and a few for language comprehension. These have only scratched the surface of what exists. There are thousands of such regularities, many are quantitative, many are parametric laws that show how one thing (say the number of items held in working memory) varies against something else (the time taken to search them).

Cognitive psychology has also developed many theories to explain these regularities. The theory that humans represent situations by models (as opposed to collections of propositions) has played a major role in theories of syllogistic reasoning (Johnson-Laird, 1983). There are currently a plethora of theories about how humans do real-time comprehension (Altmann, 1990). These particular theories are all versions of how information is processed. Often they converge on what appears to be the essentially correct discovery of the mechanisms that are dominant in the specific regularity. Soar, as an attempt at unification, incorporates many of these theories, as can be seen in the use of models in syllogisms.

But Soar also embeds all of these in a uniform theory, so the mechanisms used at one place are also used at another. The same learning mechanism is used to attain real-time language comprehension and to acquire instructions.

Linguistics has focused mostly on the structure of language, and has described it in formal schemes, e.g. for phonology and syntax. These all have the flavour of grammar-like formalisms, i.e. sets of rules whose successive application generates a structure that is predicted to be (say) a possible sentence. Language exhibits so much structure that this activity has proceeded largely autonomously. But the area called *psycholinguistics* asks all the questions of cognitive psychology but with language as the domain. The mechanisms in Soar concerning language are saturated with the results of linguistics and psycholinguistics. Though we did not do so in our story, the utterance analysis mechanisms can be related to other grammar schemes. The examples of prepositional attachment (what is the telescope with?) and the garden-path sentence are straight out of linguistics. Soar puts both cognition (syllogisms) and linguistics (comprehension) together in one theory and attempts to merge them.

The role of symbol systems

Cognitive science's central tenet is the computational view of mind. But computation is essentially the behaviour of symbol systems. This makes symbol systems central to cognitive science. However, this understates the role of symbol systems considerably. Symbol systems underlie all digital-computer technology. More correctly put, digital technology is used almost entirely to build symbol systems, namely, the digital computers so familiar to us. The amazing diversity of modern computers – word processing, data bases, graphics, animation, scientific computing, business computing, computer networks and on and on – arises because modern digital computers are symbol systems.

Most generally, symbol systems provide the ability to process a representational medium in completely flexible ways. This is usually said more mathematically as providing arbitrary functions from input to output, but it all comes to the same thing. Symbol systems obtain that flexibility, because the functions of the system are not built into its structure, but are specified by programs (our patterns-with-associations). Symbol systems permit the construction of new functions, i.e. new programs, because the programs can be the outputs of other programs (our learning).

It is easy to see why symbol systems are the foundation stone, both of computing and of human intelligence. Computers must be systems that can do any kind of information processing that its users wish to do. Analogously, humans must be capable of adaptive response to their environments, which is to say, be flexible in their responses as a function of the demands of their situation. All organisms have this requirement (more correctly, organisms are those systems that have evolved to be adaptive). Most organisms are quite limited in their adaptive capabilities, even though these play important roles in their lives. Humans, on the other hand, appear to have become unlimited in their flexibility – the diversity of ways humans operate adaptively is immense beyond description. This implies that a symbol system forms the basic technology out of which human intelligence is built.

The approach through symbols can be seen as taking its starting point for a theory of human intelligence to be the purely functional capability for extreme flexibility, and then via the basic results of computer science, being able to convert that capability to the requirement that the human system for intelligence have the structure of a symbol system. This provides sufficient constraint that, under the impact of task demands and data on human performance, theories of human intelligence emerge.

The role of the scientific approach

Let us come back finally to our story being about the approach of science in the realm of intelligence. In many areas of life the approach of science is automatic, no others are considered. But in human affairs, broadly taken, this is not yet so – in politics, education and religion. So it is with intelligence, where philosophy, literature and the other humanities all take the nature of humans as central and with that the nature of the human mind, including its functional aspect.

The choice to approach the nature of intelligence by science carries with it particular ways of operating. Most important perhaps, nothing special accrues to the fact that the phenomenon is that of intelligence. Sciences must respect their subject matter, of course, but all natural phenomena are seen as yielding to the cycle of observation, measurement, experiment, theory, prediction and analysis. Human intelligence is seen as a natural phenomenon made manifest in the behaviour evoked by doing tasks and other goal-oriented activities. The primary peculiarity of the domain, namely, that intelligence is a functional characteristic of humans that must be predicted and demonstrated by operational systems that embody the theories, lends the field a distinct flavour, but causes no ripple on the scientific character of the enterprise.

Two final remarks. First, all science builds on the accumulated prior work of earlier scientists. The way we told our story made it difficult to tell how various aspects of Soar have their roots in prior work, but in fact these roots go back three decades. Second, science, even more than politics, is the art of the possible. One does not attempt scientific problems before their time. For instance, nothing exists in the Soar theory that corresponds to *consciousness*, as that term refers to phenomenal subjective self-awareness. There are mechanisms in Soar that focus attention on parts of a situation or let Soar report what it knows. None of these seems close to answering to what consciousness should be. No one doubts that understanding the nature of consciousness is central to understanding the nature of mind, and possibly equally central to understanding intelligence. But the time is not yet.[12] In part, the art of science lies in guessing what is just barely attainable at a given point in history and placing bets accordingly. Few will bet with you, but if success is attained, then science moves forward. For Soar, the bet is not that some single new phenomenon, such as consciousness, might yield to new investigation. Rather, the bet is that unified theories can now be constructed that effectively bind together all of cognitive science.

Acknowledgements

We would like to acknowledge the entire Soar research community, which has provided the environment in which the ideas about Soar as a theory of cognition have and continue to mature. We especially acknowledge Jill Lehman and Rick Lewis, whose work on comprehension has been an important part of our story.

Notes

1 It may take intelligence to apply a theory – only some of us have learned quantum mechanics to where we can actually apply it – nevertheless, the intelligence to apply the theory is not the theory itself.

2 Often called a physical symbol system to differentiate it from other conceptions that arise in other approaches.

3 Connectionism, an important effort within cognitive science, is clearly computational. But it sometimes takes the view that connectionist systems are not instances of symbol systems. The issue is actually important, but need not divert us from generally identifying the computational theory of mind with symbol systems.

4 In fact, this is not the only possibility. The premises could be seen as referring to sets of people – the set of doctors, the set of bakers and doctors, etc. This would lead to very different reasonings. But the set-view is not at all a normal view for typical humans to take. It is almost a technical view.

5 The data was graciously made available to us by Philip Johnson-Laird, from several experiments by him and his colleagues.

6 In assessing the model, there is the standard problem of degrees of freedom from the parameters. If we use all 64 tasks to estimate the 17 parameters of the theory, then the data is overpredicted. Instead, we use part of the data (18 tasks) to set the parameters and the remainder of the tasks (46 tasks) to assess the fit.

7 This process is analogous to grammatical parsing, except that the system is comprehending the utterance, not just parsing it.

8 Language is immensely complex – enough to have an entire science, linguistics, devoted to the discovery of its structure. There is no way that the current scheme can be seen as adequate to this structure. It remains an open question whether it is, although much can be determined by analyzing the nature of the analyses that this scheme produces in the light of what other grammatical schemes do, and the scheme has exhibited competence over a modest diversity of sentences (Lehman, Lewis and Newell, 1991).

9 Again, more work has been done on parsing, rather than on comprehending language, so much of what is known of the computational complexity of language comes from the study of parsing.

10   And perception and motor behaviour as well, but it would require going too far afield to include these here (Newell, 1990) and in fact cognition is central to Soar.

11   Parts of philosophy and anthropology also contribute to cognitive science, as well as a substantial boundary area of neuroscience, now called cognitive neuroscience.

12   There need not be agreement on when a time is right. There is an increasing amount of activity in cognitive science on the topic of consciousness (Dennett, 1991).

References

Altmann, G. T. M. (ed.) 1990: *Cognitive Models of Speech Processing: Psycholinguistic and computational perspectives.* Cambridge, MA: MIT Press.

Dennett, D. 1991: *Consciousness Explained.* Boston, MA: Little, Brown.

Johnson-Laird, P. N. 1983: *Mental models: Towards a cognitive science of language, inference, and consciousness.* Cambridge, MA: Harvard University Press.

Lehman, J. F., Lewis, R. L. and Newell, A. 1991: *Natural Language Comprehension in Soar: Spring 1991* (Tech. Rep.) CMU-CS-91-117. School of Computer Science, Carnegie Mellon University.

Lewis, R., Huffman, S., John, B., Laird, J., Lehman, J. F., Newell, A., Rosenbloom, P., Simon, T., and Tessler, S. July 1990: Soar as a Unified Theory of Cognition: Spring 1990. *Proceedings of the Cognitive Science Twelfth Annual Conference.* Cognitive Science Society.

Newell, A. 1990: *Unified Theories of Cognition.* Cambridge, MA: Harvard University Press.

Polk, T. A., and Newell, A. August 1988: Modeling human syllogistic reasoning in Soar. *Proceedings Cognitive Science Tenth Annual Conference, 1988.* Cognitive Science Society.

Polk, T. A., and Newell, A. 1992: *Categorical syllogisms.* Forthcoming.

Polk, T. A., Newell, A., and Lewis, R. L. August 1989: Toward a unified theory of immediate reasoning in Soar. *Proceedings Cognitive Science Eleventh Annual Conference, 1989.* Cognitive Science Society.

3

Sub-Symbolic Modelling of Hand-Eye Co-ordination

Dana H. Ballard

Introduction

This chapter is about thinking about thinking in terms of levels of abstraction. We are very comfortable with having to deal with many different levels of abstraction in biological systems. Churchland and Sejnowski (1988) identify seven different levels used in the study of the brain in computational neuroscience: the central nervous system itself, different subsystems within that organization, cortical maps, networks of neurons within cortical maps, individual neurons, synapses of neurons and molecules used in synaptic control. The reason for using this organization is largely due to the sheer complexity of the organization of the brain. The belief is that it can be best understood as a collection of simpler systems at different levels of abstraction. In computer science, we are also accustomed to the same meta-modelling principle. The abstraction hierarchy for a computer system consists of: applications software, the operating system, assembly language, microcode, adders and memory registers, gates, pnp junctions and finally[1] doped silicon. However, in our models of human intelligence, we have not been able to appreciate the need for such an abstraction hierarchy. One reason may have been that the early work in the field has been dominated by tenets of artificial intelligence. One of the most important of these is that intelligence can be described in purely computational terms without recourse to any particular embodiment. From this perspective, the special features of the human body and its particular ways of interacting in the world have been seen as secondary to the fundamental

PICKUP(x)
  P: CLEAR(x) ∧ ONTABLE(x) ∧ ARMEMPTY
  D: ONTABLE(x) ∧ ARMEMPTY
  A: HOLDING(x)

STACK(x,y)
  P: CLEAR(y) ∧ HOLDING(x)
  D: CLEAR(y) ∧ HOLDING(x)
  A: ARMEMPTY ∧ ON(x,y)

PUTDOWN(x)
  P: HOLDING(x)
  D: HOLDING(x)
  A: ONTABLE(x) ∧ ARMEMPTY

UNSTACK(x,y)
  P: ON(x,y) ∧ CLEAR(x) ∧ ARMEMPTY
  D: ON(x,y) ∧ ARMEMPTY
  A: HOLDING(x) ∧ CLEAR(y)

Figure 3.1 A model of actions used by STRIPS, one of the most successful planning systems. In this model, the effects of actions have to be explicitly accounted for and there is no possibility of probabilistic actions. P: preconditions for action. D: predicates to be Detached. A: predicates to be added.

problems of intelligence. But when the embodiment is missing, so is the motivation for organizing it hierarchically.

In contrast to the disembodied viewpoint, our central thesis is that intelligence has to relate to interactions with the physical world, and that means that the particular form of the human body is an important constraint in delimiting the aspects of intelligent behaviour. These two views need not be at odds with each other if we see them as described at different levels of abstraction. Our central thesis is that the best model for incorporating the constraints of the human body is best framed at a level of abstraction below that traditionally used by artificial intelligence. We term this level the *sub-symbolic* level, borrowing a term used by Smolensky (1988).[2] At the sub-symbolic level, we are particularly interested in how the constraints of the physical system interact with cognition. For example, the focus of this paper is to study how the movements of the eyes interact with the coordination of the hand in problem-solving tasks. Our purpose is to show that this is not just a routine engineering endeavour but that many important features of cognition can be traced to constraints that act at this level of abstraction.

In order to understand the sub-symbolic level better, we need to develop important features of the symbolic approach. The foundation of the symbolic level is logical reasoning[3] (Genesereth and Nilsson, 1987). Thinking is modelled as logical deduction. When one reasons about the effects of actions in the world, there must be some formal account of what actions do in a logical format. Figure 3.1 shows the notation used by the most well-known of the formal systems, which goes by the acronym STRIPS, which has been extensively used to model the solution of simple block manipulation tasks. In this notation, the effects of actions are explicitly accounted for in three ways: (a) the preconditions that must be true for the action to be applicable, (b) the predicates that are to be deleted as a result of the action, and (c) the predicates that are to be added as a result of the action.

The strong point of this notation is that its generality allows arbitrary behaviour. It is 'easy' to model effects of generalization and analogies, etc. – easy in the sense that the language is express-ive. It is harder, however, to capture the uncertain effects of inter-acting in the world. There is no way of modelling actions that have uncertain outcomes. This is important as the world has a myriad of effects. If they cannot be modelled then there is no way of knowing if the simulated world is a good model for the current one.

One way to improve upon this difficulty is to adopt a model of interaction with the world that includes a much richer description of just these details. Thus, in contrast to the symbolic approach, we have been investigating models that explicitly incorporate the observed electro-mechanical systems of humans. The advantage is that we can capture aspects of behaviour that are hard to model at the symbolic level. The disadvantages are that effects that are easy in the previous sense are much more difficult to model at this level and in fact one may need an integrated system in order to understand human behaviour in any complete sense.

We will develop the viewpoint of the sub-symbolic level in three directions. First, experiments with the human visual system hint that there is a level of organization in cognition that is below conscious experience. Second, our experiments in modelling this level make some revealing suggestions about cognitive organization that challenge conventional wisdom at the symbolic level. And third and finally, we will briefly look at our own experiments in hand-eye co-ordination aimed at verifying suggestions made in the modelling work.

Structural features of human visually-guided co-ordination

To appreciate the need for a sub-symbolic approach, let us exam-ine the structure and function of eye movements in the human visual system. Our goal will be to suggest that the mechanical processing is so different from our conscious visual experience that very different models are needed for each of these two levels. Of course it could be that this peculiarity is just true for vision and by extension the sensory 'modules' as suggested by Fodor (1983). However, we will argue subsequently, in discussions of models of visuo-motor learning, that a sub-symbolic level exists for cognitive processing as well.

The human eye is distinguished from current electronic cameras by virtue of having much better resolution in a small region near the optical axis. This region is termed the fovea, and has a diameter approximately one to two degrees of visual angle. Over this region the resolution is better by an order of magnitude than that in the periphery. One feature of this design is the simultaneous representation of a large field of view and local high acuity. Figure 3.2 from a study by Sandini and Tagliasco (1980) shows graphically the kind of gains that can be achieved.

Figure 3.2 visually understates the situation for the human system, where the fovea is less than .01 per cent of the visual field area! With the small fovea at a premium in a large visual field, it is not surprising that the human visual system has special behaviours (saccades) for quickly moving the fovea to different spatial targets (Newell, 1982). The first systematic study of saccadic eye movements in the context of behaviour was done by Yarbus (1967). Subjects were given specific tasks pertaining to a familiar picture. The picture showed a room with various people in it, and a visitor entering. Subjects attempted (a) to give the ages of the people, (b) to surmise what they had been doing before the arrival of the 'unexpected visitor,' (c) to remember the position of the people and objects in the room. The traces of the eye-movements showed what has been confirmed by several other studies: subjects use scanning patterns that are highly sensitive to the particular task at hand (Noton, 1970; Noton and Stark, 1971a; 1971b).

Of the traces in this study, the last was most remarkable, since it was so similar to the task of many computer vision programs. In many popular accounts of vision, this job is assumed to be its major goal. But is this the case? We conjecture that since the eye movement traces show a specialized signature for this task as well, it is *not* done routinely. Instead, the overall impression of these

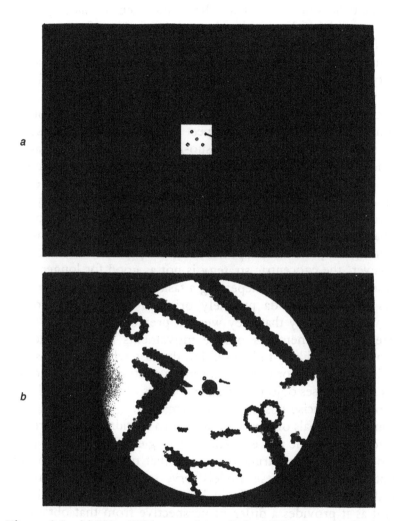

Figure 3.2 (a) 700 × 700 image taken of a backlighted scene of industrial parts. At the given resolution, the field of view is very small. (b) The same number of samples using a logarithmic decrease in resolution from the optical axis. A dramatic increase in field of view is achieved at the price of peripheral resolution (Sandini and Tagliasco, 1980).

traces was that the visual system is used to subserve problem-solving behaviours and such behaviours often do *not* require an accurate model of the world in the traditional sense of remembering positions of people and objects in a room.

Answering questions about a two-dimensional picture is a special type of behaviour, but our thesis is that one may be able to get by with reduced representations for all kinds of behaviours. A ubiquitous behaviour that we are studying is visuo-motor co-ordination, particularly with respect to the amount of representation required. Strategies for visuo-motor co-ordination can be divided into two broad classes according to the co-ordinate systems used: egocentric and exocentric. Egocentric co-ordinate systems are good for ballistic movements to targets that are acquired and remembered in the short term. Once the position of an object in space is encoded egocentrically it can be accessed quickly again, assuming its position is updated with respect to body motion. However, the egocentric strategy is not as good for longer-term memory requirements. Repeating a task on a different day rarely finds the manipulanda precisely oriented with respect to the behaver in the way that they were in previous attempts. Thus a strategy that remembers precise movements in egocentric co-ordinates is not likely to be useful in the case when body position is being changed. For this an exocentric strategy seems attractive. This strategy uses object-centred encodings of the world and does not rely on precise positioning information.

One of the goals of our laboratory is to elucidate the differences between egocentric and exocentric strategies. Our research paradigm is to build constructive models that use anthropomorphic robotic hardware. These models serve to delimit the computational requirements of different hypotheses. This information is useful as it provides a different perspective from that obtainable from animal experiments. Also it can be extremely helpful in the design of animal experiments. The laboratory currently consists of a mechanical 'head', 'body' and 'hand' (figure 3.3). The head contains two CCD cameras with approximately 400×400 pixels of spatial resolution each. These are driven independently in the yaw direction and are mechanically coupled so that they have a common pitch movement. The motors that drive them are geared to achieve a top speed of approximately 400 degrees per

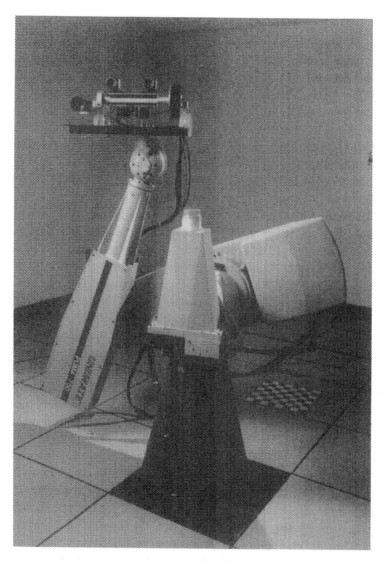

Figure 3.3 The University of Rochester's anthropomorphic vision system. The 'robot head' has three motors and two CCD high-resolution television cameras providing input to a MaxVideo® image-processing system. One motor controls pitch of the two-eye platform, and separate motors control each camera's yaw. The motors have a resolution of 2500 positions per revolution and a maximum speed of 400°/second. The robot arm has a workspace consisting of most of the volume of a sphere, with a two-metre radius, and a top speed of about one metre/second.

second. This design is sufficiently anthropomorphic so as to be an extremely good platform for studying computational problems of the human visual system (Brown et al., 1988). At the moment there are many differences from a reasonable human model, but the performance is sufficiently good to allow us to explore vision while fixating in real time. Grasping capability is provided by an ASI dextrous robot hand. This hand has three fingers and an opposable thumb, each with four degrees of motion. The control system incorporates passive compliance, which makes it a particularly good model for primate hands.

The main results of the laboratory so far show how an animal system that can fixate an environmental point can use a frame of reference centred at that point and that the calculations of early vision are greatly simplified given this ability (Ballard, 1989; Ballard and Ozcandarli, 1988; Olson and Potter, 1988; Rimey and Brown, 1990; Wixson and Ballard, 1989). Note that this is a very different assertion from that of Marr (1982), who emphasized that vision calculations were initially in viewer-centred co-ordinates. Instead, we assert that the calculations are more correctly represented as being in the co-ordinates of the frame of fixation. As shown in figure 3.4, the fixation frame is viewer-oriented, but not viewer-centred. The origin of this frame is at the point of intersection of the two optical axes. To orient this frame one axis can be parallel to the line joining the two camera centres; the other can be chosen as the optical axis of the dominant eye.

The fixation frame allows for closed loop behavioural strategies that do not require very precise three-dimensional information. For example, in grasping an object, we can first look at the object and then direct the hand to the centre of the retinal co-ordinate system. In depth the hand can be servoed relative to the plane of fixation. Informally, we refer to this behaviour as a 'do-it-where-I'm-looking' strategy, but more technically this will be referred to as a *deictic strategy* after Agre and Chapman (1987).[4] The deictic strategy of using the perceptual system to actively control the point of action in the world has precisely the right kind of invariance for a large amount of behaviours. This is particularly important as it allows these behaviours to be more easily learned over many repeated trials.

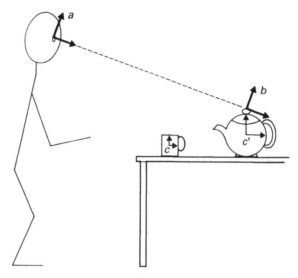

Figure 3.4 Much previous work in computational vision has assumed that the vision system is passive and computations are performed in a viewer-centred frame (A). Instead, biological and psychophysical data argue for a world-centred frame (B). This frame is selected by the observer to suit information-gathering goals and is centred at the fixation point. The task of the observer is to relate information in the fixation point frame to object-centred frames (C).

Moving the fixation frame

Deictic strategies depend critically on mechanisms for moving the eyes. One obvious value of the gaze changes arises from the fact that the spatial resolution of the retina is not homogeneous. Visual mechanisms for changing gaze are far less obvious, and although there are obvious alerting mechanisms that use motion, no compelling account of gaze change in visual problem solving has so far been found although our learning studies in the subsequent section will suggest that the change of gaze is very problem dependent, and not a general strategy for obtaining high-resolution imagery. This is very much in agreement with measurements of the human visual system dating from Yarbus (1967). Human eye movements are extremely problem dependent and operate at

Table 3.1 The biological organization of cortex into WHAT/WHERE modules may have a basis in computational complexity. Trying to match a large number of image segments to a large number of models at once may be too difficult.

| | | Models | |
		One	**Many**
Image Parts	**One**	**Manipulation**: trying to do something with an object whose identity and location are known	**Identification**: trying to identify an object whose location can be fixated
	Many	**Location**: trying to find a known object in a wide field of view	Too hard??

the rate of about three per second during concentrated problem-solving activity, such as answering questions about pictures.

One way to interpret the need for sequential, problem-dependent eye movements is as a suggestion that the general problem of associating many models to many parts of the image simultaneously is too hard. In order to make it computationally tractable within a single fixation, it has to be simplified, either into one of location (one internal model) or into one of identification (one world object). More loosely, one can either find 'the-thing-I'm-thinking-about' or extract properties of 'the-thing-I'm-looking-at'. Table 3.1 summarizes this view: a visual task can be solved by partitioning the task into two different kinds of visual subtasks.[5] We model the visual organization more crudely into a centre and a surround. The centre is 'where-I'm-looking' and the surround is a source of new gaze points. A location task is to find the image co-ordinates of a single model in the presence of many alternatives. In this task the image periphery must be searched. One can assume that the model has been chosen a priori. An identification task is to associate the foveated part of the image with one of many possible models. In this task one can assume that the location of the material to be established is at the fixation point.

The simplifications in table 3.1 constitute a broad strategy for research, as there will be many ways to exploit them. However, as a concrete example, let us consider the problem of changing gaze to fixate a specific object. One difficulty is that it is unreasonable to assume that the location of the object is known precisely, at least on the initial gaze change. Another is that whatever visual mechanism is posited must require only very low spatial resolution, since just prior to the gaze change, the target object is typically at the periphery of the visual field.

One feature that works under these circumstances is colour. Colour has been neglected recently as a useful cue, although it was used in earlier work (Feldman and Yakimovsky, 1974; Garvey 1976; Beveridge et al., 1989). One reason for this neglect may have been the lack of good algorithms for colour constancy. Recently, however, there has been great progress in correcting for both the chromaticity of the illuminant (Maloney and Wandell, 1986; Rubner and Schulten, 1989) and for geometric effects such as specularity (Klinker et al., 1988). Another reason that colour may not have been so successful is that it has been associated with a Mondrian-like view: one colour per object. But many objects are multicoloured, and this fact can prove very useful, as will be shown in the next section. A third reason for the neglect of colour may be that it is not intrinsically related to the object's identity in the way that other cues, e.g. form, are. This view is well represented by Biederman (1985):

> Surface characteristics such as colour and texture will typically have only secondary roles in primal access . . . we may know that a chair has a particular colour and texture simultaneously with its volumetric description, but it is only the volumetric description that provides efficient access to the representation of CHAIR.

but it is easily challenged. There are many examples from nature where colour is used by animals and plants to send clear messages of enticement or warning. The manufacturing sector uses colour extensively in packaging to market goods (e.g. Kodak). Animate vision systems can also use representations that are heavily *personalized* to achieve efficient behaviours, and colour is an important feature for such representations. For example, it may not be helpful to model coffee cups as being red and white, but *mine* is, and that colour combination is very useful in locating it. Another obvious example is commercial food packaging. We can readily describe the colour of food packages for the kind of eggs and milk we buy even though these colours do not generalize: they will not work for another supermarket chain.

In summary, there have been various reasons for not using colour, but most of these are now less compelling, particularly in the light of recent technical advances in colour constancy and in reconsideration of the behavioural context in which colour can be used. More importantly, colour has two very important properties that make it a useful feature. Given that reasonable colour constancy can be achieved, colour has enormous value in vision as a cue because it is a punctate property of individual photoreceptors. This means that it is a very useful cue under conditions of low spatial resolution; precisely the conditions that exist in the periphery of the retina. The second useful property is view invariance. The colours of an object typically are invariant to wide ranges in field of view and to several different kinds of occlusion.

Michael Swain has shown that colour can be used effectively to locate objects in a biologically plausible way (Swain and Ballard, 1991). Interestingly, his algorithm uses a non-retinotopic representation that shares many features with characterizations of colour found in infero-temporal cortex. His algorithm uses the colour histogram. Given a discrete colour space, the colour histogram, h(c), is obtained by integrating over the image array:

$$h(c) = \int f(c,x) \, dx$$

where c is a representation of colour space. In the referenced experiments the colour vector is the conventional $c = (r,g,b)$.[6]

In outline, Swain's algorithm uses feedback to the retinotopic representations of colour in the following way. The image colours are rated as to how helpful they are in selecting the current model. This rating gives a stronger signal in some places than in others; low-pass filtering of the signal, followed by maximum detection, is sufficient to locate the desired object.

Successful experiments have been conducted on a database of seventy articles of clothing. These are non-rigid and difficult to identify with current techniques. These experiments are preliminary and illustrate the concept of object location using top-down

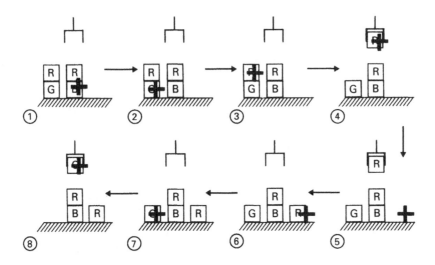

Figure 3.5 A graphical display from the output of the program after it has learned the 'Pick up the green block' task. The steps in the program use deictic references, and do not require geometrical coordinates. The program is:

Fixate (green)
Fixate (Top-of-stack)
Pickup
Fixate (Somewhere on the table)
Putdown
Fixate (green)
Pickup

feedback. Interestingly, this is a very different proposal from that of Koch and Ullman (1985), who suggested a bottom-up technique that used coincidental feature alignment to define a salience measure.

Modelling the learning of simple hand-eye co-ordination tasks

The invariance of deictic strategies has the right kind of transfer for learning many tasks. Steven Whitehead has applied these

ideas to the study of learning using a reinforcement paradigm
(Whitehead and Ballard, 1990; 1991). Whitehead has been studying
block stacking tasks. On each trial, the system, an abstracted model
of our robot, is presented with a pile of coloured blocks. A pile
can consist of any number of blocks arranged in any configuration. Each block is uniformly coloured and can be either red,
green or blue. The system can manipulate the pile by picking and
placing objects. An object can be picked up only if its top is clear,
and placed on another object only if the target object's top is
clear. When the system arranges the blocks into a successful configuration, it receives a positive reward and the trial ends. A successful configuration is some predefined set of states that represents
a desired outcome. For example, one extremely simple block
stacking task is for the system to learn to pick up a green block.
In this case, the successful configurations consist just of those
states where the system is holding a green object. The system
learns to arrange arbitrary configurations of blocks into successful
configurations. Instead of assigning an absolute symbolic name to
each item in the universe, such as 'BLOCK-44', as would be done
by a STRIPS system, the deictic system only registers objects
(and their features) according to the functional roles they play in
solving the task, such as 'THE-BLOCK-I-AM-FIXATING'.
Figure 3.5 shows how the fixation point can be manipulated in
learning to pick up a green block (Whitehead and Ballard 1989;
1990).

Most reinforcement learning systems have static sensory systems. That is, the semantics of the feature vectors that describe
the external state are defined a priori. Further, the input vector is
defined so that each state is 'sufficiently discriminable'. Unfortunately, as the complexity of the task domain increases, in particular as the number of 'possibly relevant' objects in the task grows,
the size of the static input vector (state representation) grows very
quickly even though the number of relevant objects remains small.
The problem is that with a static input vector if an object may be
relevant to the task then it *must* be represented internally.

In contrast to static systems, deictic systems that interact with
the world extensively can avoid the combinatorial explosion of
absolute representations. Again, the basic idea behind a deictic
representation is that the system shouldn't attempt to maintain an

accurate representation of every item in the universe, but instead should only register objects and aspects (features) that are relevant to the task at hand (Agre and Chapman, 1987).

Markers

The central concept underlying deictic representations is the *marker*, around which nearly all perception and action revolve (Ullman, 1984). With respect to our model, markers are the mechanism that keeps track of the system configuration. Markers are best thought of as pointers implemented by the visual-motor system; ideally, a marker points at an object in the world and registers features of that object in the internal representation. In this discussion, we assume an object can be defined by its local features, such as its shape and colour. We will describe a marker as bound to an object if the marker is pointing to it. A marker can be bound to only one object at a time, and it is assumed that the visual-motor system maintains the marker's binding at all times. Changing a marker's binding is accomplished by executing explicit actions specifically targeted for that marker. These actions index target objects in the world according to specific features that distinguish them from other objects. For example, a system might have a marker *m1* and an associated action *Move-m1-to-Red*, which is used to index and mark red objects. In this case, executing *Move-m1-to-Red* causes the visual-motor system to search the world for a red object and bind m1 to it. If a red object cannot be found, the action fails and m1's binding remains unchanged. If multiple red objects exist, the visual-motor system chooses the first one it comes to.

The moment-by-moment values of the markers define the agent's internal representation. For computational reasons, it is very important that there are only a limited number of markers, and our current model uses only two. The small number of markers and the limited number of features associated with each marker keep both the internal representation and the number of possible actions much smaller than is possible with conventional representations. If an object in the world is not marked, then it is invisible to the system (except for the effects it registers in the periphery). The emphasis is on keeping the internal representation

small and task-specific. Also, because the visual-motor system is
active, the system can dynamically track the objects that are relevant and change its focus of attention (marker bindings) as these
objects come into and fade from significance. Markers also play
an important role in motor control since actions are predomi-
nantly specified with respect to them. In this case, a marker's
binding acts to establish the reference frame in which an action is
performed. For example, the overt action *Place-at-m1* might cause
the agent to place an object it is holding at the location indicated
by marker m1. We distinguish two types of markers: overt markers and perceptual markers. A marker is overt if it has an action
that affects the state of the external world associated with it.
Otherwise, it is a perceptual marker. Overt markers are used for
establishing reference frames for actions in the world, while perceptual markers are used for collecting additional information about
the current state. Actions associated with overt markers are called
overt actions and actions associated with perceptual markers are
called perceptual actions.

Fixation and attention markers

The block manipulation system uses both a fixation frame and an
attention frame, as shown in figure 3.6. Details may be found in
Whitehead and Ballard (1990). The fixation frame is used for both
perception and action, while the attention frame is used only for
perception. Each frame has a set of local aspects associated with
it; these report the colour and shape of the marked object, the
number of blocks stacked above the marked object, whether or
not the marked object is sitting on the table and whether or not
the marked object is being held by the robot. The system has two
relational aspects – one for recording vertical alignment between
the two markers and one for recording horizontal alignment.
Peripheral aspects include inputs for detecting the presence of
colours in the scene (red, green and blue) and for detecting whether
the robot is currently holding an object. The internal motor commands available to the decision subsystem are shown on the right
in figure 3.6. In this example, all motor actions are made with
respect to the fixation frame. The two primary motor actions
are for grasping and placing objects. For grasping, the action

Sensory Inputs

(numbers in parentheses
indicate bits)

Peripheral Aspects

- (1) Red-in-Scene
- (1) Green-in-Scene
- (1) Blue-in-Scene
- (1) Object-in-Hand

Local Aspects

- (2) Fixated Colour
- (2) Fixated Shape (Block, Table)
- (2) Fixated-Stack-Height
- (1) Table-Below-Fixation
- (1) Fixating-the-Hand

- (2) Attended Colour
- (2) Attended Shape (Block, Table)
- (2) Attended-Stack-Height
- (1) Table-Below-Attention
- (1) Attending-to-the-Hand

Relational Aspects

- (1) Attention-and-Fixation-Vertically-Aligned
- (1) Attention-and-Fixation-Horizontally-Aligned

Internal Actions

Fixation Frame Commands

grasp-fixated-object
place-fixated-object
fixate-red
fixate-green
fixate-blue
fixate-stack-top
fixate-table

Attention Frame Commands

attend-to-red
attend-to-blue
attend-to-green
attend-to-stack-top
attend-to-stack-bottom
attend-to-table

Figure 3.6 The active perceptual system is divided into two parts: the fixation frame and an attention frame. The information registered in the fovea (or fixation point) can be actively controlled by executing perceptual and gaze control 'acts'. For example, fixating the block as shown causes its features to be registered in the state vector; attending to the triangle as shown causes its features to appear in the state vector. The two degrees of freedom in the state vector that can be independently controlled correspond to 'markers'. One can think of placing a special marker on an object causing its properties to appear in the appropriate place in the state vector. The system used by Whitehead is slightly more complex but still only uses 22 bits total to represent the state of the world.

grasp-fixated-object causes the robot to pick up the fixated object. The action works if the robot's hand is empty and the fixated object has a clear top. Similarly for placing, the action *place-fixated-object* causes the system to place the block it is holding on top of the fixated object. This action works if the robot is holding a block and the target object has a clear top.

Other motor actions include commands for changing fixation. Although such actions may appear to be perceptual actions, they are motor actions in the strictest sense because they affect the robot's ability to perform other motor actions. In contrast, the attention marker is a perceptual marker and has a repertoire of perceptual actions that are used exclusively for gathering additional visual information. All told the visual-motor system has a 22-bit input vector (see figure 3.6, left): 4 bits of peripheral aspects, 16 bits of local aspects, 2 bits of relational aspects; and 14 actions: 7 overt and 6 perceptual. Notice that the internal state space defined by the visual inputs, 2^{22}, or approximately 4 million, is small compared to the state space that could result if every object in the domain were represented (over 40 billion). The principal advantage is that this reduction leads to more feasible perception and simpler decision tasks. The principal disadvantage is that it limits the complexity of the problems that can be solved by the agent. For example, if during the course of a problem, a decision depends upon features of three separate blocks, then an agent with the above visual-motor system will not be capable of solving the problem because it cannot simultaneously represent features of more than two blocks. Of course, the visual-motor system could be expanded to allow the system to register features of three blocks (for example, by adding an additional marker), but in general new problems can always be defined that are beyond the scope of the current system. Our contention is that many of the problems we are interested in solving (or learning to solve) only involve keeping track of a few objects at a time (for example, see Chapman (1989)).

Again, in contrast to schemes such as STRIPS used by symbolic systems, notice that individual objects in the world are referenced not by arbitrarily assigned names, but by the features that make them relevant. For example, the action *Move-action-marker-to-stack-top* would cause the action marker to move upwards from its current position until it reaches the block at the top of the stack. What makes this top block significant is not any absolute name like 'BLOCK-43', but the relationship it holds with the rest of the world. Namely, this block is at the top of a stack and affords (Gibson, 1979) being removed and placed on the table (possibly to get at another more important block). The variety of features and properties that can be used as indices also delimits the types of problems that an agent can solve. Finally, notice that physical action in the world (e.g. picking and placing blocks) occurs relative to the reference frame defined by fixation. This is consistent with the view that objects in the world fill roles according to their features and that the control strategy learned by the decision system is specified in terms of those abstract roles.

Simulation results

Over a number of trials the system can learn to solve particular tasks. Figure 3.7 shows the number of steps used to solve the problem of picking up a green block. The disadvantage of this approach is that, so far, there is no good way to generalize it. However, that should not obscure the many important conceptual points. We contend that searching huge state spaces such as those in blocks world domains may be impossible without the incorporation of these kinds of ideas in animate vision systems. First, learning by trial and error allows the agent to amortize building a policy function over its history. Once a good policy function is learned, applying it is cheap. Second, the reinforcement learning algorithm we use has a limited attention span, so that it gives up after expending a predetermined amount of resources. This is important because (a) a real-time system *has* to respond in a timely manner, and (b) this strategy, in the context of repeated applications, causes the agent to gradually improve its competence (Blum and Blum, 1975). The third advantage of this kind of learning derives from the use of indexical representation. This allows (a) the access of items by property instead of by category, and (b) run-time indexing. *Access by property* is efficient in the following way. Consider the problem of hanging a picture where a nail has to be driven into a wall. We do not really need a hammer, but something that could serve as a hammer. *Plan access by category* forces the identification of image items, followed by a

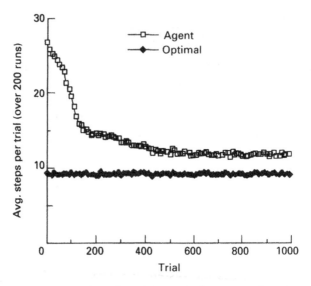

Figure 3.7 The results of applying reinforcement learning to a simple block stacking task: Pick up the green block. The system uses its fixation and attention frames to register features dynamically and thus avoid the combinatorial cost of representing large state spaces. The lower trace shows the smallest number of steps needed to solve the problem computed as the running average of the last three presentations. The upper trace shows the time taken to solve the problem, also averaged over three presentations (from Whitehead and Ballard, 1990).

check to determine the appropriate properties. *Access by properties* shortcircuits this process. Also, the fact that these properties are determined by what is in the environment at the moment filters out the consideration of strategies that would require unavailable items. Access by properties is in the spirit of Gibson's *affordances* (1979).

One problem such systems will have is the well-known credit assignment problem. If the reinforcements change, the problem of how to change the reinforcement schedule is completely open. However, such a system can search fairly cheaply local to the policy that it has and this may work for an interesting set of behaviours.

Preliminary experiments with human hand-eye co-ordination

Our experiments in reinforcement learning, particularly the use of markers, make specific predictions about how humans use eye movements in the course of solving hand-eye co-ordination tasks. We will concentrate on one of them here. Consider the primitives Place-at-Fixation Frame and Grasp-at-Action Frame used in the simulations with reinforcement learning. Do subjects use their fixation point in this way in such tasks?

To test the above hypothesis Feng Li, Steve Whitehead, Mary Hayhoe and the author designed the following experiment. A display of coloured blocks was divided up into three areas, the *source*, *target* and *model*, as shown in figure 3.8. Subjects used the cursor driven by a mouse to pick up and place blocks on the screen. Picking up a block was accomplished by moving the cursor over the block and depressing a button attached to the mouse. Placing the block was accomplished by moving the block to the desired location and releasing the button. The task was made simpler by having a set of coarse-grained, discrete locations for the blocks. This obviated the need for very precise positioning.

In the first trials that were run, fixation was reliably used in every case to pick up and drop the blocks. As a control, we asked: what would be the effect of not being able to use fixation? This was done in two ways. First, gaze was held at the centre of the screen throughout the task. Second, subjects were allowed to change gaze in between moves but had to hold gaze during the block transfer phase. In the first control, block size had to be adjusted for maximum visibility given the constraints of the eye tracker. This was approximately two degrees visual angle per block. Even at that size we were concerned that the difficulty in locating the blocks would be the decisive factor. This concern led to the second control.

The results are shown in figure 3.9 for three subjects performing two examples of each condition for a total of six data points per condition. To our surprise, the fixation condition was extremely debilitating, taking approximately three times longer than the unrestricted condition. The second control takes even longer, with subjects requiring approximately four times the amount of

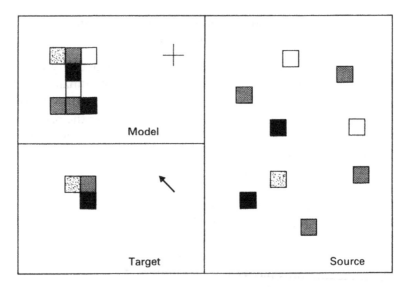

Figure 3.8 Display used in the hand-eye co-ordination experiments. The subject's instructions are to build a copy of the model in the target area using blocks from the source area. Blocks are moved using the cursor (arrow) that is controlled by the Macintosh Mouse™. The right eye is used in the experiment and its position (cross) is tracked by the SRI Dual-Purkinjee eye tracker.

time as in the unrestricted case. This result is perhaps even more surprising, as here the subjects are allowed to see clearly in between block moves. One explanation for this result is that there is overhead associated with changing between states where fixation is held and where it is not. However, in the light of our learning experiments, we can offer another explanation at the sub-symbolic level. When the fixation marker is restricted, the program to do the task has to have additional instructions. The additional program length accounts for the increased time.

Conclusions

To summarize the technical material, there are three main thrusts. The first is to suggest how objects in the world could be associated

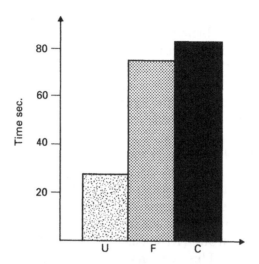

Figure 3.9 Preliminary results from the hand-eye co-ordination experiment. The times shown are for three different conditions. In the case marked U, the eyes were allowed to move freely throughout the experiment. In the case marked F, subjects performed the task while holding gaze at the centre of the screen. In the Conditional case (C), subjects could look at the screen while not moving the blocks, but had to fixate the centre point before moving.

with an internal variable, or 'marker', using colour as a feature – in other words, a *modus operandi* for a deictic instruction. Given a world of multicoloured objects, knowing the colours of a given object allows the speedy identification of the location of that object. The second thrust shows that this primitive could plausibly be part of a sequence of deictic instructions that accomplish a goal, such as picking up a coloured block. Furthermore, the program for doing so is succinctly expressed in terms of deictic instructions, as these have transfer to novel situations. Finally, our first attempts at verifying these ideas in humans demonstrate the tremendous premium associated with being able to foveate objects in the course of a task. This result certainly does not prove that deictic strategies are used, but it is consistent with the economies that are attendant with their use.

All of the above work was motivated by human saccadic data. This data forces us to accept how dynamic a process visual behaviour must be. Saccades at the rate of three per second are routine in visual problem solving. Furthermore, most of the brain structures that represent visual information are retinally indexed. This means that their state is changed with each eye movement. If the data-collecting process is so dynamic, how can the world appear to be stable? In the light of our examination of sub-symbolic structures, we believe that this question must have a surprising answer: the visual system provides the illusion of three-dimensional stability by virtue of being able to execute fast behaviours. This point may be very difficult as it is so counter-intuitive, but it has been arrived at in different forms by many different researchers. For example, Rosenschein has stressed the importance of implicit knowledge representation by a behaving 'situated automaton' (Rosenschein, 1985; Rosenschein and Kaelbling, 1986). This may have been the point of Gibson's 'affordances' (Gibson, 1979). O'Regan and Lévy-Schoen empha-size the use of the world as a 'memory buffer' that can be accessed by visual behaviours (1983). Dickmanns' self-driven car makes extensive use of a dynamic model of the roadway (1989). At any rate, having a particular embodiment forces one to deal with performance issues: one has to act in a timely manner under re-source constraints. One way to do this would be to have an elaborate internal representation as a form of 'table look-up'. But in a dynamic world, the cost of maintaining the correspondence between the representation and the world becomes prohibitive. For this reason, particularly at the sub-symbolic level, the human cognitive system may depend on highly adaptive behaviours that can quickly discover how to use current context.

The main thesis of this paper is that an understanding of intel-ligence will require models at different levels of abstraction. To motivate at least two levels, we have cast the traditional symbolic level in juxtaposition with a sub-symbolic level that explicitly models body mechanisms. The sub-symbolic level has a very different modelling emphasis than the symbolic level. This differ-ence in emphasis is summarized in table 3.2.

In summary, we have attempted to motivate the development of models at lower levels of abstraction that specifically model body mechanisms. This is because traditional models that have been described at the symbolic level have proved insufficient to

Table 3.2 Comparing the symbolic and sub-symbolic levels.

Symbolic	Sub-symbolic
Logical deduction	**Probabilistic inference**
Maintain distinctions	**Blur distinctions**
Logical inference demands that constants used to denote entities in the world be distinct. This leads to expensive representations.	Probabilistic inference explicitly allows representations to confuse external world symbols. This leads to representational economies.
Decoupled sensory-motor apparatus	**Integrated sensory-motor apparatus**
The sensory-motor apparatus is modelled as separate from the logical reasoning process. The task of vision is seen as one of translating pixels into predicates in a task-independent way.	The sensory-motor apparatus is integral to the probabilistic reasoning process. In particular, anthropomorphic gaze control systems can be modelled with two variables.
One-shot learning	**Repeated trials**
Solve new problems without much transfer from previously encountered problems of a similar type.	Model situations where tasks of the same or similar type are encountered repeatedly.
Cost of deduction	**Cost of inference**
Proportional to the size of the representation.	Proportional to the difficulty of the task.

capture important features of intelligence. One way to understand this is to use conventional computers as a metaphor. Consider the way virtual memory works on a conventional workstation. Virtual memory allows the applications programmer to write programs that are larger than the physical memory of the machine. What happens is that prior to the running of the program, it is broken up into smaller pages, and then at run time the requisite pages are brought into the memory from peripheral storage as required. This strategy works largely because conventional sequential programs are designed to be executed sequentially, and the information required to interpret an instruction is usually very localized. Consider now two very different viewpoints. From the applications programmer's viewpoint, it appears that a program of unlimited length can be written. But the system programmer's viewpoint is very different. The environment is very dynamic as individual pages are moved in and out of physical memory. It is just this difference that captures the difference between the symbolic approach and the approach we are terming sub-symbolic. At the symbolic level, which neglects the details of the machine, the world appears seamless and stable. It is only at the sub-symbolic level that we find that this must be an illusion, as the human's real-time visuo-motor system has many creative ways to interact with the world in a timely manner.

All the work reported above represents rather modest progress in modelling human intelligence in the light of the enormous capabilities that we have. Nonetheless we believe that they are an important stepping stone that shows that the mechanisms of human perception and action play a very important part in understanding intelligence.

Acknowledgements

I would like to thank my colleagues Christopher Brown and Randal Nelson for critiquing these ideas. I am also especially grateful to the University of Rochester team of researchers, Tim Becker, David Coombs, Nat Martin, Ray Rimey, Michael Swain, Steve Whitehead, Lambert Wixson and Brian Yamauchi, all of whom have greatly helped refine the ideas herein. The perspective of the paper in terms of the symbolic/sub-symbolic dichotomy is new, but other technical results are drawn from the work of research projects at Rochester. The colour examples are derived from research projects headed by Michael Swain and Lambert Wixson. Michael Swain now has a post-doctoral appointment at the University of Chicago's Computer Science Department. The learning example comes from a research project headed by Steve Whitehead, who currently has a post-doctoral appointment in the

Center for Visual Science at Rochester. The eye movement results are from experiments currently being done in collaboration with my faculty colleague Mary Hayhoe, Feng Li and Steve Whitehead. Peggy Meeker is responsible for the pleasing format of the manuscript.

Notes

1   Apologies to physicists for stopping here.
2   Smolensky uses the term to refer to purely computational systems; thus our use of the term to refer to a modelling level that explicitly acknowledges the electro-mechanical features of the human body is slightly different from his original intention, but the juxtaposition of sub-symbolic with symbolic is the main idea.
3   There are many current attempts to integrate probabilistic formalisms at the symbolic level, e.g. Pearl (1988), but the tenets of logical reasoning still represent the central position.
4   This cursory account of grasping finesses many important issues but it is probably the case that these can be dealt with independently (Jeannerod and Decety, 1990)
5   A major feature of the gross organization of the primate visual brain is the specialization of the temporal and parietal lobes of visual cortex into WHAT/WHERE functions. The parietal cortex seems to be subserving the management of locations in space, whereas the temporal cortex seems to be subserving the identification of objects in the case where location is not the issue.
6   The r-g-b value obtained from the tri-chromatic receptor array can be sensitive to gross lighting changes such as the $1/r^2$ falloff from a point source. One way to compensate for this, observed in biological systems, is to use an opponent colour space $c' = (r-g, b-(r+g)/2)$.

References

Agre, P. E. and Chapman, D. 1987: Pengi: An implementation of a theory of activity. *Proc., AAAI 87*, 268–72.

Aloimonos, J., Bandopadhay, A. and Weiss, I. June 1987: Active vision. *Proc., 1st Int'l. Conf. on Computer Vision*, 35–54. Also in 1988: *Int'l. J. Computer Vision 1*, 4, 333–56.

Arbib, M. A. 1981: Perceptual structures and distributed motor control. In V. B. Brooks (ed.), *Handbook of Physiology – The Nervous System II. Motor Control*, Bethesda, Maryland: Amer. Physiological Society, 1449–80.

Bajcsy, R. and Allen, P. Nov. 1984: Sensing strategies. *U.S.-France Robotics Workshop*, U. Pennsylvania, Philadelphia.

Ballard, D. H. 1981: Generalizing the Hough transform to arbitrary shapes. *Proc., Int'l. Conf. on Computer Vision and Pattern Recognition.*

Ballard, D. H. Feb. 1989: Behavioural constraints on computer vision. *Image and Vision Computing 7*, 1.

Ballard, D. H. and Ozcandarli, A. December 1988: Eye fixation and early vision: Kinetic depth. *Proc., 2nd IEEE Int'l. Conf. on Computer Vision.*

Bandopadhay, A. 1987: A computational study of rigid motion. Ph.D. Thesis, Computer Science Dept., U. Rochester.

Beveridge, J. R., Griffith, J., Kohler, R. R., Hanson, A. R. and Riseman, E. M. January 1989: Segmenting images using localized histograms and region merging. *Int'l. J. Computer Vision 2, 3*, 311–47.

Biederman, I. October 1985: Human image understanding: Recent research and a theory. *CVGIP 32*, 1.

Blum, L. and Blum, M. 1975: Toward a mathematical theory of inductive inference. *Information and Control 22*, 125–55.

Brooks, R. A. 1986a: Achieving artificial intelligence through building robots. TR 899, Massachusetts Inst. of Technology.

Brooks, R. A. 1986b: A robust layered control system for a mobile robot. *IEEE J. Robotics and Automation RA-2*, 14–23.

Brown, C. M. May 1990a: Gaze controls with interactions and delays. *IEEE Trans. Systems, Man, and Cybernetics 20*, 3.

Brown, C. M. May 1990b: Prediction and cooperation in gaze control. *Biological Cybernetics 63*, 61–70.

Brown, C. M. (ed.), with Ballard, D. H., Becker, T. G., Gans, R. F., Martin, N. G., Olson, T. J., Potter, R. D., Rimey, R. D., Tilley, D. G. and Whitehead, S. D. August 1988: The Rochester Robot. TR 257, Computer Science Dept., U. Rochester.

Chapman, D. 1989: Penguins can make cake. *AI Magazine 10*, 45–50.

Chen, C. H. and Kak, A. C. 1989: A robot vision system for recognizing 3-d objects in low-order polynomial time. *IEEE Trans. SMC* (Special Issue on Computer Vision).

Churchland, P. S. and Sejnowski, T. J. 1988: Perspectives on Cognitive Neuroscience. *Science, 242*, 741–45.

Clark, J. J. and Ferrier, N. J. December 1988: Modal control of an attentive vision system. *Proc., 2nd Int'l. Conf. on Computer Vision*, Tampa, Florida, 514–523.

Cutting, J. E. 1982: Motion parallax and visual flow: How to determine direction of locomotion. *4th Meeting, Int'l. Soc. for Ecological Psychology*, Hartford, Connecticut.

Dickmanns, E. D. August 1989: Real-time machine vision exploiting integral spatio-temporal world models. Invited presentation, *11th Int'l. Joint Conf. on Artificial Intelligence*, Detroit, Michigan.

Erkelens, C. J. and Collewijn, H. 1985: Eye movements and stereopsis during dichoptic viewing of moving random-dot stereograms. *Vision Research 25*, 1689–1700.

Feldman, J. A. and Yakimovsky, Y. 1974: Decision theory and artificial intelligence I: A semantics-based region analyzer. *Artificial Intelligence 5*, 349–71.

Fodor, J. A. 1983: *The Modularity of Mind*. Cambridge, Mass. MIT Press.

Garvey, T. D. September 1976: Perceptual strategies for purposive vision. Technical Note 117, SRI Int'l.

Genesereth, M. and Nilsson, N. 1987: *Logical Foundations of Artificial Intelligence*. San Mateo, California: Morgan Kaufmann.

Gibson, J. J. 1979: *The Ecological Approach to Visual Perception*. Boston: Houghton Mifflin.

Hinton, G. E. August 1981: Shape representation in parallel systems. *Proc., 7th Int'l. Joint Conf. on Artificial Intelligence*.

Huttenlocher, D. P. and Ullman, S. April 1988: Recognizing solid objects by alignment. *Proc., DARPA Image Understanding Workshop*.

Jeannerod, M. and Decety, J. 1990: The accuracy of visuomotor transformation: An investigation into the mechanisms of visual recognition of objects. In M. A. Goodale (ed.), *Vision and Action: The Control of Grasping*, Norwood, New Jersey: Ablex Pub. Corp.

Klinker, G. J., Shafer, S. A. and Kanade, T. 1988: The measurement of highlights in color images. *Int'l. J. Computer Vision 2*, 7–32.

Koch, C. and Ullman, S. 1985: Shifts in Selective Attention Y – Y Towards the Underlying Neural Circuitry. *Human Neurobiology*, 4, 219–27.

Komatsu, H. and Wurtz, R. H. August 1988: Relation of cortical areas MT and MST to pursuit eye movements. III. Interaction with full-field visual stimulation. *J. Neurophysiology 60*, 2, 621–44.

Krotkov, E. 1988: Focusing. *Int'l. J. Computer Vision 1*, 3, 223–38.

Lowe, D. December 1989: Fitting parameterized 3-d models to images. Technical Report 89–26, Computer Science Dept., U. British Columbia.

Lowe, D. 1985: *Perceptual Organization and Visual Recognition*. Boston: Kluwer Academic Publishers.

Maloney, L. T. and Wandell, B. A. January 1986: Color constancy: A method for recovering surface spectral reflectance. *J. Optical Society of America A 3*, 1, 29–33.

Marr, D. C. 1982: *Vision*. San Francisco: W. H. Freeman and Co.

Maunsell, J. H. R. and Van Essen, D. 1986: The topographic organization of the middle temporal visual area in the macaque monkey: Representational biases and the relationship to callosal connections and mylo-architectonic boundaries. *J. Comparative Neurology 266*, 535–55.

Maunsell, J. H. R. and Newsome, W. T. 1987: Visual processing in monkey extrastriate cortex. *Ann. Rev. Neurosci. 10*, 363–401.

Mishkin, M. 1982: A memory system in the monkey. *Phil. Trans. Royal Soc. London B298*, 85–95.

Mishkin, M., Ungerleider, L. G. and Macko, K. A. 1983: Object vision and spatial vision: Two cortical pathways. *Trends in Neurosciences 6*, 414–17.

Moravec, H. P. August 1977: Towards automatic visual obstacle avoidance. *Proc., 5th IJCAI*, 584.

Nakayama, K. August 1988: Presentation. *Woods Hole Workshop on Computational Neuroscience*, Woods Hole, Mass.

Nelson, R. C. 1991: Qualitative detection of motion by a moving observer. To appear, *Int'l. J. of Computer Vision 7*, 1, 33–46.

Nelson, R. C., and Aloimonos, J. October 1989: Obstacle avoidance using flow field divergence. *IEEE Trans. PAMI 11*, 10, 1102–6.

Newell, F. W. 1982: *Ophthalmology: Principles and Concepts*. St. Louis: The C. V. Mosby Co.

Noton, D. October 1970: A theory of visual pattern perception. *IEEE Trans. on Systems, Science & Cybernetics SSC-6*, 349–57.

Noton, D. and Stark L. 1971a: Eye movements and visual perception. *Scientific American 224*, 6, 34–43.

Noton, D. and Stark, L. 1971b: Scanpaths in saccadic eye movements while viewing and recognizing patterns. *Vision Research 11*, 929.

Olson, T. J. and Coombs, D. J. June 1990: Real-time vergence control for binocular robots. TR 348, Computer Science Dept., U. Rochester.

Olson, T. J. and Potter, R. D. November 1988: Real-time vergence control. TR 264, Computer Science Dept., U. Rochester.

O'Regan, J. K. and Lévy-Schoen, A. 1983: Integrating visual information from successive fixations: Does trans-saccadic fusion exist? *Vision Res. 23*, 8, 765–8.

Pearl, J. 1988: *Probabilistic Reasoning in Intelligent Systems: Networks of Plausible Inference*. San Mateo, California: Morgan Kaufmann.

Pentland, A. August 1985: A new sense of depth of field. In *Proc., Int'l. Joint Conf. on Artificial Intelligence*, 988–94.

Pentland, A. December 1988: Shape from shading: A theory of human perception. In *Proc., Int'l. Conf. on Computer Vision*, Tarpon Springs, Florida.

Ramachandran, V. S. September 1987: Interactions between motion, depth, color and form: the utilitarian theory of perception. *Proc., Conf. on Visual Coding and Efficiency.*

Raviv, D. and Herman, M. Dec. 1989: Towards an understanding of camera fixation. Technical Report, Robot Systems Div., National Inst. of Standards and Technology.

Rimey, R. D. and Brown, C. M. February 1990: Selective attention as sequential behavior: Modeling eye movements with an augmented hidden Markov model. TR 327, Computer Science Dept., U. Rochester.

Rosenschein, S. J. September 1985: Formal theories of knowledge in AI and robotics. Technical Note 362, AI Center, SRI International.

Rosenschein, S. J. and Kaelbling, L. March 1986: The synthesis of digital machines with provable epistemic properties. *Proc., 1986 Conf. on Theoretical Aspects of Reasoning about Knowledge,* Monterey, California.

Rubner, J. and Schulten, K. 1989: A regularized approach to color constancy. *Biological Cybernetics 61,* 1, 29–36.

Sandini, G. and Tagliasco, V. December 1980: An anthropomorphic retina-like structure for scene analysis. *CVGIP 14,* 4, 365–72.

Shapiro, S. (ed.) 1987: *Encyclopedia of Artificial Intelligence.* New York: John Wiley and Sons.

Smolensky, P. 1988: On the Proper Treatment of Connectionism. *The Behavioral and Brain Sciences,* 11, 1–74.

Swain, M. J. November 1990: Color Indexing. Ph.D. Thesis and TR 360, Computer Science Dept., U. Rochester.

Swain, M. J. and Ballard, D. H. 1991: Color indexing, to appear, *Int'l. J. of Computer Vision 7* (Special Issue), 1, 11–32.

Tsotsos, J. June 1987: A complexity level analysis of vision. *Proc., IJCCV,* London.

Ullman, S. 1984: Visual routines. *Cognition 18,* 97–157. Also in S. Pinker (ed.) 1984: *Visual Cognition,* 97–160, Cambridge, Mass.: Bradford Books.

Whitehead, S. D. and Ballard, D. H. 1990: Active perception and reinforcement learning. *Neural Computation 2,* 409–19.

Whitehead, S. D. and Ballard, D. H. 1991: Learning to perceive and act by trial and error. *Machine Learning 7,* 45–83.

Whitehead, S. D. and Ballard, D. H. June 1989: A role for anticipation in reactive systems that learn. *Proc., 6th Int'l. Workshop on Machine Learning,* Cornell U., Ithaca, New York.

Wixson, L. E. and Ballard, D. H. November 1989: Color histograms for real-time object search. *Proc., SPIE Sensor Fusion II: Human and Machine Stategies Workshop,* Philadelphia, Pennsylvania.

Yamauchi, B. June 1989: JUGGLER: Real-time sensorimotor control using independent agents. *Proc., Optical Society of America Image Understanding and Machine Vision Conf.* (N. Falmouth, MA, June 1989), *1989 Technical Digest Series 14*, 6–9.

Yarbus, A. L. 1967: *Eye Movements and Vision*. New York: Plenum Press.

Yeshurun, Y. and Schwartz, E. L. March 1987: Cepstral filtering on a columnar image architecture: A fast algorithm for binocular stereo segmentation. Robotics Res. TR 286, Courant Inst., New York U.

4

Networks in the Brain

Edmund T. Rolls

Introduction

The aim of this chapter is to show how some cognitive phenomena, for example memory, can be understood in terms of *how* the brain actually computes. Ballard (1990; see chapter 3 of this volume) has shown the importance of analysing *what is computed* to lead to an understanding of Human Intelligence. For example, when visuo-motor functions such as arm reaching to a seen object are performed, it appears that instead of trying to fully analyse the information across the whole visual scene about the objects present and their relationships, humans instead fixate and pay attention to a small part of the scene, with respect to which the movement can be planned and made. A lesson here is that problems may be solved by humans in rather more limited, but nevertheless effective, ways than the general purpose solutions attempted in some cases in investigations of Artificial Intelligence. A part then of understanding Human Intelligence is to understand *what* is computed by humans.

In this chapter I shall consider some examples of *how* the brain computes, and will show that many properties of Human Intelligence arise from the particular style of computation used naturally by the brain. It is for this reason that another important way forward for the understanding of Human Intelligence is to analyse *how*, not only *what*, the brain computes.

The analysis of how the brain computes is an area in which rapid advances are being made now. It is now becoming possible to understand the operation of networks of neurons (brain cells)

(a) because of advances in anatomical methods which allow the connections between neurons and therefore the architecture of the neuronal networks to be described; (b) because of advances in physiology and pharmacology which allow investigation of the rules which describe how the strengths of synapses between neurons can be altered by experience, both in the mature animal and during development; (c) because of advances in theoretical analyses of the operation of such neuronal networks; and (d) because of advances in relating the operation of the networks analysed in this way to the function they perform in the context of the whole brain (i.e. at the systems level) and behaviour, using neurophysiological, neuropsychological and psychological methods. The ways in which these methods can be combined will be illustrated in this chapter by considering recent advances in our understanding of memory.

The particular type of memory considered will be declarative memory, that is memory about which we can make declarations. One type of this memory is episodic memory, that is, memory for past episodes, such as where one ate lunch yesterday, what was eaten and with whom. The other aspect of declarative memory is semantic memory, that is memory about facts, for example that Wolfson College is one of the colleges of Oxford University.

Memory

Neuropsychology: systems level analysis of the role of the hippocampus in episodic, semantic and recognition memory

Damage to the posterior parts of the temporal lobe of the human brain produces amnesia evident as a major deficit in learning new episodes, and new facts (e.g. that the hippocampus is in the temporal lobe), that is in episodic and semantic memory. In addition (particularly if the damage is extensive), there is a deficit in recognition memory (e.g. if you are shown a series of objects, you may not recognize later which objects you have seen previously). The amnesia is anterograde, in that new information cannot be learned after the brain damage, but patients with anterograde amnesia can remember memories formed before the brain damage, particularly old memories. (That is, any retrograde amnesia can be relatively minor.) The anterograde amnesia has been attributed to damage to the hippocampus, which is within the temporal lobe, and to its associated pathways such as the fornix, but it is possible that severe deficits on recognition memory are only found when there is also damage to overlying cortical areas such as the entorhinal cortex. In humans, there is some lateralization of the function of this brain region, in that verbal learning (e.g. paired associate learning) is impaired by left damage, and spatial learning is impaired by right damage (see Weiskrantz, 1987; Squire, 1992). In animals, impairment of spatial memory is evident. For example, in monkeys hippocampal damage produces an impairment in remembering the positions of objects, and in rats there is a deficit in learning about places visited (see Rolls 1990a).

Anatomy: the connections of the hippocampus, and the architecture of its neuronal networks

In order to understand how the hippocampus operates to enable it to play a role in memory storage, we must now consider its connections, and how its synapses alter their strength during learning so that it can store information.

The hippocampus receives extrinsic inputs via the entorhinal cortex (area 28) and the parahippocampal gyrus from many areas of the cerebral association cortex, including the parietal cortex which is concerned with spatial functions, the visual and auditory temporal association cortical areas and the frontal cortex (figure 4.1). There are also subcortical cholinergic inputs from the septum. The hippocampus in turn projects back via the subiculum, entorhinal cortex and parahippocampal gyrus (area TF-TH), to the cerebral cortical areas from which it receives inputs (Van Hoesen, 1982), as well as to subcortical areas such as the mammillary bodies (see figure 4.1).

Schematic diagrams of the internal connections of the hippocampus are shown in figure 4.2. One feature is that there is a sequence of stages, in each of which there is a major set of input axons which connect via a form of matrix of synapses with the output neurons of that stage. (Note: the receiving surface of a

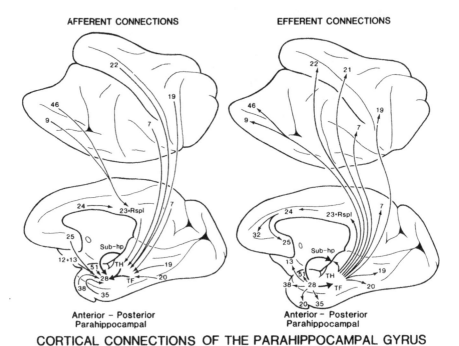

CORTICAL CONNECTIONS OF THE PARAHIPPOCAMPAL GYRUS

Figure 4.1 Connections of the primate hippocampus with the neocortex (from Van Hoesen, 1982). A medial view of the macaque brain is shown below, and a lateral view is shown inverted above. The hippocampus receives its inputs via the parahippocampal gyrus, areas TF and TH, and the entorhinal cortex, area 28. The return projections to the neocortex (shown on the right) pass through the same areas. (The hippocampus is behind area 28 in the diagram.) Cortical areas 19, 20 and 21 are visual association areas, 22 is auditory association cortex 7 is parietal association cortex and 9, 46, 12 and 13 are frontal cortical association areas.

neuron of a brain cell is the dendrite; effects from the axons which connect to a dendrite reach the cell body, which fires a spike whenever its inputs have exceeded a threshold; and this spike is carried from the cell body via the axons to influence other cells via synapses on to their dendrites.) The two stages which most clearly exemplify this feature are the dentate granule (FDgc in figure 4.2b) and the CA1 stages. The CA3 stage has recurrent collateral axons which return to make synapses with the dendrites of the

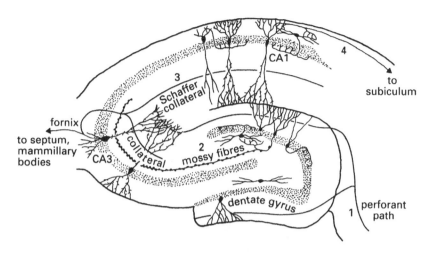

Figure 4.2a   Representation of connections within the hippocampus. Inputs reach the hippocampus through the perforant path (1) which makes synapses with the dendrites of the dentate granule cells and also with the apical dendrites of the CA3 pyramidal cells. The dentate granule cells project via the mossy fibres (2) to the CA3 pyramidal cells. The well-developed recurrent collateral system of the CA3 cells is indicated. The CA3 pyramidal cells project via the Schaffer collaterals (3) to the CA1 pyramidal cells, which in turn have connections (4) to the subiculum.

other CA3 cells, as shown in figure 4.2. The contact probability of an axon with one of the dendrites is relatively high, 4 per cent in the rat, calculated on the basis that there are 300,000 CA3 cells and that approximately 12,000 synapses per CA3 pyramidal cell are likely to be devoted to recurrent collaterals (Rolls, 1989; 1990a). It is remarkable that the CA3 recurrent collateral axons travel so widely in all directions that they can potentially come close to almost all other CA3 neurons. The significance of this is considered later.

Long-term potentiation as an indicator of the synaptic
modification important in learning

Studies of an effect called long-term potentiation provide evidence that the strengths of synapses in some parts of the hippocampus

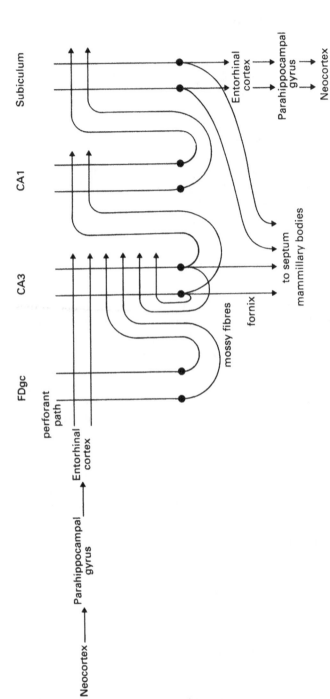

Figure 4.2b Schematic representation of the connections of the hippocampus, showing also that the cerebral cortex (neocortex) is connected to the hippocampus via the parahippocampal gyrus and entorhinal cortex, and that the hippocampus projects back to the neocortex via the subiculum, entorhinal cortex and parahippocampal gyrus. FDgc – dentate granule cells.

are modifiable, and that learning is implemented by this modifiability. In particular, these synapses become stronger when there is strong conjunctive postsynaptic activation (i.e. of the dendrite or cell body) and presynaptic activity (i.e. activity in the synaptic terminal of the axon of another cell that contacts the dendrite) (Brown et al., 1990).

Long-term potentiation (LTP) is a use-dependent and sustained increase in synaptic strength that can be induced by brief periods of synaptic stimulation. It is usually measured as a sustained increase in the amplitude of electrically evoked responses in specific neural pathways following brief trains of high frequency stimulation (see figure 4.3). For example, high frequency stimulation of the (Shaeffer collateral) inputs to the hippocampal CA1 cells results in a larger response recorded from the CA1 cells to single test pulse stimulation of the pathway. LTP is *long-lasting*, in that its effect can be measured for hours in hippocampal slices, and in chronic *in vivo* experiments in some cases may last for months. LTP develops rapidly, typically in less than one minute. LTP is in some brain systems *associative*. This is illustrated in figure 4.3, in which a weak input to a group of cells (e.g. the commissural input to CA1) does not show LTP unless it is given at the same time as (i.e. associatively with) a strong input to the cells. This associative property is shown very clearly in experiments in which LTP of an input to a single cell only occurs if the cell membrane is depolarized by passing current through it at the same time as the input arrives at the cell. The depolarization alone or the input alone are not sufficient to produce the LTP, and the LTP is thus associative. Moreover, in that the presynaptic input and the postsynaptic depolarization must occur at about the same time (within approximately 500 ms), the LTP requires *temporal contiguity*. LTP is also *synapse-specific*, in that for example a weak input to a cell does not show LTP when a strong input to a cell is activated sufficiently for the strong input to show LTP, unless the weak input is stimulated conjunctively with the strong input (see figure 4.3).

The rule which underlies associative LTP is thus that synapses connecting two neurons become stronger if there is conjunctive presynaptic and (strong) postsynaptic activity. This learning rule for synaptic modification is sometimes called the Hebb rule, after

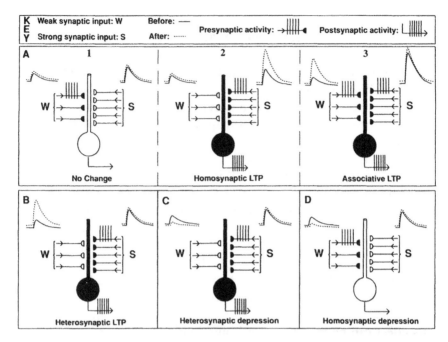

Figure 4.3 Illustration of several varieties of use-dependent synaptic changes. Each neuron is shown receiving two sets of non-overlapping synaptic inputs, one weak (W) and the other strong (S). The difference between these two sets reflects the number of afferent fibres. The waveforms above each input illustrate schematically the excitatory postsynaptic potential produced by a single stimulation of that input before (*solid curve*) and after (*broken curve*) tetanic (high-frequency) stimulation of one or both inputs. *Filled elements* indicate activity during the conditioning (tetanic) stimulation. A. Associative LTP. A1. Tetanic stimulation of W alone does not cause LTP in either input. A2. Subsequent tetanic stimulation of S may cause homosynaptic LTP (synaptic enhancement in the stimulated input) but not heterosynaptic LTP (enhancement in the unstimulated input). A3. Concurrent tetanic stimulation of W and S causes associative LTP (enhancement in W). Further, LTP in the S input may also occur under these conditions (but is not illustrated). B. Heterosynaptic LTP. Tetanic stimulation of the S input alone causes LTP in the unstimulated W input. Homosynaptic LTP in the stimulated S input may also occur under these circumstances (but is not shown). C. Heterosynaptic depression. Stimulation of the S input alone causes depression in the unstimulated W input. Homosynaptic LTP in the S input may also occur under these conditions (but is not shown). D Homosynaptic depression. High frequency stimulation of W alone causes depression in the W input. In principle, homosynaptic depression could also occur in the S input if tetanic stimulation of this input did not cause homosynaptic LTP. (Reproduced with permission from the Annual Review of Neuroscience, vol. 13, © 1990 by Annual Reviews Inc.)

Donald Hebb of McGill University who drew attention to this possibility, and its potential importance in learning, in 1949.

In that LTP is long-lasting, develops rapidly, is synapse-specific and is in some cases associative, it is of interest as a potential synaptic mechanism underlying some forms of memory. Evidence linking it directly to some forms of learning comes from experiments in which it has been shown that the drug AP5 infused so that it reaches the hippocampus to block NMDA receptors blocks both LTP and spatial learning mediated by the hippocampus (see Morris, 1989). The task learned by the rats was to find the location relative to cues in a room of a platform submerged in an opaque liquid (milk). Interestingly, if the rats had already learned where the platform was, then the NMDA infusion did not block performance of the task. This is a close parallel to LTP, in that the learning, but not the subsequent expression of what had been learned, was blocked by the NMDA receptor antagonist AP5.

Operation of the neuronal networks in the hippocampus

The operation of one part of the hippocampus, the CA3 network, will be described to show how the hippocampus may be involved in learning. The anatomy of this network is that the CA3 neurons have recurrent collateral axons which make connections with other CA3 neurons. This is shown in figure 4.4. The connections made from one CA3 neuron to another are believed to show associative LTP of the type described above which has been analysed in detail for the perforant path to dentate granule cell connections and for the CA3 to CA1 connections. This functional anatomy suggests that this operates as a particular form of memory called an auto-associative memory, the operation of which is described next.

Consider a neuronal network with the architecture shown and with Hebb modifiable synapses. Consider a pattern of activity which represents the input stimulus present on the input axons i. This input is applied to the dendrites such that D1 and D3 are active (state = 1), and the other dendrites are inactive (state = 0). Then axons A1 and A3 will be active as they are recurrent collaterals, and the synapses from A1 to D1 and to D3 (i.e. A1-D1 and A1-D3) become strengthened (the state initially 0 becomes 1). Similarly synapses A3-D1 and A3-D3 are strengthened

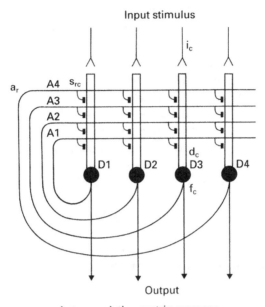

Autoassociation matrix memory

Figure 4.4 The architecture of an autoassociative neuronal network (see text).

to 1. The two signals present conjunctively on D1 and D3 have now been associated together to form a new memory. This is how a new memory becomes stored in the autoassociation network memory.

Recall of memories from the network is performed by applying an input stimulus again through input axons i. A very important property of the recall is that the whole of the memory can be recalled by presenting only part of it as the input. For example, if D1 occurs as a memory key, then the strengthened synapse A1-D3 results in D3 becoming active as well as D1. Thus the whole of the memory is recalled. This property is called completion. It is also an important property of our own episodic and semantic memories, and this property of our memories appears to arise very naturally because of the way in which memories are stored in these types of neuronal network in the brain. Imagine for example that the recall key was simply the excellent meal you ate at lunch yesterday, and that this is being applied to neuron D1 (or in practice in the brain, a set of neurons D1). Then the place where you ate the meal can be recalled via the collateral of D1 which makes contact with the set of neurons D3, which originally, during learning, provided the input about spatial location. Part of the importance of this neuronal network approach to brain function is that many of the properties of our cognitive function, such as the completion of memories from a partial input, or the generalization from a present input to a similar input seen previously, can be understood in terms of the details of the operation of the neuronal networks in the brain.

Another useful property of such an associative memory is that it shows graceful degradation, in that if some synapses or neurons are damaged in the network, then the network can still operate reasonably. This property arises because the representation of each memory is distributed over many neurons in the network (see further Rolls, 1987; Rolls and Treves, 1990; Amit, 1989). This form of fault tolerance is again a crucial property of such neuronal networks, for it means that if some neurons or synapses in the network become damaged, or do not develop perfectly, then nevertheless the system as a whole can still continue to operate reasonably. This is of course a property of our own memories, and again we see how a property of Human Intelligence can be understood by analysing the neuronal network properties of the brain.

It is possible, with suitable thresholds set for the neurons in the network, to store very many memories in the network (see Rolls and Treves, 1990; Treves and Rolls, 1991; Amit, 1989). Moreover, the fact that the signals can recirculate for several times round the network can improve the accuracy of the recall.

Systems level theory of hippocampal function

As indicated in figure 4.4, a network of the type found in one part of the hippocampus, the CA3 cells, could form part of a memory system which could link together different signals which occur together. The actual signals that are linked together by the net can be understood by considering the types of memory that are disrupted by damage to the hippocampus, the signals that reach the hippocampus through its afferent pathways and neuronal activity recorded in the hippocampus. The type of learning impaired by damage to the hippocampus is, as described above, episodic and semantic. In these memories, arbitrary events or facts must be linked together, and this may be what the hippocampus allows. For example, the components of an episodic memory, forced onto different CA3 cells, might be what one ate for lunch yesterday, where and with whom. The CA3 cells would then link these components together, to form an episodic memory, the whole of which could be recalled by any of the parts. The input connections of the hippocampus are consistent with this, for, via the parahippocampal gyrus and the entorhinal cortex, (area 28), the hippocampus receives from many high order areas of the cerebral cortex, for example from the visual association cortex (areas 20 and 21), the auditory association cortex (area 22), the parietal cortex (area 7), and even the olfactory cortex (see figure 4.1). Thus the hippocampus receives highly processed information from the ends of each of our sensory processing systems, and provides a way for the high level representations to be linked. There are not many places in the brain where, given brain anatomy, this could occur, and the hippocampus provides one place with a simple associative network which would enable such memories to be formed.

In addition to this systems level anatomy, systems level neurophysiological findings show that combinations of events received by the hippocampus from different parts of the cerebral cortex do activate single hippocampal neurons, as predicted. For example some hippocampal neurons in the monkey respond in memory tasks to a combination of information about a visual stimulus being shown (reflecting information processed in the temporal lobe cortical visual areas) and about its position in space (reflecting information processed in the parietal cortex) (Rolls, 1989; 1990a).

Damage to the hippocampus impairs the ability to form new memories, but not necessarily the ability to recall old memories. Now the hippocampus has projections, via the entorhinal cortex and parahippocampal gyrus, to the neocortical areas from which it receives inputs. These backprojections may enable the hippocampus, having formed a linkage between different events, to take part in the laying down of a very long term trace in the cerebral cortical areas connected to the hippocampus (see Rolls, 1990a).

Other memory systems in the brain

It should be emphasized that the hippocampus implements one type of memory, required for episodic, semantic and recognition memories. There are other brain regions, with different internal architectures, and connections to different brain regions, which implement other types of memory. For example, the amygdala is involved in associating previously neutral stimuli, such as the sight of an object, with its rewarding or punishing consequences, which might arise for example because of its taste. In that the amygdala is involved in learning about rewards and punishments it is of great importance for the learning of emotional states (see Rolls, 1990b, 1991a). As a further example, the orbitofrontal cortex is involved in reversing this type of learning, and without it responses to previously rewarding stimuli (including emotional stimuli) become inappropriate (see Rolls, 1990b). It is one of the current challenges in neuroscience to understand in detail the operation of these other brain regions in memory in terms of the neuronal networks they contain.

Coding of information in sensory systems that interface to memory systems

Towards the ends of each sensory processing system in the brain, it sends connections to structures such as the hippocampus, amygdala and orbitofrontal cortex that are involved in memories. The way in which information is represented as a pattern of firing of a reasonable number of neurons, which nevertheless are quite finely tuned, in these parts of the sensory systems appears to be due to the utility of such a sparse distributed representation for memory systems (see Rolls and Treves, 1990). For example, in the temporal cortical parts of the visual system there are neurons that are relatively finely tuned in that not only do they respond primarily to faces, but they also respond differently to the faces of different individuals (Rolls, 1992). Nevertheless, the representation of the face of a particular individual is distributed, in that many neurons respond (with slight differences between the neurons) to the face of a given individual.

This type of sparse distributed representation is what is required

for the input to many types of associative neuronal networks (Rolls
and Treves, 1990). The advantage in sparse encoding (as compared
with fully distributed encoding) in that this increases the number
of learned patterns that can be stored, by decreasing the noise
effects due to the storage of a large number of patterns. Further,
in some types of associative nets there is an advantage in sparse
encoding in that this increases the number of independent associations that can be stored, by not allowing interference during recall
(for details see Rolls and Treves, 1990). Nevertheless, encoding
which is partly distributed and uses at least an ensemble of active
neurons to represent a pattern has the advantages of graceful
degradation and generalization to near patterns, where nearness is
measured by the correlation between the test input and an input
learned previously. It also has the advantage that (with non-linear
neurons) more patterns can be stored than when only one neuron
is firing (because the combination of inputs is stored). We thus see
that in general, as noted previously (Rolls, 1987; 1989a,c), the
representation of information in an associative net will in many
cases be a compromise between rather sparse representations with
relatively few neurons active in each pattern to increase the number
of patterns stored, and rather more distributed encoding to allow
generalization and graceful degradation. This theoretical analysis
thus provides at least a partial account of why the tuning of
neurons at the end of sensory systems becomes relatively, but
not extremely, sharp.

Synthesis

I have shown in the above how analyses of neuronal networks
provide a way to link anatomical, physiological, pharmacological,
computational and systems level (e.g. psychological) analyses
to produce an integrated, multi-level understanding of how our
memories are stored in the brain. It is by investigations of the
neural networks in the brain that the operation of each brain
region can be understood, and a neuronal network perspective
shows that certain types of evidence are required from neuroscience
to lead to such an understanding. This type of approach has
only relatively recently become possible, and is likely to lead to

rapid advances in understanding brain function, and thus Human Intelligence.

The properties of the networks analysed have properties which are very similar to those of some aspects of Human Intelligence. These properties include generalization, completion, graceful degradation and speed of operation. These properties arise from the style of computation in neuronal networks. Because of these very close relations between the details of the operation of neuronal networks and of some aspects of human cognition, it is likely to advance our understanding greatly of human cognition to understand the computations actually being performed by the parts of the brain involved in different cognitive functions. The essence of the computational style is that there are many, relatively simple (e.g. threshold-linear, neuron-like) nodes, each connected to many other nodes by connections (synapses) that can alter in strength during learning.

Consideration of the types of computation that could be performed by neurons has led to connectionist analyses of cognitive function, in which the properties of different types of network in performing different types of cognitive function are analysed. These connectionist models are revolutionizing cognitive science, and our understanding of Human Intelligence (see Rumelhart and McClelland, 1986).

How the computations are performed thus seems to have an important influence on *what* computations are performed. The neuronal networks in the brain are very good at functions such as associative memory, as shown above. They are less good at syntactic operations, involving relations between features, for example that if A B C and D are active, then A and B form one pair, and C and D form another pair. Special properties of networks, such as synchronized firing of groups of neurons, must be invoked if such processing is to be performed (Malsburg, 1990). It may well be that Human Intelligence uses a computational style which minimizes the degree of syntactic processing, and, at the expense of using large numbers of neurons, uses instead processes in which association and competition are important. Examples of how this could be applied to vision have been described elsewhere (Rolls, 1992).

These considerations lead to the view that, when considering the simulation of Human Intelligence, it is becoming possible to perform a simulation on a large computer in which the number of neurons, and the number of connections each neuron has, as well as the computational properties of each neuron, are of the same order of magnitude as those found in real brains. This is possible now for the hippocampus, and I and my colleagues are involved in such a simulation. When the computation is simulated on a computer in this way, the dividing line between the operation of the network in the brain, and how it operates in the computer, becomes quite thin.

The approach to Human Intelligence using neuronal networks is not only useful for the reasons given above, but also because one can start to understand dysfunctions of human cognitive processing by understanding how those processes are implemented in the brain. For example, in Alzheimer's disease one class of neuron that degenerates is the population of cholinergic neurons that projects into the hippocampus. Without this cholinergic input, it is likely that the thresholds of hippocampal neurons are not set correctly, and this may underlie some of the cognitive memory deficits found in Alzheimer's disease.

Lastly, it is the case that the hippocampus has a relatively regular structure which has made it particularly amenable to the neuronal network approach. It is now an exciting challenge for neuroscience and cognitive science to understand the operation of other, more complicated, brain regions such as the cerebral neocortex (see Rolls, 1989a; 1991b; 1992).

Acknowledgements

The author has worked on some of the investigations described here with P. Cahusac, G. C. Littlewort, R. P. Kesner, R. Payne and A. Treves, and their collaboration is sincerely acknowledged. This research was supported by the Medical Research Council, PG8513790.

References

Amit, D. J. 1989: *Modelling Brain Function: The World of Attractor Neural Networks*. Cambridge: Cambridge University Press.

Ballard, D. H. 1990: Animate vision uses object-centred reference frames. In R. Eckmiller (ed.), *Advanced Neural Computers*, Amsterdam: North-Holland, 229–36.

Brown, T. H., Kairiss, E. W. and Keenan, C. L. (1990): Hebbian synapses: biophysical mechanisms and algorithms. *Ann. Rev. Neurosci. 13*, 475–511.

Malsburg, C. von der 1990: A neural architecture for the representation of scenes. In J. L. McGaugh, N. M. Weinberger and G. Lynch (eds), *Brain Organization and Memory: Cells, Systems and Circuits*, New York: Oxford University Press, chapter 18, 356–72.

Morris, R. G. M. 1989: Does synaptic plasticity play a role in information storage in the vertebrate brain? In R. G. M. Morris (ed.), *Parallel Distributed Processing*, Oxford: Oxford University Press, chapter 11, 248–85.

Rolls, E. T. 1987: Information representation, processing and storage in the brain: analysis at the single neuron level. In J.-P. Changeux and M. Konishi (eds), *The Neural and Molecular Bases of Learning*, Chichester: Wiley, 503–40.

Rolls, E. T. 1989a: The representation and storage of information in neuronal networks in the primate cerebral cortex and hippocampus. In R. Durbin, C. Miall and G. Mitchison (eds), *The Computing Neuron*, Wokingham: Addison-Wesley, chapter 8, 125–59.

Rolls, E. T. 1989b: Functions of neuronal networks in the hippocampus and neocortex in memory. In J. H. Byrne and W. O. Berry (eds), *Neural Models of Plasticity: Experimental and Theoretical Approaches*, San Diego: Academic Press, chapter 13, pp. 240–65.

Rolls, E. T. 1989c: Parallel distributed processing in the brain: Implications of the functional architecture of neuronal networks in the hippocampus. In R. G. M. Morris (ed.), *Parallel Distributed Processing: Implications for Psychology and Neurobiology*, Oxford: Oxford University Press, chapter 12, pp. 286–308.

Rolls, E. T. 1990a: Functions of the primate hippocampus in spatial processing and memory. In D. S. Olton and R. P. Kesner (eds), *Neurobiology of Comparative Cognition*, Hillsdale, N.J.: L. Erlbaum, chapter 12, 339–62.

Rolls, E. T. 1990b: A theory of emotion, and its application to understanding the neural basis of emotion. *Cognition and Emotion 4* 161–90.

Rolls, E. T. 1991a: Neurophysiology and functions of the primate amygdala. In J. P. Aggleton (ed.), *The Amygdala*, New York: Wiley-Liss.

Rolls, E. T. 1991b: Research directions in the neural basis of memory.

In W. Singer and G. Orban (eds), *Research Directions in Cognitive Science: European Perspective: Cognitive Neuroscience*, Hillsdale, N.J.: L. Erlbaum.

Rolls, E. T. 1992: Neurophysiological mechanisms underlying face processing within and beyond the temporal cortical visual areas. *Philosophical Transactions of the Royal Society 335*, in press.

Rolls, E. T. and Treves, A. 1990: The relative advantages of sparse versus distributed encoding for associative neuronal networks in the brain. *Network 1*, 407–21.

Rumelhart, D. E. and McClelland, J. L. 1986: *Parallel Distributed Processing*. Cambridge, Mass.: MIT Press.

Squire, L. R. 1992: Memory and the hippocampus: a synthesis from findings with rats, monkeys and humans. *Psychological Review*, *99*, 195–231.

Treves, A. and Rolls, E. T. 1991: What determines the capacity of associative memories in the brain? *Network, 2*, 371–97.

Van Hoesen, G. W. 1982: The parahippocampal gyrus. New observations regarding its cortical connections in the monkey. *Trends in Neurosciences 5*, 345–350.

Weiskrantz, L. 1987: Neuroanatomy of memory and amnesia: A case for multiple memory systems. *Human Neurobiol.*, *6*, 93–105.

5

Computational Vision

Michael Brady

Introduction

Ordinarily, I introduce work on computational vision by stressing its engineering applications: inspection of manufactured products, parts localization to enable them to be grasped by a robot, visual guidance for an automatic vehicle, remote sensing from aeroplanes or satellites and medical applications such as monitoring the growth of cataracts, glaucoma or breast cancer. Our purpose here, however, is to consider the way in which computational methods can be used to model aspects of human vision, such as detecting intensity changes, determining the colour and lightness of surfaces, measuring the image flows generated by object motions, determining the layout of space surrounding the observer by stereo vision, perceptual grouping of image 'tokens' and the control of attention and eye movements. The claim that is most relevant to the collection of articles in this volume is that there has been a rewarding interaction between engineers and biologists based on computer vision:

- building computational models provides precision and powerful insight into the human visual system;
- modelling the exquisite abilities of the human system can guide the engineer to make useful, adaptable artificial systems.

Starting with the late David Marr, an effective champion of the interaction of engineering and biology in computer vision, vision has become a torch bearer for what might be true more generally for intelligence. The common-sense view of intelligence equates it with 'pure thought', with cognitive abilities that are divested of perception and motor control. According to this conventional view, perception and motor control are peripheral to, or are specialized parts of, the real core of intelligence. We take a different view, one that is closely related to that advanced by Dana Ballard elsewhere in this volume: the need to deal with the uncertain, changing, incompletely perceived, noisy world that continually confronts us is not only what necessitates 'smart' robots, but also what necessitates, and shapes, intelligence of human order. According to this view, perception and motor control are crucial to a study of intelligence. Self-protection, searching out food, shelter or a mate are the essence of intelligence. Pure problem solving is a luxury we have gradually grafted on the base of our perception and motor control system.

The remainder of this chapter elaborates on these ideas by sampling a number of topics that have been studied in computational vision:

- the interpretation of 2D images as 3D scenes;
- the representation and recognition of shapes;
- 'model-based' recognition;
- the crucial, though hard, problems of early visual processing;
- the computation of an estimate of global state (or interpretation) given only local information (or constraint);
- 3D vision;
- the integration of vision with motor control to build systems that have a 'continuing existence'.

Interpreting 2D images as 3D scenes

Look for a moment at figure 5.1(a). Most people instantly interpret the image *not* as an arrangement of straight lines drawn on a flat page (which it assuredly is), but as an oblique view of a solid L-shaped piece that is lying on the ground. Why do we prefer the 3D interpretation? Is there only one such? If not, why do we see the one we do? It is important to realize the limitations of a purely

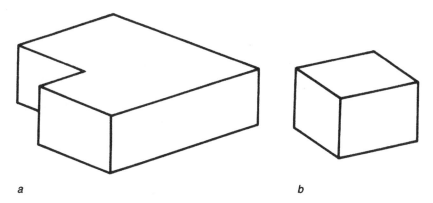

a   *b*

Figure 5.1 (a) A line drawing on a planar piece of paper that is instantly interpreted as a solid L-shaped piece lying on the ground. (b) Perspective distortion means that the image of a rectangular brick never has parallel sides.

geometric approach to this problem: we are perfectly content that the image shown in figure 5.1(b) depicts a rectangular block, but in reality we never see it because of perspective distortions.

To interpret line drawing images such as those in the figures, computational vision has uncovered a number of constraints, and devised a number of processes in which they can be mobilized for recognition. The first constraint is illustrated in figure 5.2: *junctions formed from a number of image lines arise as the projections of a limited set of 3D vertices.* The Y-shaped junction shown can arise in only a few ways, two being shown, certainly far fewer than the full combinatorial set of possible combinations of line interpretations. An image line might (for example) be the projection of a concave or convex edge, both of whose flanking surfaces are visible, or only one of the flanking surfaces may be visible. These are depicted in figure 5.2, in which the occluding edge is shown with both senses of occlusion. Combinatorially, a three-line junction has 3^4 possible interpretations (labellings), but of these only four are physically realizable.

A second constraint is that *a straight edge can have only one interpretation along its length.* (The artist Escher has often explored the possibilities of violating this constraint; see Gregory, 1970 for

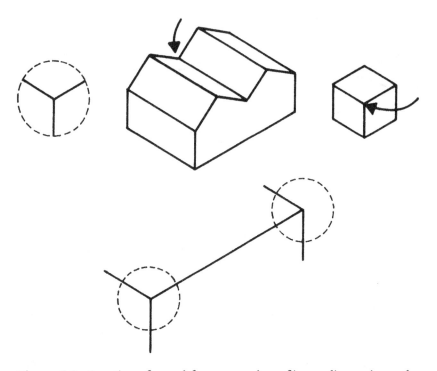

Figure 5.2 Junctions formed from a number of image lines arise as the projections of a limited set of 3D vertices. The Y-shaped junction shown can arise in only a few ways, two being shown.

examples.) Constraints 1 and 2 lead to the 'jigsaw algorithm': initially a set of legal junction pieces are placed beside each junction, then constraint 2 is applied repeatedly to cut out those that do not give rise to a consistent edge interpretation. That these 'local' constraints are insufficient is illustrated in figure 5.3: the notched pyramid isn't planar.

Constraint 3 requires *each image region to be associated with a single surface orientation*. This constraint rules out the notched pyramid as a possible 3D volume.

Mathematical aside:
The gradient space representation is useful in enforcing this constraint. Formally, the normal of a surface ñ is parallel to the vector

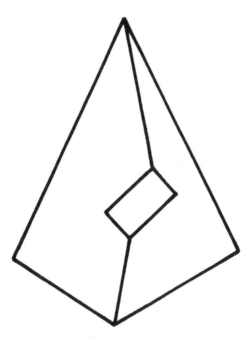

Figure 5.3 The notched pyramid isn't planar but satisfies the first two constraints.

$$\bar{n} = \begin{bmatrix} \dfrac{\partial z}{\partial x} \\ \dfrac{\partial z}{\partial y} \\ -1 \end{bmatrix}$$

Gradient space has axes $p = \frac{\partial z}{\partial x}$, $q = \frac{\partial z}{\partial y}$. It has many interesting properties (see e.g. Horn, 1986). For our purposes, one such is shown in figure 5.4: the line g_l in gradient space joining the gradients g_A, g_B of image regions A and B is orthogonal to l. If the order of g_A, g_B along g_l is the same as A, B across l, then l is convex, else concave. To see this, first place g_A arbitrarily in gradient space, then try to place g_B using the constraints provided by lines l_1, l_2. First, g_B lies along the line perpendicular to l_1. But it also lies along the line perpendicular to l_2. Since l_1

Figure 5.4 In the gradient space representation, the line *l* shown at left is transformed to the gradient line g_l that is orthogonal to *l*.

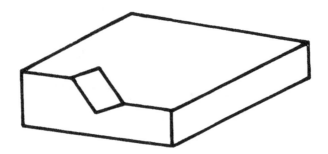

Figure 5.5 The gradient space constraint is insufficient to rule out 'impossible' line drawings.

is not parallel to l_2, g_B must coincide with g_A: the only consistent interpretation of the image is that it is planar – and of course we know this is acceptable since we drew the figure on a plane piece of paper!

Figure 5.5 shows that the gradient space constraint is insufficient. A fourth constraint states simply that *one straight line in space is nearer the observer than another, or further away, but not both*, that is, it makes explicit the relative depths of surfaces. We omit the details (see Sugihara, 1986) and content ourselves with two remarks:

1   Look at figure 5.6, in particular at the marked junction. A long edge and a trihedral junction are 'accidentally' aligned. It turns out that it is possible to use the relative depth constraint to spot the presence of such accidental alignments.

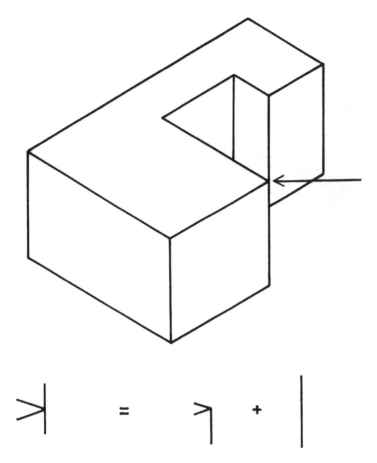

Figure 5.6 The view direction has led to an accidental alignment of spatially separated edges.

2 Reasoning about relative depths enables a program to figure out that figures such as that shown in figure 5.7(a) are 'impossible', by rediscovering that the only consistent non-planar interpretation is an accidental alignment as shown in figure 5.7(b).

To conclude this brief introduction to line drawing interpretation: the isolation, and explicit representation, of a set of constraints, and their mobilization in algorithms explains some of the observed

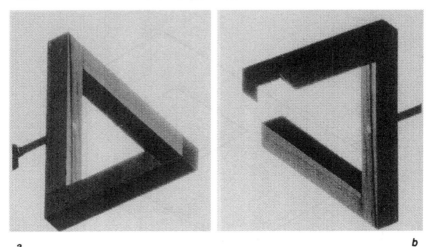

a   b

Figure 5.7 (a) A well-known 'impossible' figure. (b) Richard Gregory's construction pointed out that the impossible figure in (a) could arise from accidental alignment. A computer vision program has found this construction. (By permission of Prof. R.L. Gregory, from *The Intelligent Eye*, London: Weidenfeld & Nicolson, 1970.)

competence that humans display in preferring 3D interpretations of line drawings. Koenderinck's (1990) recent book extends the approach to drawings of curved objects, and makes particular use of modern differential geometry and singularity theory.

The representation and recognition of shapes

There is not enough space here to present other than a skeletal, and selective, account of shape representation (see Brady, 1983; Brady and Asada, 1984; Brady and Scott, 1988 for more discussion). Unfortunately, the accounts of shape representation in the psychology literature have been quite imprecise, certainly insufficiently detailed to support implementation in a computer program that can use the representation to achieve a variety of tasks. What has computer vision taught us?

First, you don't need to recognize an object to determine its position and pose. Second, you don't need to attend to detail to recognize large classes of objects. Indeed, gross representations have the advantage of suppressing the many kinds of noise that

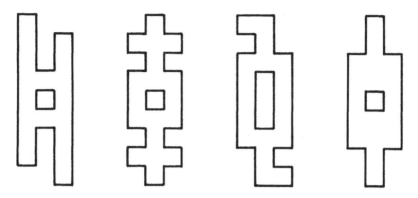

Figure 5.8 A set of four shapes that are difficult to distinguish on the basis of gross features such as area, number of holes, etc.

afflict real images. Horn's (1986) Extended Gaussian Image is based on the observation, originally due to Minkowski, that the pattern of surface normals of a shape, represented on the Gauss sphere and weighted by Gaussian curvature, uniquely specifies the shape of a convex object. Grimson's (1990) recent book sketches another approach in which shape is represented by pairwise constraints between points (or surface facets) on the boundary of the shape. Neither of these representations, however, is useful for detailed inspection, for learning or generalizing about shapes, or in applications in which fine distinctions need to be made between one shape and another, or between a shape instance and its model.

Look at the shapes shown in figure 5.8. One approach to shape representation is to compute a set of statistical parameters such as the area, the height/width (aspect ratio), the number of holes, dimensionless measures of compactness such as the square of the perimeter divided by the area. Unfortunately, these four measures are identical for the shapes in figure 5.8, the shape representation is too coarse to distinguish between them. Suppose, instead, you are asked to find the shape that is 'a rectangle with a coaxial rectangular hole, with two arms attached at opposite ends and with the arms bent at 90 degrees in opposite directions'.

Is it possible for a program to generate such a shape representation (for the third shape in figure 5.8), and to use such a

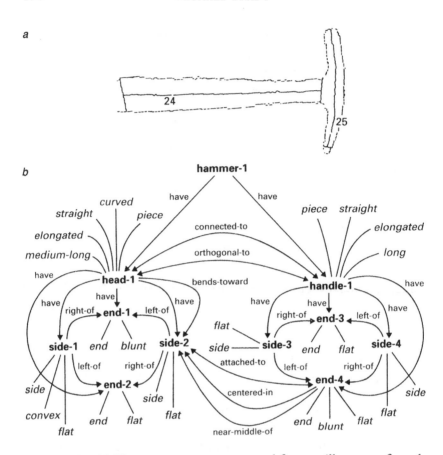

Figure 5.9 (a) The symmetry set computed from a silhouette of a tack hammer. (b) The 'semantic network' representation of the shape computed by the author and Jon Connell.

representation to recognize instances, perhaps when parts of it are occluded? The answer is that it is indeed possible. Over the past eight years the author and his colleagues have been developing 2D and 3D representations with a useful redundancy to handle as many cases of recognition despite occlusion as possible. The redundancy is that both the boundary and the region occupied by the (2D) shape are represented. The boundary representation makes curvature changes explicit, as explained in more detail later. The region representation is based on computing local symmetries. Figure 5.9 shows the symmetry set computed for a tack hammer,

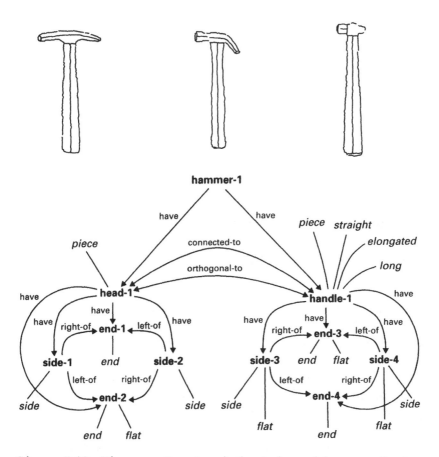

Figure 5.10 The semantic network that is learned by generalization from the three hammer shapes shown.

and a semantic network representation for the shape. Figure 5.10 shows how such a representation can be generalized by showing hammers of different sorts and weakening the representation so that it applies to all of them. Connell and Brady (1987) give more details. Brady and Scott (1988) analyse the representation and the algorithms by which it is computed. We are currently working on a generalization of the scheme that explores the idea of modal decomposition suggested in Brady and Scott (1988), and which is invariant under skew. Altogether, this provides a third lesson to add to the two above: one can generate, and learn, an inconclusive

Figure 5.11 Shape recognition based on a representation of a planar shape that is invariant under skew of the shape.

shape representation that has many of the characteristics of specific exemplars, and one can use this representation to recognize further instances of the shape, even when they are partially hidden by other objects.

Recently, Rothwell, Zisserman, Forsyth, Mundy and their colleagues (Forsyth et al., 1990a,b; Zisserman et al., 1990; Rothwell et al., 1992) have explored the use of invariants as a basis for a shape representation. The challenge posed by skew is that the appearance of a shape depends on its orientation relative to the viewer. A single feature, such as a curve, provides insufficient constraint to disentangle the effects of skew. However, a pair of curves does provide sufficient constraint, at least for planar shapes. Roughly, the way one curve distorts is mathematically related to the way a second curve distorts. From the two curves can be computed an invariant, a quantity that is independent of the orientation from which the shape is viewed: figure 5.11 shows an example. So far, only a beginning has been made on the elucidation of invariants; much remains to be done. Interestingly, the mathematics used to date in the development of invariants was developed in the nineteenth century by mathematicians exploring abstract representations of space and transforms that preserve symmetries.

Model-based recognition

The recognition schemes described in the previous section are addressed primarily to the question 'what is in the scene?' We saw that it is possible to compute representations which resemble, in some respects at least, the 'mental schemes' proposed by Bartlett (1932) in his classic study of remembering. In many practical cases, there are strong contextual constraints on the kinds of objects we expect to see. For example, if the task is aerial reconnaissance of airfields, we may expect to see aeroplanes, aircraft hangars and runways. On the other hand, camels and submarines are unlikely. Since we may suppose that we have a vast number of mental representations of objects, a task of considerable practical import, and, according to Bartlett and others of direct relevance to human perception, is enshrined in the task 'find the aeroplanes'.

The key insight in such approaches is that putative matches between image and model fragments must conform to constraints imposed by the model. For example, if two edges e_1 and e_2 are found in the image, and it is hypothesized that e_1 forms part of the front of a wing while e_2 forms part of the back of the wing, then the image distance between e_1 and e_2 constrains the distance to the aeroplane, and the slope of the wing relative to the camera. The image position of a fragment matched subsequently must conform to the constraints imposed by the model, e.g. the relative length and width of the wings and the length and width of the fuselage.

Many variations on this theme have been explored in working programs. They differ in what constitutes a model, what information is extracted from the image to initiate the constrained match process, and how the model constraints are propagated. Dickson (1990) and Grimson (1990) give good overviews of model-based vision. Figure 5.12 is representative of results obtained by programs of this sort. Here the features extracted are 'corners', sharp changes in edge direction, the model fragment consists of a pair of such vertices, and the match process is by voting in an accumulator array (see Thompson and Mundy, 1987 for details).

Early visual processing

The first stage of visual processing is to convert the continuous light energy distribution reaching the eye or TV camera to a form that the brain or computer can use. In the case of a TV camera this amounts to digitizing the image (sampling it into an array, typically 512 × 512, of brightness values), and quantizing the brightnesses to one of, typically, 256 values. The computer's

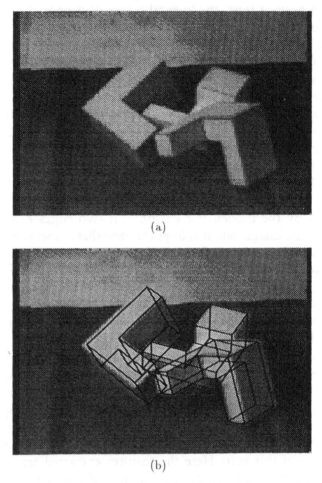

(a)

(b)

Figure 5.12 A typical example of 'model-based' recognition, by a program constructed by Ian Reid at Oxford.

earliest representation of an image fragment looks like figure 5.13(a); equivalently it can be plotted as a piece of image surface, figure 5.13(b). Studies of early visual processing in the human system stress the importance of intensity changes, which conforms with the engineer's view that a constant signal carries no information. The first question to be addressed is how are intensity changes detected? In 1962, Hubel and Wiesel discovered that visual cortex contains populations of cells whose response to intensity changes differs according to the relative direction of the intensity a *Grey levels*

```
161 162 162 162 163 163 163 158 139 110   96 102 110 116 121 126 126 128 132 136 139
161 161 161 159 159 159 159 156 136 107   95 101 109 113 121 129 131 131 134 137 139
160 160 161 161 162 162 161 156 136 106   94 101 109 113 119 126 129 131 134 137 138
159 159 159 159 159 159 160 154 132 101   92 101 108 110 114 121 126 128 131 134 137
160 160 161 161 161 161 161 156 134 103   92 101 108 110 114 119 124 128 130 132 136
159 159 159 160 159 159 159 155 133 102   91 100 107 109 112 117 122 124 128 132 137
160 162 162 161 161 160 160 156 136 105   93 100 107 109 112 117 121 125 129 130 134
158 158 159 159 159 159 159 155 136 106   93 100 108 110 110 114 120 123 127 129 132
147 149 151 152 153 155 156 153 134 104   92 102 109 109 110 113 118 123 127 129 132
109 112 114 117 121 125 128 128 118  98   90 100 106 108 111 113 116 118 122 125 130
 78  79  81  82  84  86  89  91  89  84   87  97 105 103 101 104 111 114 116 117 122
 62  63  63  64  65  66  68  69  72  75   85  95 103 101  95  95 100 102 103 106 113
 55  55  56  56  56  57  59  60  64  73   84  95 103 103  96  95  97  98  98 101 107
 57  57  58  58  58  58  58  58  62  72   85  95 103 103  98  95  98 100 100 102 108
 58  58  58  58  58  58  58  58  63  73   84  95 103 104  98  94  98  99  98 100 107
 58  58  58  58  58  58  58  58  63  73   85  96 103 105  99  95  98  99  99 101 108
 56  56  57  57  58  58  58  58  63  74   85  96 104 105  99  95  99 100 101 103 109
 57  57  57  58  58  58  58  59  64  74   86  96 104 106  99  95  98  99 101 104 110
 57  58  58  58  58  58  58  59  64  73   86  97 106 108 101  96  99 101 101 103 108
 57  57  58  59  59  59  59  60  64  74   86  96 104 106 100  97 100 100 101 105 111
 58  58  58  59  59  59  59  60  65  75   87  97 106 108 101  98 101 101 101 104 111
 60  59  59  59  59  59  60  60  64  74   86  97 106 109 101  97  99 101 101 103 109
 60  60  60  60  60  60  60  61  64  73   86  98 109 111 103  99 101 102 103 104 109
 60  61  61  61  61  61  61  62  66  75   86  97 106 109 103  99 101 101 102 104 109
```

b *Intensity surface*

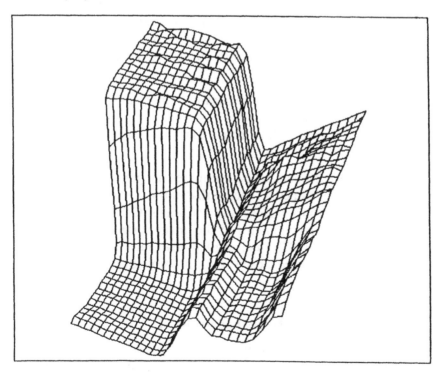

Figure 5.13 (a) The computer's earliest representation of an image fragment is a large array of sampled intensities. (b) Equivalently, the image fragment can be plotted as a piece of image surface.

change and of the cell's preferred orientation. They are 'orientation tuned'. We now believe that such cells essentially compute first and second directional derivatives of the image surface. Later work has explored operations such as a difference-of-Gaussians (approximately, the Laplacian after Gaussian smoothing), though this performs poorly in practice, and directional Gaussian modulated sine waves (Gabor filters).

Computational studies from image processing suggest non-linear, idempotent operators, such as those pioneered in mathematical morphology (Serra, 1982; Noble, 1990) see figure 5.14 and Owens' local energy model (Owens and Venkatesh, 1989).

Fleck has adapted a number of ideas from algebraic topology in her development of the 'Phantom' model of edge detection. Figure 5.15 shows a typical result of her implemented algorithm, which has recently been extended to extract texture boundaries.

Early information-theoretical approach to psychology in the 1950s included a study by Attneave (1954) of the role of corners (more precisely, curvature discontinuities). The brief presentation by psychologists (using devices called tachistoscopes) of images such as that shown in figure 5.16 were not significantly more difficult to interpret than smooth curve line drawings. The message seems to be:

- edges provide tighter constraint than regions of uniform brightness, and
- corners provide tighter constraint than smooth portions of edges.

But how are corners to be computed in practice? Asada and Brady (1986) developed a scheme that extracts curvature changes along image contours at several spatial scales. Others have studied the local differential geometry of the image surface. Koenderinck and van Doorn (1987) have argued that such mathematically-based approaches agree closely with physiological data from cell responses.

Global from local

Many processes, particularly those of early vision, provide only local information that does not completely constrain the parameter

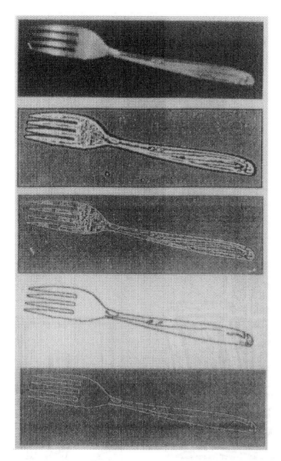

Figure 5.14 An image of a fork and the intensity changes discovered by a program by Alison Noble at Oxford. Note in particular the ends of the tines, which are missed by most edge detection algorithms.

of interest. The human visual system is remarkable for its ability to combine such locally computed information to yield one (or at any rate a small number of) globally consistent values. As an example, consider the motion (optic flow) field first studied by the psychologist Gibson (1950).

Mathematical aside: A first order Taylor's series expansion of the time-varying image $I(x, y, t)$ yields the 'motion constraint equation'

Figure 5.15 A typical result from Margaret Fleck's *Phantom* edge
detection algorithm at Oxford. (a) The image. (b) The 'cartoon' in which
edges correspond to transitions between black and white. (c) An image
reconstructed from the cartoon shows that most information has been
preserved by the edge detector.

$$\bar{\mu}(s) \cdot \bar{n}(s) = -\frac{\partial I/\partial t}{\|\nabla I\|}$$

Where $\bar{n}(s)$ is the unit vector $\nabla I/\|\nabla I\|$ in the direction of the
image gradient, $\bar{\mu}(s)$ is the optic flow we seek to compute and
$\partial I/\partial t$ is the partial derivative of the image with respect to time.
The motion constraint equation tells us two things.

Figure 5.16 Brief presentation of line drawings, such as that shown, reliably elicited recognition.

1. to first order, only the component of $\bar{\mu}(s)$ in the direction of the brightness gradient can be estimated locally. There is no estimate for the tangential component.
2. even so, the estimate of $\bar{\mu}(s) \cdot \bar{n}(s)$ is likely to be worthless unless $\|\nabla I\|$ is quite large, which it is, typically, either in textured regions or at intensity changes (edges).

Now consider a shape such as that shown in figure 5.17 that is translating and rotating. The arrows indicate the size of $\bar{\mu}(s) \cdot \bar{n}(s)$ for sampled points along the curve.

A local (myopic) detector for motion works primarily for edges and similar features, and can detect only motion perpendicular to the edge it is observing. The problem of global-from-local amounts, in this case, to piecing together the estimates to find the missing tangential component, hence the whole optic flow $\bar{\mu}(s)$.

Mathematical aside: One popular approach is to use a variant to constrained least squares, variously variational and regularization methods. For example, Hildreth (1984) supposed that the

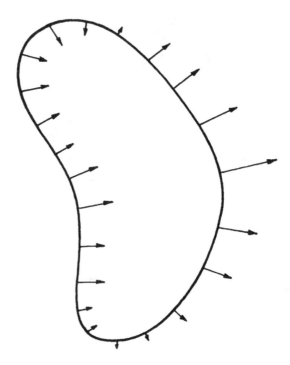

Figure 5.17   Image of a curve that is translating and rotating. The arrows indicate the direction and magnitude of the 'optic flow'.

measured values of $\bar{\mu}(s) \cdot \bar{n}(s)$ are denoted by $\bar{\mu}^{\perp}(s)$ and computes the flow field $\bar{\mu}(s)$ that minimizes

$$\oint \left(\frac{\partial \bar{\mu}_x}{\partial s}\right)^2 + \left(\frac{\partial \bar{\mu}_y}{\partial s}\right)^2 ds + \lambda \oint (\bar{\mu}(s) \cdot \bar{n}(s) - \bar{\mu}^{\perp}(s))^2 ds$$

In this expression, the second term enforces the motion constraint equation and agreement with the data, while the first term imposes a smoothness constraint on $\bar{\mu}(s)$ along s. The constant λ controls how much the data is believed relative to smoothness. The constrained least squares problem can be discretized and solved numerically using a locally parallel implementation of a suitable algorithm. There are many possible approaches.

Hildreth was particularly concerned to relate the behaviour of her algorithm to psychophysical results concerning the human motion system. Constrained least squares computations have the advantages of being fast to compute and have well-understood convergence proofs. They have the major disadvantage that they assume a convex energy function, so that the result they compute will be the nearest local minimum, which may, or may not, be the global minimum depending on the problem.

A number of techniques have been developed to escape local minima to compute the global minimum. These include simulated annealing (also called stochastic relaxation), an algorithm that provably, in some cases, attains the global minimum but takes forever to do so (or so it seems to the programmer)! Blake and Zisserman (1987) have pioneered the technique of graduate non-convexity that works in polynomial time, and heuristically works well in many cases. All these techniques can give good results, but we should avoid being seduced by general methods. Often, a problem can be posed differently to overcome the difficulty.

Optic flow is a good case in point. A second-order Taylor's expansion of the flow field suggests that the full flow $\bar{\mu}(s)$ can be estimated accurately near corners. This suggests a two stage process:

1. Estimate $\bar{\mu}(s) \cdot \bar{n}(s)$ everywhere, and $\bar{\mu}(s)$ where it can be estimated reliably (e.g. at corners)
2. Propagate the $\bar{\mu}(s)$ values between corners.

Gong and Brady (1990) report such an algorithm. Wang and Brady (1990) have implemented it in parallel on a network of transputers. Figure 5.18 shows a result computed by the method. It would be interesting to build on Hildreth's psychophysical experiments to see whether the Brady-Gong-Wang algorithm is related to human vision.

Three-dimensional vision

A single 2D image $I(x,y)$ depicts, typically, a fully 3D world. We interpret flat (planar, two-dimensional) photographs and paintings as depicting a fully three-dimensional world populated by

Figure 5.18 The 'optic flow' computed by a parallel implementation of an algorithm developed by the author, Siaogang Gong and Han Wang. The full flow is estimated at image 'corners' and propagated between such points using the motion constraint equation by a wave process.

curved objects lying at various distances from the viewer. The reduction in dimension, from three in the scene to two in the world, arises directly from the imaging process (confounded by perspective distortion but that is not of immediate interest). The dimensional reduction is even more remarkable when motion is added: cinema and TV exploit the fact that we quickly (a few tens of milliseconds to be precise) interpret an image stream $I(x,y,t)$ (three dimensions) as objects in motion (it requires six numbers to specify the translation and rotation of a moving object). These dimensional reductions, with their corresponding loss of information, are easily undone by our visual system, at least when it is taken out of the psychological laboratory to view the real world! How is this done?

The puzzle was well formulated by Helmholtz (1963) in viewing a room:

> Looking at the (normal) room with one eye shut, we think we see it just as distinctly and definitely as with both eyes. And yet we should get exactly the same view in case every point in the room were shifted arbitrarily to a different distance from the eye, provided they all remained on the same lines of sight.

Evidently, we do not treat every line of sight independently, or the room would look rather strange. Some time later, the American psychologist Ames built such a room and it can be seen at the Smithsonian Institution! Instead of treating each line of sight independently, we need to mobilize additional constraints, or knowledge, about the world. One such constraint reared its head in the discussion of optic flow above: mostly depth varies smoothly, with occasional sharp changes.

In a landmark contribution to the theory of human perception in 1950, James J. Gibson (1950) emphasized the rich variety of 'cues' for depth that are to be found in images in the real world, including the overlap of one object by another, texture gradients (as shown for example in figure 5.20), smooth shading, the relative motions of objects (called motion parallax), and stereo vision.

Stereo (two-eyed) vision is the technique for computing three-dimensional layout of the world most intensively studied by psychologists, and in computational vision. Early algorithms matched patches of the left image against likely patches in the right image. Such schemes work only when there is a close photometric relationship between the images, for example when the scene has an appearance rather like matt monochrome paint. A good example of this is in remote sensing of tree-covered mountains, indeed such algorithms are in regular and successful use in aerial photogrammetry.

An important constraint (called epipolarity) was uncovered by nineteenth century photogrammetrists, and underpins most computer vision stereo algorithms and studies of human stereo vision. As pointed out by Helmholtz, we know that each point of an image defines an optic ray which together with the line joining the optic centres of the two eyes defines a plane. The plane intersects the other image plane in a line (the epipolar line) along which matches for the point in the first image must lie. This constraint reduces the number of putative matches to a single line. Many algorithms were developed in computer vision with additional constraints such as smoothness: the disparities between neighbouring left-right matches should not change 'too quickly'. Following the psychophysical investigations of Burt and Julesz (1980) a new constraint, the disparity gradient limit, was uncovered,

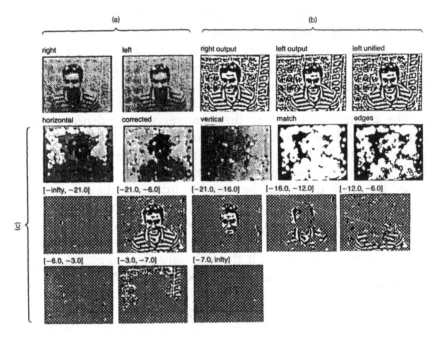

Figure 5.19 (a) A stereo pair of images. (b) The intensity changes found in the images in (a). (c) Slices at different depths after stereo matching.

then refined and implemented in a computer program PMF by Pollard, Mayhew and Frisby (1985). This is one of the most powerful stereo algorithms to have been developed to date. Here we see an example of computer vision leaning directly on a study of human vision to produce a practical system. Of course, PMF has its limitations. Techniques for overcoming them, and their implications for human vision, is an active area of research.

Figure 5.19(a) shows a stereo pair of images. With practice, you may be able to cross your eyes to look at the left image with your right eye, and the right image with your left eye. Then you may find that the person 'jumps out' of the image and stands in front of the wallpapered background. Figure 5.19(b) shows the output from Margaret Fleck's (1988) PHANTOM intensity change detector for the left and right images. You may find it easier to match the images in figure 5.19(b) than those in figure 5.19(a).

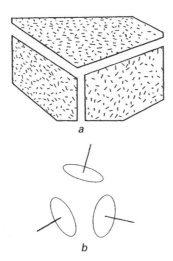

Figure 5.20 (a) Line segments extracted from an image of a box sprinkled with rice grains. (b) Surface orientations computed by Blake and Marinos' program for each of the regions shown in (a).

Figure 5.19(c) shows a series of slices through the depth map computed by Fleck's program. The person has clearly been separated from the background.

Over the past twenty years, computational models for most of the three-dimensional 'cues' that appear to be used by the human visual system have been proposed, in fact, many models for each cue. We do not have space here to do justice to the subject, and content ourselves with two examples. Figure 5.20(a) shows three textured regions computed by a program developed by Blake and Marinos (1990) from an image taken of three sides of a black rectangular box that has been sprinkled with rice grains. The short lines indicate the directions of the individual grains. The program rests on the assumption that the rice grains are randomly scattered on the box and that no orientation is preferred. Figure 5.20(b) shows the surface orientations computed by Blake and Marinos' program for each of the regions shown in figure 5.20(a). Blake and Marinos explore a number of statistical assumptions and propose a powerful computational framework for shape from texture.

It is well known by make-up artists that the *perceived* shape of a surface, for example a human face, can be altered radically by the appropriate use of powder, paint and lines. A face can look thinner or a jaw can become more prominent. The way that surfaces reflect light is remarkably complex (see for example Horn and Brooks, 1989). Often, simple models can give qualitatively correct results. For example, a shape-from-shading program developed recently by Frankot and Chellappa (1990) can be applied to a shaded image of the moon's surface, and construct a reasonable estimate of the actual contours.

James J. Gibson emphasized that in most practical, real world, viewing conditions, several 'cues' are present, each of which offers some estimate of the three-dimensional structure of the environment. But what do such representations of 'structure' contain? And, equally importantly, how are they combined to provide the perceiver with a more reliable percept than could be expected if only one 'cue' were relied upon? A number of proposals have been made, each of them amounting to a model of the uncertainty that attends upon any individual 'cue', and each a model of full surface reconstruction (see Blake and Zisserman, 1987 and the special issue volume 7 (1988), part 6 of the *International Journal of Robotics Research*. One recent example of 'cue integration' by the author and Simon Lee (1991) combined shape-from-shading and stereo to estimate the size of the optic disk, as part of a program to assist ophthalmologists to monitor the development of glaucoma.

Vision plus motion control

The first 25 years of research in computational vision concentrated on static images. In part this was because it proved remarkably difficult to develop algorithms that could reliably compute a perceptually satisfying set of intensity changes, that could perform shape recognition for naturally occuring shapes, etc. But mostly it was because computer vision researchers were intimidated by the massive volume of information that arises in natural vision, given that computer memory was so expensive and processors so slow. Of course, judged from the perspective of ten years from now (seemingly a timeless statement!) today's computers are still expensive and slow, but things have improved sufficiently for us to be a bit more confident, and to begin to tackle the construction of algorithms that have a continuing existence. This has raised a whole series of fresh tough problems! First, most control theory has developed for one-dimensional signals (time is typically the dimension) and there are technical reasons why many of its methods do not extend simply to the three dimensions that arise in image sequences. Second, and more importantly, we are having to rethink the whole basis of many of our algorithms as we unfold them to take advantage of novel parallel computer architectures. However, there are opportunities too, not least the extra constraint that is provided by temporal coherence (smoothness) over and above the spatial coherence referred to earlier.

Several exploratory systems have been built, including a system that can play a creditable game of ping-pong, one that can reach out and touch balls suspended from the ceiling as they swing to and fro, and several that generate depth maps as a robot vehicle moves through an environment. This is an area of intense research and excitement at present.

Where have we reached?

Let me sketch what I consider to be a realistic assessment of where we have reached. First, there has been considerable progress, not least on low-level image processing, spatio-temporal aggregation of information, stereo, shading and surface reconstruction. I am reminded of the old joke about the person who has climbed a tree, and points excitedly at the ground below, as evidence of massive progress to reach the moon. At the very least, I think we have climbed a tall tree!

More significantly for the current volume, there has been strong interaction between engineers and physiologists/psychologists, to their mutual benefit. Such interactions seem to be growing in volume and strength. Engineers have obviously benefited, for example in the case of stereo, by adapting results and theories about human vision. Engineers have returned the compliment, not least by introducing a new level of mathematical rigour into the study of perception, as well as the rigour that derives from building working implementations of whole systems on unforgiving computers.

What can we *not* do?

Plainly, there is a vast amount to learn about vision. Current computer models too often resemble a house of cards whose responses degrade disgracefully whenever they are presented with an input that differs slightly too much from what is expected. Change the lighting and the program won't work! Again, the convenient mathematical assumption that the scene is composed of polyhedral objects is strained if a program has an uncontrived glimpse of the real world. Worse, such an assumption may encourage mathematically elegant, but ultimately irrelevant, work. Vision programs dimly perceive purpose or threat, other than that which has been written into them, and most programs serve no social or ecological benefit. It will be a long while before we build a program remotely as smart as a sheep.

Acknowledgements

My professional life in Oxford has been enriched by discussions with my colleagues, particularly Andrew Blake, Hugh Durrant-Whyte, Ron Daniel, David Murray, Stephen Cameron, Lionel Tarassenko, Penny Probert, Andrew Zisserman, David Forsyth, Margaret Fleck, Brian Rogers, Andrew Parker, Roberto Cipolla, and my graduate students who continue to provide the high spots of my weeks. Donald Broadbent read my draft manuscript carefully and offered many welcome suggestions for improvement, especially to avoid my natural temptation to lapse into mathematics!

References

Asada, H. and Brady, Michael 1986: The curvature primal sketch. *IEEE Trans. PAMI*, 8–1, 2–4.

Attneave, F. 1954: Informational aspects of visual perception. *Psychol. Review*, 61, 183–193.

Bartlett, F. C. 1932: *Remembering*. Cambridge: Cambridge University Press.

Blake, A. and Marinos, C. 1990: Shape from texture: estimation, isotropy, and means. *Artificial Intelligence*, 45, 323–80.

Blake, A. and Zisserman, A. 1987: *Visual Reconstruction*, Cambridge, Mass.: MIT Press, 1987.

Brady, Michael 1983: Criteria for representations of shape. In A. Rosenfeld, B. Hope and J. Beck (eds), *Human and Machine Vision*, San Diego: Academic Press.

Brady, Michael and Asada, Haruo 1984: Smoothed local symmetries and their implementation. *Int. J. Robotics Research*, **3**.

Brady, Michael and Scott, Guy 1988: Parallel algorithms for shape representation. In I. Page (ed.), *Parallel Architectures and Computer Vision*, Oxford: Oxford University Press.

Burt, P. and Julesz, 1980: A disparity gradient limit for binocular fusion. *Science*, 208, 615–17.

Connell, J. H. and Brady, Michael 1987: Generating and generalizing models of visual objects. *Artificial Intelligence* 31, 159–83.

Dickson, J. W. 1990: Image Structure and Model-based Vision. D.Phil thesis, Oxford University Dept. Engineering Science.

Fleck, M. M. 1988: Boundaries and Topological Algorithms. PhD Thesis, MIT Artificial Intelligence Laboratory.

Forsyth, D. et al. 1990a: Invariance: a new framework for vision. 3rd Int. Conf. Computer Vision Osaka, Japan.

Forsyth, D. et al. 1990b: Transformational invariance: a primer. *Proc. Brit. Mach. Vision Conf.*, Oxford, 1–6.

Frankot, R. T. and Chellappa, R. 1990: Estimation of surface topography from SAR imagery using shape from shading techniques. *Artificial Intelligence*, 43, 271–310.

Gibson, J. J. 1950: *Perception of the the visual world*. Boston: Houghton Miflin.

Gong, S. and Brady, Michael 1990: Parallel computation of optic flow. In O. D. Faugeras (ed.), *Proc. 1st European Conf. Computer Vision*, Antibes, Heidelberg: Springer Verlag.

Gregory, R. L. 1970: *The Intelligent Eye*. London: Weidenfeld and Nicolson.

Grimson, W. E. L. 1990: *Object Recognition by Computer: the Role of Geometric Constraints*. Cambridge, Mass.: MIT Press.

Helmholtz, H. 1963: *Handbook of Physiological Optics*. New York: Dover.

Hildreth, E. C. 1984: Computations underlying the measurement of visual motion. *Artificial Intelligence* 23, 309–53.

Horn, B. K. P. 1986: *Robot Vision.* Cambridge, Mass.: MIT Press.

Horn, B. K. P. and Brooks, M. J. 1989: *Shape from Shading.* Cambridge, Mass.: MIT Press.

Koenderinck, Jan J. 1990: *Solid Shape.* Cambridge, Mass.: MIT Press.

Koenderinck, Jan J. and van Doorn, A. 1987: Representation of local geometry in the visual system. *Biol. Cyb.,* 53, 383–96.

Lee, Simon, and Brady, Michael 1991: Integrating stereo and photometric stereo to monitor the development of glaucoma. *Image and Vision Computing.*

Mayhew, J. and Frisby, J. P. 1991: *3D Model Recognition from Stereoscopic Cues.* Cambridge, Mass.: MIT Press.

Noble, J. A. 1990: Descriptions of Image Surfaces. D.Phil thesis, Oxford University Dept. Engineering Science.

Owens, R., and Venkatesh, S. 1989: A robust scheme for isolating and classifying features. Int. Conf. Artificial Intelligence in Industry and Government, Hyderabad, India, 664–76.

Pollard, S. B., Mayhew, J. E. W. and Frisby, J. P. 1985: PMF: A stereo algorithm using a disparity gradient limit. *Perception,*14, 449–70.

Rothwell, C. et al. 1992: Canonical frames for planar object recognition. *Proc. 2nd European Conf. Computer Vision,* Genoa.

Serra, J. 1982: *Image Analysis and Mathematical Morphology.* London: Academic Press.

Sugihara, K. 1986: *Machine Interpretation of Line Drawings.* Cambridge, Mass.: MIT Press.

Thompson, D. W. and Mundy, J. L. 1987: Three-dimensional model matching from an unconstrained viewpoint. *GE Computer Science Branch, Corporate Research and Development.* Also in Bolles and B. Roth (eds), *Proc. 4th Int. Symp. on Robotics Research,* Santa Cruz.

Wang, Han, Brady, Michael and Page, Ian 1990: A fast algorithm for computing optic flow and its implementation on a Transputer array. *Proc. Brit. Mach. Vision Conf.,* Oxford, 175–9.

Zisserman, A. et al. 1990: Relative motion and pose from invariants. *Proc. Brit. Mach. Vision Conf.,* Oxford, 7–12.

6

The Handling of Natural Language

Gerald Gazdar

Introduction

Human beings make use of a variety of languages, some of them artificial (algebraic expressions, predicate logic, knitting patterns, FORTRAN, etc.) whereas others are natural (English, Japanese, Dyirbal, etc.). Some of the artificial languages can be understood by computers just as effectively as they can be by humans. But, in 1991, none of the natural languages can be as well understood by computers as they can be by those humans who speak the languages natively. This chapter provides an account of how researchers have been trying to get computers to handle natural language texts in insightful and useful ways. It begins by looking at the structure and recent history of the academic discipline whose territory this is, gives an indication of where the problems are and the progress that has been made, and concludes by looking at some of the practical applications that the satisfactory handling of natural language is leading to.

The academic discipline that studies computer processing of natural languages is known as Natural Language Processing (NLP) or Computational Linguistics.[1] Although a few writers make a distinction, most researchers use these two names for the field interchangeably. NLP is most conveniently seen as a branch of Artificial Intelligence (AI), although it is a branch into which many linguists and a few psycholinguists have moved. In Europe, NLP is dominated by ex-linguists but this is not so in the USA where there is a tradition of people moving into the field from Computer Science.

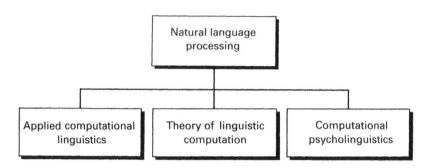

Figure 6.1   The structure of the field.

NLP itself breaks down into three main sub-areas with respect
to the goals of the researchers involved (see figure 6.1).[2] The core
area is theory of linguistic computation which is the area in which
computational linguists examine what it is like to compute natural
language, what it is like to process it, what its computational properties are, what sort of algorithms are appropriate for processing
it, what kinds of representations are appropriate for its analysis in
a computational context, and what sort of theoretical problems
the analysis of natural language by computer throws up. It is a
fairly abstract area of study and it is not one that makes particular
commitments to the study of the human mind, nor indeed does
it make particular commitments to producing useful artefacts.
These latter concerns are the concerns of computational psycholinguistics and applied computational linguistics, respectively.

Although the bulk of work in NLP falls under the theoretical
or applied headings, for at least the last 15 years or so, there have
been computational linguists who have been shooting for specifically psychological goals. And, in more recent years, there have
been psycholinguists who thought that the way to study how the
mind processes language was via the tools and models that they
could get out of NLP. Typically, work in this area begins by
building a computational model of some psychologically plausible account of human natural language processing. This computer
model can be used to generate interesting hypotheses and detailed
sets of predictions about behaviour. These can then be tested
experimentally using standard psycholinguistic techniques.

As the name suggests, applied computational linguistics is the application of NLP techniques to produce systems that are potentially useful for some purpose, often for a commercial purpose. I will end this chapter by considering a number of examples of such applications.

To conclude this introduction, we need to note one further distinction, and that is a dichotomy between language interpretation and language generation. If you are trying to process natural language by computer, then there are really two main things that you could do or would want to do. One of them is to understand natural language and the other is to produce or generate natural language. There are other tasks like learning natural language which are plainly of interest but the two main tasks as they have been seen by the field are interpretation and generation. In fact, the large bulk of work in NLP has been on interpretation. However, in the last few years, generation has shown signs of coming into its own, although it is still a minority pursuit. Of course, some NLP tasks involve both operations, most obviously machine translation. A machine translation system has to both understand text in one language and generate text in the other.[3] But there are also other systems that involve both. Abstracting systems, for example, are systems that attempt to understand the text and then give you an abstract of it, and that involves both interpretation and generation. A very specialized kind of abstracting system will be presented at the end of this chapter.

In the following sections, I will examine the issues that have preoccupied NLP during the 1980s, give some special attention to the problem of ambiguity, present a sketch of the architecture of contemporary NLP systems, venture some speculations as to the issues that will dominate NLP in the 1990s, and conclude by looking at the practical applications that research in NLP is leading us towards.

Key issues in the 1980s

Parsing and syntax
Morphological processing
Declarativeness
Portability
Ambiguity

These five issues do not have the same ontological status: the first two are subdomains of the object of study, the second two are desiderata for (components of) NLP systems, and the last is a problem that all NLP techniques and systems have to face.

These five issues were in vogue for much of the 1980s and a great deal of work was done on them. That is not to say, of course, that no other important work was done or that other issues were seriously neglected, but simply that these five topics provide the flavour of the decade. It might appear, to a rational outsider, that parsing, syntax and morphological processing are so central to NLP that they would, of necessity, feature on the key list of topics for any decade of work in NLP. But this is not the case. In the 1970s, these areas were all deeply unfashionable in NLP: there was virtually no work on morphological processing, for example. Likewise, 'procedural' was a positive attribute in the 1970s, and 'declarative' was barely used at all. In the 1980s, 'declarative' became the positive attribute and 'procedural' became a term of abuse. So there was a big shift in the 1980s in terms both of the domains that were being investigated in depth and also the spirit in which they were being investigated.

The 1980s were a period when computational linguists realized that they actually needed to have grammars of languages in order to be able to do NLP. To the rational outsider, that may seem a surprising comment to make. How on earth can you process a language unless you have a grammar for it? Nonetheless, in the 1970s there were many people in NLP who argued vociferously that you did not need grammars to process natural language and that you were probably better off without them. Even those who rejected those arguments and thought that syntactic processing was essential did not think that writing computational grammars of natural languages was an especially important thing to do. That all changed in the 1980s and, along with the interest in grammars, an interest in parsing returned. Parsing, for the computational linguist, means attempting to discover what the syntactic structure of a sequence of words is with a view to finding a way station from which you can infer the semantic structure and thus the meaning.

A whole family of formal languages for representing computationally interpretable grammars of natural languages known as the unification grammars emerged in the 1980s. This family of grammars gets its name from an operation for putting information together called unification: it is this operation that provides the basis for all of these formal languages.

In parallel with the emergence of the unification grammars, a new family of parsers became the standard way to do syntactic processing. The chart parsers represented a very significant advance for the field because their key characteristic was the way they stored intermediate results and thus removed the need to waste time doing the same thing again and again. Once a chart parser recognizes that a certain sequence of words could be, say, a noun phrase, it remembers that fact: if at a later time it is relevant to identify that noun phrase then the work has been done and the results have been recorded. The parsers that were widely used in the 1970s did not store intermediate results and, as a consequence, they could quite often recalculate the existence of a particular noun phrase dozens or even hundreds of times, with obvious consequences for the efficiency of the overall process.

Another approach to parsing also attracted a lot of attention in the 1980s: deterministic parsers never retrace their steps, they become irrevocably committed to every decision they make. Deterministic parsing was originally motivated by computational psycholinguistic considerations: computer parsers get bogged down in ambiguities but humans do not. Although the most strictly deterministic parsers are probably not a satisfactory solution to any problem in NLP, the thinking that led to them has proved to have an enduring legacy and less radically deterministic devices continue to be an active research area in both computational psycholinguistics and in NLP more widely (see, e.g. Faisal and Kwasny, 1990).

Just as sentences are made up of words, so words are made up of morphemes (*reactivated = re-active-ate-ed*). Linguists standardly distinguish between inflectional morphology, which concerns those morphemes which signal syntactic properties of words (such as tense, person, gender, number and so on), and derivational morphology, which concerns those morphemes that change the syntactic category of the meaning of a word (thus the suffix *-ate* can convert an adjective to a verb and the prefix *re-* can change the meaning of a verb). With very few exceptions, computational linguists have always ignored derivational morphology and regarded it as a matter for lexical listing (thus *active, activate* and *reactivate* would all be separately listed in the lexicon, typically with no link made between them). Prior to 1980, computational linguists had also largely ignored inflectional morphology, a topic that was dealt with *ad hoc*, or consigned to exhaustive lexical listing. Surprisingly, perhaps, one can get away with this neglect if one restricts attention to a language like English. English inflectional morphology is pretty minimal: the suffixes -*s*, -*ing* and -*ed* almost exhaust the topic. In the 40 year history of NLP, the vast bulk of the work done has been done on English – hence the neglect of inflectional morphology processing. However, when computational linguists turn their attention to a language like Finnish, they find that each verb has several thousand morphologically distinct inflectional forms. The problem can no longer be treated *ad hoc* or consigned to the lexicon. In the 1980s, for the first time, the computational processing of inflectional morphology got on to the research agenda and valuable work was done, both in terms of the algorithms needed to tease words into their components and in terms of the representations needed to describe the nature of a language's inflectional morphology in a way that a computer program can understand.

Faced with a group of tourists at Oxford station who wish to get to Linacre, you can give them a set of instructions: 'Go down to the main road, turn left and then immediately left again, bear right and then keep walking straight for nearly a mile until you hit a T junction, turn left and continue for six hundred yards until you find the college on your right'. Or you can simply hand them your map of Oxford and run for the train. The first alternative is a procedural solution; you are giving them a set of instructions that, if followed, will result in their achieving the goal they have. The second alternative is a declarative solution: you are giving them a detailed description of Oxford and leaving it to them to use it howsoever they will to achieve their goal. Apart from enabling you to catch your train, the declarative approach has many advantages. It makes it easier for the tourists to find their way back from Linacre to the station; it will make it possible for them to deal with the fact that the whole of Broad Street has been sealed off by the police because of a bomb scare, and it will enable them to get from Linacre to the Ashmolean without further interaction with natives.

The computational linguists of the 1970s had been excited by algorithms and procedures and so they wanted to reconstruct natural languages in terms of algorithms and procedures. Curiously enough, within computer science proper, things were moving in the opposite direction and theoretical computer scientists were trying in the 1970s and through into the 1980s to say what they were doing in a declarative rather than in an algorithmic manner. In the 1980s, this change of emphasis had begun to affect NLP and, by the end of that decade, the development of what are known as declarative semantics for grammars and other computational linguistic formalisms had become a major research area. Giving a declarative semantics for a grammar formalism is very like providing a semantics for a logic (as truth functions, for example, provide a semantics for the propositional calculus). Work of this kind would really have been unthinkable in the context of 1970s NLP.

One of a number of motivations for the move away from proceduralism towards declarativeness was what has come to be known as 'portability'. It was realized that some of the largest and most successful natural language systems of the 1970s were essentially cul-de-sacs. They were very impressive at doing what they did but you could not transfer what they had done to another domain. These 1970s NLP systems were not portable: they were special purpose systems that you could develop in their own terms but then they just came to an end. You could not do anything else with them other than what they had been designed for. For applied computational linguistics, portability is an important issue because of the cost of constructing things like lexicons and grammars for natural languages. They are extremely costly to produce, so if they are not portable, if you cannot move them from one application to another, then the chances are that what you want to do is simply uneconomic. Portability is related to declarativeness because if you have declarative representations of various kinds of linguistic knowledge then that knowledge will be much more portable than if the knowledge is inextricably bound up with algorithms and bits of code that do processing of various kinds.

Ambiguity

The last item on my list of 1980s concerns is ambiguity, a topic which appeared in passing in the discussion of deterministic parsing, above. Ambiguity has always been a major issue for NLP and there is no immediate prospect of its dropping off the research agenda. In many ways, it is *the* problem of NLP. Ambiguity is pervasive at all levels of description in an NLP system. From the lexicon and the morphology through the syntax and semantics right through to the pragmatics, ambiguity problems appear at every point. Ambiguity can be local, which means that, ultimately, it can be resolved by the linguistic context at the relevant level of analysis. Or it can be global, which means that it cannot be resolved by reference to the current level of analysis. Even local ambiguity can seriously slow processing as the search space becomes cluttered with options that turn out to lead nowhere. Global ambiguities are, if anything, worse: they multiply against each other and they can lead to very large numbers of potential interpretations that have, somehow, to be resolved at a subsequent stage of analysis.

Ambiguity is often seen as a problem for interpretation but it is also a problem for generation. The fact that a sentence you have generated has a particular interpretation is not, in itself, a guarantee that it does not have dozens or hundreds of other interpretations. The problem the generation program then faces is that of ensuring that the intended interpretation is the one that the reader picks up. Thus, even in generation, one has to worry about ambiguity because one cannot be sure that what one has produced is unambiguous, or, at least, that the intended reading is the (humanly) preferred reading of those available.

I will illustrate the ambiguity issue by reference to a couple of old chestnuts familiar to anyone that has ever done a course in NLP, but none the worse for that. Consider the following sentence: 'The police were ordered to stop drinking after midnight.' Now, ask yourself these questions: Who was drinking? Was it the police? When were they drinking? When was drinking supposed to stop? When was the order given? A few moments reflection will convince you that you cannot answer any of these questions since you cannot know what this sentence is intended to mean. It is globally ambiguous and has many possible interpretations, most of which are quite sensible. Without knowing something of the context in which the sentence was uttered, you simply cannot determine which of these interpretations was intended by the speaker. Notice that the ambiguity has little to do with any of the words in the sentence being ambiguous: the ambiguity is structural rather than lexical. One factor in the structural ambiguity of this sentence is the point at which the prepositional phrase *after midnight* is attached: whether to *drinking*, to *stop drinking* or to *ordered to stop drinking*.

The next example illustrates lexical as well as structural ambiguity: 'Flying planes made her duck.' Unlike the previous example, this sentence only has one sensible plausible interpretation and it may therefore be rather hard for the reader to see that it is, in fact, four ways ambiguous. The word *duck* is lexically ambiguous between a verb indicating a particular kind of movement and a noun referring to a species of aquatic waterfowl. The word *her* is ambiguous between a possessive pronominal determiner and a pronominal object noun phrase (cf. *his/him*). The word *make* is ambiguous between the verb that just takes an object noun phrase as in *I made a cake* and a verb which takes a noun phrase and a following verb phrase as in *I made Sally leave*. Finally, *flying* is ambiguous between an adjectival sense and a verbal sense. Although you are probably still having difficulty establishing exactly what the four interpretations are supposed to be, a 1980s NLP system would have no such difficulty. Unfortunately, it would probably also have no way of choosing between them.

Most of the ambiguity that shows up in the parsing of English is caused by constructions that put things together in pairs so as to form an object that is of the same syntactic type as one or both of the items in the pair. That is, in fact, one of the things that happens in the police example, above. The three main English constructions that have this property are co-ordinate constructions, noun-noun compounds and the attachment of modifiers such as adverbial phrases, prepositional phrases and the like. These are the three major sources of structural ambiguity in English text. Ambiguities with this property proliferate in number according to a series known to mathematicians as the Catalan series. The numbers in this series grow to be very large very quickly (1, 1, 2, 5, 14, 42, 132, 469, 1430, 4862, . . .). To illustrate this, here is an artificial and idealized example (adapted from Church and Patil, 1982) which is meant to give you some quantitative sense of just how big the ambiguity problem is:

1   Kim (1)
2   Kim and Sue (1)
3   Kim and Sue or Lee (2)
4   Kim and Sue or Lee and Ann (5)
5   Kim and Sue or Lee and Ann or Jon (14)
6   Kim and Sue or Lee and Ann or Jon and Joe (42)
7   Kim and Sue or Lee and Ann or Jon and Joe or Zak (132)
8   Kim and Sue or Lee and Ann or Jon and Joe or Zak and Mel (469)
9   Kim and Sue or Lee and Ann or Jon and Joe or Zak and Mel or Guy (1430)
10 Kim and Sue or Lee and Ann or Jon and Joe or Zak and Mel or Guy and Jan (4862)

Example (1) is a simple one-word noun phrase that has but a single interpretation. Example (2) is a simple co-ordinate noun phrase that also has only one interpretation. Example (3) contains both conjunction and disjunction and has two possible interpretations (the conjunction embedded as a disjunct or the disjunction embedded as a conjunct). In example (4), the number of available interpretations is five and, when we reach example (10), there are nearly 5000 possible interpretations of a noun phrase that is less then 20 words long.

You should not let the artificiality of the examples deceive you into thinking that this kind of ambiguity is unlikely to be a problem in naturally occurring texts. Consider noun-noun compounds: although they look different and play a different role in language from co-ordinate constructions, the mathematics of their combinatorial ambiguity is just the same as that illustrated above. You do not have to search hard to find noun-noun compounds like *judiciary plea bargain settlement account audit date*. You can find such things in pretty much any official governmental document you care to look it. That one expression has 132 distinct structural

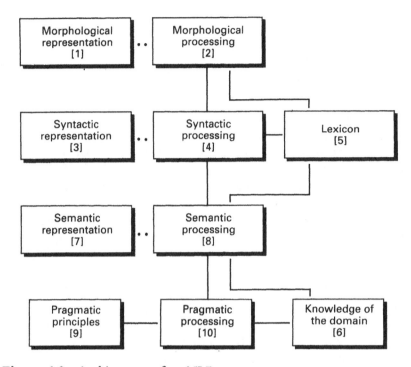

Figure 6.2 Architecture of an NLP system.

interpretations. If you come across a sentence with a couple of these in it, then you are looking at over 17,000 different structurally distinct interpretations for the sentence as a whole. As a human reader, you probably have little or no problem arriving at the intended interpretation for such sentences. But for NLP they constitute a formidable unsolved problem.

My discussion of ambiguity has concentrated on lexical and syntactic examples, but, as indicated above, ambiguity is pervasive at all levels of analysis. It has been, is, and is likely to remain the key problem in natural language processing.

The shape of the art

Figure 6.2 is intended to show a roughly consensus view of what the majority of researchers take to be the architecture of a full NLP system. The dotted lines link a representation to the processing component that operates on that representation. The continuous lines indicate flow of information: the directionality may vary here depending on whether one is dealing with a system that interprets or generates a natural language. Thus, for example, in an understanding system, the syntactic processing component [4] will combine information from the lexicon [5] and the output of the morphological processor [2] and transmit its results to the semantic processing component [8]. Note that the box for knowledge of the domain [6] is not really a part of NLP proper, but rather a component that NLP must hope to borrow from the area of knowledge representation in AI.

The lexicon [5] has become increasingly important over the last five years or so. The reason for that increasing importance is that it has absorbed much of the rest of NLP. The style these days is to put enormous amounts of linguistic information in the lexicon and very little elsewhere. So it is not uncommon now to see grammars that only contain two or three rules. All the information that used to be in the grammar has been shifted into the lexicon. Likewise with the semantics, rather than having a lexicon that said almost nothing about semantics, you see lexicons that are full of elaborate lambda calculus representations. In consequence, the semantic processor may well have rather little to do.

I think it is fair to say that, for many practical purposes, computational linguists now know how to handle components [1] to [4]. This comment needs to be rather carefully hedged: I do not mean that all known problems are solved or that there are no interesting research topics left in these components. There are masses of interesting research topics and people will go on actively working on these for many more years. What I mean by my comment is that there are solutions to the problems addressed by these components that you can more or less pick off the shelf. And, if you do not particularly care about the sort of ideological or technical niceties that distinguish these solutions from each other, then you can just grab one and go away and use it if you are, say, an applied computational linguist. The available solutions do what they are supposed to do quite well.

By contrast, components [8] to [10] remain deeply problematic. These are areas in which understanding is not well advanced, where there are no standard solutions, and where the existing literature does not provide techniques that you can just adopt and use and be confident that they will work well enough for practical purposes. Components [5] to [7] fall somewhere between the two categories of component just considered.

Key issues in the 1990s

Ambiguity
Probabilistic techniques
Robustness
Scale
Reuse of extant knowledge

This is a speculative section and I shall keep it short. One thing we can be confident of is that the ambiguity problem is not about to go away. However, people are becoming much more adventurous in the range of possible solutions that they are prepared to countenance. In particular computational linguists of all ideological persuasions are increasingly inclined to tolerate probabilistic techniques for reducing the ambiguity problem. In essence, the hope now is that considerable amounts of knowledge can be boiled down to numbers. These numbers show up in a variety of forms, including probabilistic grammars, neural network techniques and trigrams. Trigrams are statistics about the co-occurrences of three items, often three words. It is a technique that IBM has been working on for more than a decade, to the mirth of much of the rest of the field. But, around 1988, people stopped laughing and began to take such probabilistic techniques very seriously. There is every reason to believe that they will continue to be taken seriously throughout the 1990s. In contrast to Speech and several other areas of AI, neural network techniques have yet to prove their worth in the NLP area, but so much work is being done with them that they are almost bound to find a use in NLP by the end of the decade.[4]

The problem of robustness is that users of NLP systems do not offer such systems perfect input. The input they offer is, from the point of view of a pedantic grammarian, deviant and unacceptable in a variety of ways. Although the 1980s NLP advances in morphology and syntax made an enormous contribution to the field, they did not make any contribution to the problem of robustness. The canonical 1980s morphological processor, syntactic parser, grammar or lexicon just falls over completely if it is given something that is in any way deviant. Probabilistic techniques are widely thought to have a role to play here also.

Much of the most exciting work in the 1980s was illustrated by what people in the field called toy systems, systems whose lexicons have only a few dozen words in and whose grammars have rules for only the most basic constructions. Such experimental systems were never intended to deal with the huge variety of constructions and the tens or hundreds of thousands of words that a real natural language contains. The problem of scale arises because researchers have found that toy systems cannot, in general, simply be enlarged by adding more of the same. Size poses a whole collection of problems of its own and these problems will have to be addressed in the 1990s if the theoretical advances of the 1980s are going to lead to useful applications.

As I have already noted above, one of the things that the 1980s has taught us is that it is extremely expensive to write realistic size grammars or realistic size lexicons from scratch. The work is painfully slow and requires a highly skilled labour force with postgraduate qualifications in linguistics or NLP. This fact has led to an energetic search for ways of achieving the same end more cheaply, either by automating the process or by getting a free ride on some body of extant knowledge, already expensively acquired for another purpose. The 1990s will thus see an increasing emphasis on techniques for processing existing bodies of text (known as corpora) in order to gather usage statistics, infer grammars, bootstrap parsers and so on. There will also be a steadily increasing use of other existing machine readable resources, such as typesetting tapes from dictionary publishers, and knowledge bases built for other AI systems. So, for example, a knowledge base that has been built for some expert system might be called into use to do double duty for a natural language system working on the same domain. By the end of the 1990s, we may even see machine readable encyclopaedias being invoked. There is a chicken and egg problem here, of course: before a computer can use the knowledge in a machine readable encyclopaedia to help interpret a natural language, the computer has to be able to understand the natural language in which the encyclopaedia is written.[5]

Applications of NLP

Introduction

Arguably the hardest part of applied computational linguistics is finding applications that are both doable and useful. There are many things that are doable and there are many things that would be useful if we could do them. Finding the intersection is not just a matter of searching two lists and looking for common members. We cannot be sure, in advance of trying to build them, which NLP projects are doable and which are not. And we cannot be sure, in advance of trying to market them commercially, which NLP products are useful and which are not. There is an analogy here with expert systems technology. That technology undoubtedly works for a variety of domains and yet many commercial attempts to use expert systems fail. Often they fail for reasons largely irrelevant to the capabilities of the technology.

Despite these observations, there is already a commercial market for NLP products, albeit a fairly small one.[6] The available evidence suggests that this market is doubling in size every couple of years (Johnson and Guilfoyle, 1989). The main NLP areas in which we can expect to see further commercial products appear in the 1990s are listed below:

Machine translation
Natural language information generation
Natural language interfaces
Message understanding
Hybrid systems

I will not say anything about machine translation except that it is the NLP application with the longest pedigree and the one that has attracted the most investment over the years (not least from the EEC which has spent millions of pounds on the EUROTRA project).[7]

Natural language information generation is a relatively new area and it may well be ripe for commercial exploitation.[8] One class of application involves machines that explain themselves. Consider the humble photocopier. At the moment, when you press the print button, a tiny LCD screen blinks *Paper jammed*. Faced with this message you go and look for help, rummage around for the long-lost instruction book, or start opening covers and pulling levers at random. But if the photocopier could talk to you, it might say: *I am sorry, there seems to be a problem. I think a sheet of paper is jamming my mechanism. Please open the cover above the main paper feed tray and pull the green handle.* You then open the wrong cover and it says: *No, not that cover, the one below.* And so on. The machine monitors what you are doing and talks you through a diagnostic and repair routine. In many cases, to be useful, the output of natural language information generation systems will need to be routed through speech synthesis technology rather than a visual display unit. At their simplest, such devices will simply utter canned text that is triggered by particular states of the microprocessor that controls the machine (as is the case with the English error messages that appear on the LCD screen of the contemporary photocopier).

But the sheer complexity of modern machines, which may need to communicate any one of a thousand or a hundred thousand different internal states, and the virtually unlimited range of ways in which humans may err in their interactions with such machines, make a canned text approach infeasible in general. Advances in natural language generation research are making it possible to go a good deal further than canned text and to produce utterances *de novo* to fit the situation at hand. The hard problem here is not that of producing semantically correct grammatical English, but that of producing English utterances that come across as natural, fluent, coherent and tuned to what has been said before.

Natural language interfaces

Natural language interfaces to databases have been seen as a primary application for NLP for most of the history of the discipline (see Copestake and Sparck Jones (1990) and Perrault and Grosz (1986) for discussion and references). Existing PC-based commercial products such as Clout (Microrim), Guru (MDB), HAL (Lotus), NLMenu (Texas) and Q&A (Symantec) began to appear in 1985 and several have been successful in the market.[9] Academic work in this area has generally made use of the power of mainframes, minicomputers or, more recently, AI workstations. Commercial products aimed at such platforms have also been available for a number of years from such US companies as AI Corporation and Carnegie Group.

In 1990, the computer on the desk of someone accessing a business database contained an 8088, 8086 or 80286 chip running at between 5MHz and 12MHz. In 1994, that same person will be sitting in front of a machine that contains an 80486 or 80586 chip running at 33MHz to 100MHz. The dramatic increase in processing power that this change represents, together with the availability of AI language compilers and development environments that target Intel-based computers, will make it possible to deliver the (AI workstation-based) NLP technology of the 1980s on the average office desk in the mid-1990s. Here are some examples of the kind of questions that can be understood and answered by this technology:

What products is Jane Carter selling next quarter?
Which staff are being supervised by Dr. Gantry?
Can you tell me who Sam Hart's manager is?
How many of the new technicians were given a bonus last month? Which ones?

Successful natural language interfaces will allow occasional and novice users to employ everyday terminology to get the information they need, without having to concern themselves with the way that information is stored and without having to be trained in the use of the standard interface or access language. Even for experienced database users, they will allow certain types of query to be made much more compactly than would be possible with a standard interface (e.g. follow-up queries that are expressed elliptically).

We can expect the canonical 1990s commercial natural language database interface to be highly modular. It will use a unification grammar and standard parsing techniques. The parser will translate the natural language input into an intermediate representation language based on first-order logic. Inferencing on its knowledge base will then induce the construction of queries in a standard database query language such as SQL.

The system will deal with ambiguity largely by avoiding it. Modifier attachment will be done deterministically (by fiat), multiple co-ordination likewise, and only binary noun-noun compounds (and application-specific noun compounds) will be permitted.

This kind of ambiguity minimization strategy runs the risk that users will mean one thing and yet be interpreted as meaning something different. Thus such systems will offer a natural language paraphrase of their query – 'evaluative feedback' in the sense of Boguraev and Sparck Jones (1984). If the paraphrase fails to reflect the users' intent then they will have the option to rephrase their query. Although such systems will have access to a model of the database domain in which they operate, they will not have a model of the user, nor will they be able to deal with interesting pragmatic phenomena. The standard meanings of standard 'indirect' speech act forms (such as *can you tell me* or *I need to know*) are likely to be hardwired into the syntax-to-database-query mapping. However, queries that embody certain false presuppositions can be flagged (e.g. *how many of the April payments to IBM were returned*? in a world in which no payments had been made to IBM in April) since such functionality can be provided at relatively little cost.

One key reason why restricted systems of the kind just sketched can work is explained by the NLP researcher whose own work led to Q&A: 'Users of English interfaces are remarkably forgiving of natural language limitations and are often content to find *any* English phrasing that will retrieve the data they need, and don't seem too bothered if the most natural way of phrasing a request doesn't work' (Hendrix, 1986, pp. 164–5). This observation provides an important insight for all real world natural language processing systems. Users do not expect natural language processing systems to behave as well as people and they are flexible enough to cope with something that performs much less well.

Message understanding systems

The last decade has seen an exponential increase in the amount of electronic text that can be readily accessed. The most dramatic contributor to this increase has been that of CD-ROM – a 5″ disk of plastic and foil costing less than $2 to reproduce can hold 70 minutes of Mozart or more than 50 million words of text. But faster, cheaper optical character recognition, the ubiquity of computer based typesetting, and the spread of older technologies such as network access, news-wire services, teletext and Prestel have all contributed, separately or in combination, to an avalanche of largely unstructured textual data. This avalanche includes the full texts of many reference books, newspapers, magazines, court reports and official publications of all kinds, and the abstracts of hundreds of thousands of academic and professional publications. For example, the fifth edition of *The CD-ROM Directory* (Mitchell, 1991) lists 1522 disks, whereas the fourth edition (1990) only listed 816.[10]

Unfortunately, the potential users of such electronic text do not have access to good ways of handling it. You cannot just sit down with a CD-ROM and browse your way through 50 million words. For the most part, users are stuck with methods of information retrieval that have changed little over 15 years (boolean string search and indexing by keyword or content word root, essentially). As one recent discussion points out, such methods 'cannot figure out that users interested in sheep husbandry are probably interested in lamb raising' (Nutter, Fox and Evens, 1990, p. 129).

There are two different standard processing tasks that relate to electronic text databases. One is what one might call the data recovery task in which one simply wishes to identify and isolate all and only those portions of the text which deal with some topic. Traditional information retrieval (IR) techniques use indexes to get at documents (e.g. using keywords that have been associated with the document) but much (probably most) of the flood of textual data now available is not indexed (indexing is expensive). And material which has been indexed is quite likely to have been indexed with different purposes in mind from those of the user. The alternative to indexing is string search: text fragments are recovered if they contain some boolean combination of words. But the latter technique is notoriously unsatisfactory. Depending on the job in hand, these IR techniques may or may not be useful: given an unindexed database of newswire reports, (a) boolean string search can produce good results if all you want to do is recover the stories that make reference to terrorism, but (b) if your aim is to identify exactly those stories in which a terrorist attacks a court officer (judge, prosecutor, magistrate, etc.) but is not apprehended, then traditional IR will provide very limited help.

The other task, which is much more ambitious than the recovery task, is one that we might call the database mapping task. The problem here is to map all and only the relevant fragments of the electronic text into the data structures of a conventional database. Traditional IR has almost nothing to offer here. Note that machinery which can deal with the database mapping task can, *ipso facto*, deal intelligently with recovery tasks.

The US military is currently investing large amounts of money in stimulating commercial, government and academic research institutions to provide robust solutions to the database mapping task. The name that has emerged for implementations of such solutions is 'message understanding systems' and there have been three recent conferences dedicated to them, along with a full-scale comparative evaluation of existing systems. A typical military application would be a system that maps prose reports of equipment failures into a standard relational database representation of the information they contain. Such a system does not, of course, do anything that cannot be done by a clerk, but the expectation is that it will do the job more quickly, more cheaply, more reliably and with acceptable accuracy.

SCISOR is a fairly typical instance of a state-of-the-art message understanding system. Its designers claim that it can process Dow Jones financial news stories at more than 500 per hour, correctly identify 90 per cent of those that deal with takeovers, and map 80 per cent of those identified into appropriate database entries (Jacobs and Rau, 1990).

A hybrid application example

I will conclude this chapter by looking in some detail at a particular applied hybrid NLP system. It is a hybrid because it combines

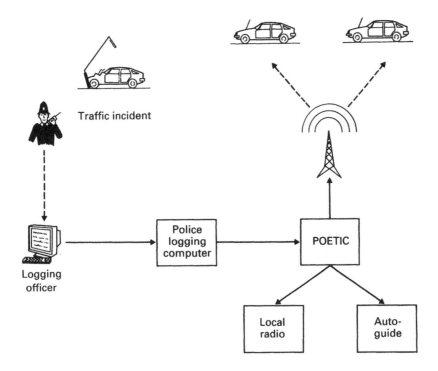

Figure 6.3 An automatic traffic information system.

a large message understanding component, an expert system and a small information generation component. As an example, it provides a pretty good indication of what is possible in NLP applications in 1991. This system has been under development at the University of Sussex for the last six years and rejoices in the most inappropriate acronym: POETIC (Portable Extendable Traffic Information Collator).[11]

POETIC is a system which reads police reports of traffic incidents and, when relevant to do so, automatically generates appropriate warning messages for motorists. It does this by monitoring everything that is typed into a police logging computer and searching for those items which relate to traffic incidents. It ignores all the other material that gets logged by the police. As it collects and interprets relevant items, it uses them to build up a picture of the incident, works out what the likely effects are, formulates suitable advisory messages and arranges for their

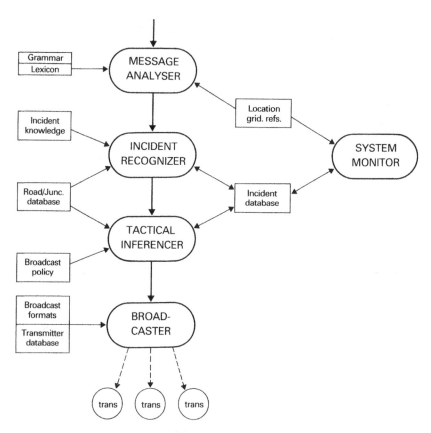

Figure 6.4 The architecture of the POETIC system.

delivery to motorists. Since the system is still a prototype, it uses historical police log records and message delivery to cars is simulated, either on the computer, or via the commercial pager network. If the system were to be made publicly available, then message delivery would be via cellular radio or the Radio Data System.

The overall architecture of POETIC is shown in figure 6.4. The message analyser is a robust parser which identifies those messages that relate to traffic incidents (as opposed to those that relate to burglaries, civil disorder, suspicious persons, lost budgerigars and the like), and maps them into sets of semantic representations (the messages are often ambiguous at this level of analysis).

The incident recognizer uses the incident database to help it decide on the most likely of any competing interpretations supplied by the message analyser. It also seeks to establish co-reference between expressions in successive messages and exploits various kinds of knowledge it has about the likely time course of incidents (for example, a trapped driver will be released *before* the vehicle is towed away). Having established the most likely meaning of the message, the incident recognizer updates the incident database. The tactical inferencer then uses the information in this database to decide whether to disseminate information, what to say, how often to say it and what area to direct the messages at. The other components in the diagram need not concern us here.

The police log takes the form of a more or less verbatim transcription of oral reports received from the police officers in the field. These reports are expressed in a specialized sub-language of English that is telegraphic in character and makes heavy use of a variety of abbreviations (e.g. *rqst* for *request*, *hgv* for *heavy goods vehicle*, *ic* for *incident closed*, and so on). The following example shows a typical sequence of timed messages relating to a particular incident (the log itself would contain dozens of other messages not related to this incident, but these are omitted for the sake of clarity here):

1   0807 a281 at henfield lorry blocking road
2   0809 rqst tow for hgv
3   0814 garage en route
4   0822 garage now attending
5   0824 road will have to be closed
6   0827 recovery will take approx 5 mins
7   0828 diversions in force
8   0929 ic

Input 1 prompts POETIC into the following message, broadcast by transmitter 1 at 0815, and transmitter 2 at 0820:

There is a blockage on the A281 at Henfield. The road is partially blocked. Drivers are advised to reduce speed.

Input 5 alters the message to the following, but it is overtaken by events and never gets broadcast:

There is a blockage on the A281 at Henfield. The road is totally blocked. Drivers are advised to avoid the area.

Input 7 changes the message again. The following message is broadcast by transmitter 1 at 0830, 0845 and 0900, and by transmitter 2 at 0835, 0850 and 0905:

There is a blockage on the A281 at Henfield. The road is totally blocked. Diversions are in force. Drivers are advised to avoid the area.

Notes

Many of the topics raised in the early sections of this paper are covered in much greater depth in Gazdar & Mellish (1989) which also provides a full bibliography. The POETIC project discussed in the final section is supported by a grant from the SERC. I am grateful to Roger Evans for help with that section.

1 It is tempting to say that NLP is the academic discipline that studies computer processing of the written form of natural languages. But that would be a misrepresentation. The discipline that studies computer processing of the spoken form of natural languages is known as Speech Processing or just Speech. Surprisingly, perhaps, Speech and NLP are really rather separate disciplines: there is minimal overlap in the personnel involved, the journals and conferences are different, and the theoretical approaches and methods used have little in common. Speech research studies the problems that are peculiar to processing the spoken form of language whereas NLP research, in principle at least, studies problems that are common to the processing of both spoken and written forms of natural languages. Speech research will not be considered further in this chapter.

2 The terminology is due to Thompson (1983) and the trichotomy is essentially that of Bundy (1990).

3 Although note Somers, Tsujii & Jones (1990) for an approach to machine translation in which the source text is, at most, implicit.

4 The use of a neural network as an 'oracle' in an otherwise conventional parser is one promising line of research (Faisal and Kwasny, 1990).

5 This is much less of a problem with machine readable dictionaries because dictionary entries are written in a highly restricted and highly

structured fashion – almost in a formal language. In addition, the elaborate typographical conventions used by lexicographers make it relatively easy to determine the roles of the various components of an entry (see Boguraev and Briscoe, 1989).

6 See Shwartz (1987) and Obermeier (1989) for discussion of commercial NLP products.

7 Hutchins (1986) provides a near exhaustive history of machine translation research from its beginnings after the second world war until the early 1980s.

8 Bourbeau et al. (1990) report a commercial text generation system that converts meteorological data into marine weather forecasts in English and French.

9 Q&A has been one of the best-selling products in the PC market.

10 Among many other things, the 1991 edition lists disks containing the full text of newspapers and magazines, law reports and/or statutes from many countries, European Community Law and the Official Journal of the European Communities, daily economic wire stories, dozens of dictionaries and encyclopaedias, numerous national patent listings, government press releases, along with vast amounts of textual material that deal with medical and scientific matters.

11 POETIC, as described here, is the creation of David Allport, Lynne Cahill, Roger Evans, Robert Gaizauskas, Anthony Hartley and Chris Mellish. Further details are provided by Cahill and Evans (1990), Evans and Hartley (1990) and Evans, Gaizauskas and Hartley (1990). The project involves a consortium consisting of Racal Research, the AA, the IBA and the University of Sussex, with co-operation from the Sussex Police, the Metropolitan Police and the Road Research Laboratory. Financial support is provided by SERC and the DTI.

References

Bourbeau, L., Carcagno, D., Goldberg, E., Kittredge R. and Polguere, A. 1990: Bilingual generation of weather forecasts in an operations environment. *COLING-90*, Vol. 3, 318–20.

Boguraev, Branimir and Briscoe, Ted 1989: *Computational Lexicography for Natural Language Processing*. London: Longman.

Boguraev, Branimir and Jones, Karen Sparck 1984: A natural language front end to databases with evaluative feedback. In G. Gardarin and E. Gelenbe (eds), *New Applications of Databases*, New York: Academic Press, 159–82.

Bundy, Alan 1990: What kind of field is AI?. In Derek Partridge and Yorick Wilks (eds), *Foundations of AI: A Source Book*, Cambridge: Cambridge University Press.

Cahill, Lynne and Evans, Roger 1990: An Application of DATR: the TIC lexicon. In *Proceedings of the 9th European Conference on Artificial Intelligence*, Stockholm, 120–5.

Church, Kenneth W. and Patil, Ramesh 1982: Coping with syntactic ambiguity or how to put the block in the box on the table. *American Journal of Computational Linguistics* 8.3/4, 139–49.

Copestake, Ann and Sparck Jones, Karen 1990: Natural language interfaces to databases. *Knowledge Engineering Review* 5.4, 225–49.

Evans, Roger and Hartley, Anthony 1990: The traffic information collator. *Expert Systems* 7.4, 209–14.

Evans, Roger, Gaizauskas, Robert and Hartley, Anthony 1990: POETIC – the portable extendable traffic information collator. In Jamsa Heikki (ed.), *OECD Workshop on Knowledge-based Expert Systems in Transportation*, Volume 1 (VIT Symposium 116), Espoo: Technical Research Centre of Finland, 171–84.

Faisal, Kanaan A. and Kwasny, Stan C. 1990: Design of a hybrid deterministic parser. *COLING-90*, Vol. 1, 1–6.

Gazdar, Gerald and Mellish, Christopher S. 1989: *Natural Language Processing in Prolog: An Introduction to Computational Linguistics*. Wokingham: Addison-Wesley.

Hendrix, Gary G. 1986: Q & A: already a success?. *COLING-86*, 164–6.

Hutchins, W. John 1986: *Machine Translation: Past, Present, Future*. Chichester: Ellis Horwood.

Jacobs Paul S. and Rau, Lisa F. 1990: SCISOR: Extracting information from on-line news. *Communications of the ACM* 33(11), 88–97.

Johnson, Tim and Guilfoyle, Christine 1989: Commercial markets for NLP products. In Jeremy Peckham (ed.), *Recent Developments and Applications of Natural Language Processing*, London: Kogan Page, 1–7.

Mitchell, Joanne 1991: *The CD-ROM Directory* (5th Edition). London: TFPL Publishing.

Nutter, J. Terry, Fox, Edward A. and Evens, Martha W. 1990: Building a lexicon from machine-readable dictionaries for improved information retrieval. *Literary and Linguistic Computing*, 5.2, 129–37.

Obermeier, Klaus K. 1989: *Natural Language Processing Technologies in Artificial Intelligence*. Chichester: Ellis Horwood.

Perrault, C. Raymond and Grosz, Barbara J. 1986: Natural-language interfaces. In Joseph F. Traub (ed.), *Annual Review of Computer Science*

1., Palo Alto: Annual Reviews Inc. Reprinted in Howard E. Shrobe
(ed.) 1988: *Exploring Artificial Intelligence*, San Mateo: Morgan
Kaufmann, 133–72.

Shwartz, Steven P. 1987: *Applied Natural Language Processing*. Princeton:
Petrocelli Books.

Somers, Harold L., Tsujii, Jun-ichi and Jones, Danny 1990: Machine
translation without a source text. *COLING-90*, Vol. 3, 271–6.

Thompson, Henry S. 1983: Natural language processing: a critical analysis
of the structure of the field, with some implications for parsing. In
Karen Sparck Jones and Yorick A. Wilks (eds), *Automatic Natural
Language Parsing*, Chichester/New York: Ellis Horwood/Wiley, 22–
31.

7

The Impact on Philosophy

Margaret A. Boden

The philosophy of mind has been deeply problematic ever since the seventeenth century, when Descartes put a metaphysical chasm between mind and body. There have been many attempts to cross the chasm, starting from one side or the other, or to stay adamantly on only one side of it. Those who favour the materialist (as opposed to the idealist) side are typically influenced by their respect for the natural sciences – including neurophysiology and psychophysics.

In terms of William James' familiar distinction, such philosophers are tough-minded rather than tender-minded. The tough-minded typically believe that the fundamental realities are described by physics (since modern physics deals with energy as well as mass, they are termed 'physicalist' rather than 'materialist'). They may also believe that the higher-level sciences are reducible to physics, so that psychology is in principle dispensable (because its theories could be systematically mapped onto, or even translated into, theories of physics). The tender-minded spurn such reductionism. They regard mental categories as no less real than physical ones, and may even regard them as philosophically fundamental.

These two intellectual types have a low opinion of each other. As James himself put it: 'The tough think of the tender as sentimentalists and soft-heads. The tender feel the tough to be unrefined, callous, or brutal' (1907, p. 13). Evidently, these are not purely disinterested arguments. On the contrary, they relate to some of our deepest human values.

In my experience, the computer simulation of intelligence tends to bring out the tenderness in even the toughest of one's acquaintance. Most people who know little or nothing about this work take for granted that it must involve a thoroughly reductionist account of mind. Where, they ask, is there any room for meaning, purpose, subjectivity, creativity, consciousness? Assuming that the answer can only be 'Nowhere!', they dismiss the very idea of thinking of mental processes in computational terms. 'Unrefined', 'callous' and 'brutal' are mild, compared with the insults they hurl in the debate: 'When men write whole volumes of such stuff, are they not mad, or intend to make others so?' (Robinson, 1972 (after Hobbes)).

In fact, the impact of computer simulation on philosophy is largely due to the hope of a reconciliation between the tough and the tender, to the promise that we can have our science and eat our humanism too.

As we shall see, some philosophers are not persuaded: they argue that no such reconciliation can be effected by computational means. If they are right, then computational psychology is deeply flawed, not to say fraudulent, in that it promises to do something which simply cannot be done. Before addressing this issue, let us see why the initial philosophical impact of this work was so great.

During the first half of the twentieth century, two philosophies of mind were especially popular with those who prided themselves on being tough-minded. One was epiphenomenalism, the other behaviourism. Both, however, had serious flaws.

Epiphenomenalism, initiated by Thomas Henry Huxley in the late nineteenth century (Huxley, 1893), is the view that brain-events cause other brain-events, and sometimes mental events too – but these are a mere by-product, and have no causal powers themselves. Mental events were likened to the smoke given off by a steam-engine: we may see only the puffs of smoke above the hedgerows, but all the work is being done by the engine. Like Descartes, Huxley could not explain how mental states can possibly be caused by physical ones. Moreover, epiphenomenalism goes against our intuition that mental states can have both mental and physical effects. Othello's jealousy, we normally say, caused him both to disbelieve what Desdemona said about her missing handkerchief, and to kill her with his bare hands.

Behaviourism, which took various philosophical forms after the psychologist John Watson's original manifesto (Watson, 1913), not only allowed no causal power to internal mental states – it seemed to deny them altogether. Gilbert Ryle (1949), for example, scoffed at the Cartesian 'Ghost in the Machine', and analysed all psychological concepts in terms of dispositions to behave. To say that Othello is jealous, for instance, is to say that in certain circumstances he will probably behave in certain ways; even 'itches' and 'tickles' are to be similarly understood. However, this strongly reductionist programme is infeasible. In general, one cannot specify the behaviour corresponding to one mental predicate except by using others. Othello's jealousy, for example, involved his believing or suspecting that Desdemona was lying, and his decision to punish her by death.

In the 1950s, a third approach appeared to tempt the tough-minded: the identity-theory (also known as 'central-state materialism') (Place, 1956; Smart, 1959). Most psychological concepts were analysed as behavioural dispositions caused by specific brain-states, while sensations – such as itches and tickles – were regarded as *identical* with some brain-state. The identity was said to be empirical, not conceptual: a matter of scientifically discoverable fact (like the fact that lightning is identical with electrical discharge). 'Othello is jealous' or 'Desdemona feels pain' are true if and only if such-and-such brain-states are present, and it is for the neurophysiologists to discover the relevant 'such-and-such'.

Of the various objections raised against the identity-theory, two concern us here. First, it is highly implausible that exactly the same brain-states underlie all cases of jealousy, or all cases where someone wants to catch the 3.30 train. (A Parisienne can want to catch the 3.30 train, but she thinks of it by using French numerals, not English ones; presumably, the activity in the language-area of her brain is different also.) Indeed, Karl Lashley (1950) had shown that *an individual organism* need not rely on the very same neurones in remembering a particular task. Second, it is conceivable that there might be intelligent Martians, meriting many of the same psychological descriptions as we do, but with a very different bodily form. To say 'No Martian can be jealous' on the grounds that Martians do not form exclusive personal relationships would be in order. But to say 'No Martian can be jealous' merely because they have a different physiology seems unwarranted.

During the heyday of the identity-theory, the first AI-programs were already being developed. Indeed, computational ideas had been related to various philosophical issues in the 1940s (McCulloch, 1965). But few philosophers knew of this work. The provocative term 'artificial intelligence' – guaranteed to raise philosophical hackles – was not coined until 1956, the more anodyne 'computer simulation' being used well into the 1960s. Alan Turing's paper on 'Computing Machinery and Intelligence' had appeared in the philosophical journal *Mind* (Turing, 1950), but it was primarily focused on whether intelligence could be defined in behavioural terms. So far as the mind-body problem was concerned, the identity-theory was the loudest song to be heard – discordant though it might be.

In 1960, then, each of the most widely accepted physicalist philosophies of mind was inadequate. To be tough-minded was to abandon some of our deepest psychological intuitions, without putting a coherent account in their place. Small wonder, then, that Hilary Putnam's papers of the 1960s had such an impact (Putnam, 1960; 1967).

Putnam's paper introducing 'functionalism' was the first systematic application of computational ideas to the mind-body problem. He used the abstract notion of a Turing machine, and the program-hardware distinction (then being made by people working with computers), to argue that mental states can be defined in functional terms, abstracted from their specific embodiment.

For the functionalist, mental states are defined in terms of their causal relations with other mental states, and with sensory input and motor output. These causal relations are abstract functions, as opposed to physical energy-exchanges, and they are in principle specifiable as a machine-table for a Turing machine. Both minds and Turing machines are abstract computational systems, which might be embodied in many different material machines. Some 'new' mental states might be discovered previously unknown to common sense. For example, computational theories might refer to many non-introspectible processes involved in speaking, seeing or grasping. But familiar folk-psychological categories such as jealousy, so it was assumed, could be functionally defined and accepted within a coherent psychological science.

Functionalism had many attractions, in terms of 'saving' our common-sense intuitions. It posited internal, hidden, mental states.

It allowed that these have causal powers. It allowed that they are essentially connected with behaviour and with other mental states (so it is not a mere matter of fact that jealousy can lead to suspicion, but a conceptual truth). Like the identity-theory, it saw each individual instance of a mental state as, at base, identical with some physiological state. But unlike the identity-theory, it allowed varying embodiments to the several instances of a given type, or class, of mental event. (As Putnam pointed out, two computers running 'the same' function, or algorithm, may do so in physically very different ways.) Accordingly, it not only saved our intuition that other species too might have mental states, but also saved the autonomy of psychology. If various instances of jealousy can each have a different embodiment, there is no possibility that neurophysiology alone could ever describe or explain jealousy *as such*.

At last, it seemed, the tough-minded could be tender-minded as well. Jealousy is a real phenomenon, with real effects, and psychology is the science suited to deal with it. Speaking, seeing and grasping – all taken for granted in the drama concerning Desdemona's handkerchief – are psychological phenomena too, to be studied in abstract computational terms. Moreover, Putnam's abstract philosophical argument appeared to be backed up by a new area of empirical research: the computer-modelling of mental processes. To cap it all, some of the leading figures in this young science were theorizing about the mind in terms very like those employed by functionalism.

Specifically, an approach similar to Putnam's was being taken throughout the 1960s by Allen Newell and Herbert Simon (whose theory is presented in chapter 2) (Newell and Simon, 1961; 1972). They pioneered many technical advances in AI: list-processing and means-end analysis in the 1950s, production systems in the late 1960s, and the SOAR architecture in the 1980s. They applied these techniques within various computer-models of thinking, starting with the 'Logic Theorist' and 'General Problem Solver' of the 1950s. They justified their programs by reference to their extensive psychological experimentation on human subjects. And they drew on their empirical work in arguing a bold philosophical claim about the nature of intelligence.

Newell and Simon claimed that symbols and computations

are embodied as physical patterns and processes: brains and computers alike are 'physical symbol systems' (Newell and Simon, 1972, pp. 21–2; Newell, 1980). However, their psychological theory described these systems in abstract information-processing terms, the details of the underlying hardware or physiology being irrelevant.

They defined symbols and computations in terms of a causal semantics. In a causal semantics, meaning is defined in terms of causal relations (involving the organism, its environment, and information-processes within the organism itself). An expression *designates* an object, they said, 'if, given the expression, the system can either affect the object itself or behave in ways depending on the object'; and the system can *interpret* an expression 'if the expression designates a process and if, given the expression, the system can carry out the process.' The *meaning* of a symbol is identified as the set of changes which it enables the information-processing system to effect, either to or in response to some other object or process.

Like Putnam, Newell and Simon admitted unobservable mental states, for they stressed that the 'objects' and 'processes' could be internal to the system. Unlike Putnam, they complemented philosophical discussion with empirical hypotheses about specific computational processes that might be involved.

The 1960s cocktail of functionalism and computer-modelling was heady stuff. Cognitive science grew apace (and is growing still), the functionalist position widely accepted as its philosophical base. At the same time, functionalist views gained ground within the philosophy of mind. The old philosophical puzzle of intentionality was discussed in terms that allowed (some conceivable) computers just as much right to be described in psychological terms as their human designers (Dennett, 1987). Mind, intelligence, rationality, meaning: all of these – and creativity, motivation, and emotion too (Boden, 1972; 1977, ch. 11; 1990; Simon, 1979; Sloman, 1987) – were seen as grist to the computational mill.

But, here as in other areas of life, the first fine careless rapture did not last. Worried or dissenting voices were raised against functionalism, folk-psychology and the 'formalist' methodology of cognitive science. Some came from within the computational camp (e.g. Fodor, 1980; Stich, 1983), some from outside it (e.g. Nagel, 1974; Block, 1978; Dreyfus, 1979; Searle, 1980). Even Putnam, the high-priest of functionalism, has recently recanted (Putnam, 1988).

The two main areas for philosophical debate (both of which are still highly problematic) concern consciousness on the one hand, and meaning or understanding on the other. Let us consider these briefly, in turn.

As for the problem of consciousness, there is no such thing. That is to say, there is no *one* problem of consciousness. The words 'conscious', 'consciously' and 'consciousness' are used to mark many different psychological distinctions, which call for different theoretical explanations.

Some puzzles about consciousness have already been illuminated by functionalist ideas. Consider, for example, the case of so-called multiple personality in which 'Eve Black' apparently had full access to the conscious thoughts of 'Eve White' (thoughts which Eve Black refused to admit as her own), yet Eve White was unaware even of the existence of Eve Black. We can understand how such non-reciprocal co-consciousness is possible if we liken the mind to a computer program, whose modules can influence each other, and/or share different memory-stores, to varying extents. In general, a functionalist approach can illuminate those philosophical and psychological puzzles where the pure Cartesian 'unity' of the mind seems somehow to be in question.

Explaining conscious experience *as such*, however, is more difficult – not least because we do not really know what is meant by 'consciousness as such'. Many attacks on functionalism have argued that causal-computational relations between abstractly-defined mental states simply cannot account for – or even describe – our felt experience (Nagel, 1974; Block, 1978). In short, functionalism leaves experience on one side.

We can imagine, these critics claim, that all the functional relations were as the functionalist says, but without any conscious sensation (any *qualia*) at all. Or we can imagine the accompanying qualia being systematically different, so that one mind experiences red whenever another (functionally identical to it) experiences green. Since we can imagine these things, there is something

– namely, conscious experience – which is not captured by a functionalist philosophy.

The functionalist may (and in my opinion should) reply that perhaps we *cannot* imagine these things. An anatomically-ignorant person may think that he or she can imagine a mermaid. If by this they mean not merely a viable creature with the external appearance of half-woman-half-fish, but also one with the internal anatomy of half-woman-half-fish, then they are mistaken. Knowledge of comparative anatomy (not to mention physiology) forbids us to posit such a creature. The two sets of nerves, blood-vessels and respiratory organs cannot be combined at the mid-plane to give a biologically credible organism. Likewise, the functionalist may say, it is our current scientific ignorance of the detailed functional anatomy of the mind that tempts us to believe, for instance, that the inverted (red-for-green) spectrum is possible. If only we knew the scientific facts underlying colour-vision, we would see that it is not.

The 'eliminative materialist' will add that future scientific knowledge could lead us to say that the experience of red, or the taste of coffee, *just is* the spiking of certain neurones at certain frequencies. Moreover, our experiences of different colours, or of tastes, will be systematically inter-related within a structured space, whose dimensions are defined in neural and functional terms (Churchland, 1986). (As for jealousy, we shall no longer hope to see it given a place in a theoretical psychology, because we shall know that – like most folk-psychological categories – it cannot be mapped systematically onto any specific neural, or even computational, process (Churchland, 1981). The eliminativist, then, denies the assumption made by many functionalists, that folk-psychology will turn out to be a good approximation to the scientific truth.)

Each of these tough-minded positions on consciousness is a promise rather than an achievement. Eliminative materialism is a more discriminating, and more scientifically-informed, version of the mid-century Identity Theory. However, like the functionalist reply citing the inconceivability of mermaids, it appeals to *future* scientific knowledge and *future* intuitions about what is or is not conceivable. To that extent, it demands an act of faith.

More conceptual analysis is needed, too, on the many meanings of 'conscious' and 'experience'. These matters are still highly controversial. But the point of interest here is that computational work *may* help to explain consciousness – the thing which most people assume to be furthest from its remit.

The other item widely felt to be beyond the computationalist's grasp is meaning, or understanding (sometimes called 'intentionality'). This is the rock on which Putnam's functionalist faith has foundered (Putnam, 1988). And this is the focus of John Searle's influential attack on functionalism, and on AI and cognitive science as conceived of by Newell and Simon (Searle, 1980; Boden, 1988, ch. 8).

On Searle's view, AI-based cognitive science is fundamentally fraudulent, because it promises to explain something – understanding, or intelligence – which it is in principle incapable of explaining. By implication, he also rejects functionalism as a philosophy of mind. He offers two arguments, of which one concerns what computers are made of, the other what they do.

Searle's first argument is that whereas neuroprotein is a kind of stuff which can support intelligence, metal and silicon are not. (Searle uses the term 'neuroprotein' as a convenient shorthand for the many biochemical substances active in the central nervous system.) He claims that this is obvious.

But it is not obvious at all. Certainly, neuroprotein does support intelligence and meaning. But we understand almost nothing of how it does so, *qua* neuroprotein – as opposed to some other chemical stuff. Indeed, insofar as we do understand this, we focus on the neurochemistry of certain basic *computational functions* embodied in neurones: message-passing, facilitation, inhibition, and the like.

Neurophysiologists have discovered the 'sodium-pump', for instance. This is the electrochemical process, occurring at the cell membrane, which enables an electrical signal to pass (without losing strength) from one end of a neurone to the other. And they have studied the biochemistry of neurotransmitters, substances (such as acetylcholine) that can make it easier – or harder – for one nerve-cell to cause another one to fire. In a few cases, they have even been able to say something about how a cell's chemical properties (and connectivities) enable it to code one sort of information rather than another: picking up colours, light-intensity gradients, or sounds of varying pitch.

For the psychologist, as for the philosophical functionalist, it is these functions which are important. If the neurophysiologist can tell us which cells and chemical processes are involved, all well and good. But any other chemistry would do, if it enabled these functions to be performed. Likewise, any chemical processes would do at the cell-membrane, and at the synapse, provided that they allowed a nerve-cell to propagate a message from one end to the other and pass it on to neighbouring neurones.

The fact that we cannot see how metal and silicon could possibly support 'real' intelligence or consciousness is irrelevant. For, intuitively speaking, we cannot see how neuroprotein – that grey mushy stuff inside our skulls – can do so either. *No* mind-matter dependencies are intuitively plausible. Nobody who was puzzled about intelligence (as opposed to electrical activity in neurones) ever exclaimed '*Sodium* – of course!'. Sodium-pumps are no less 'obviously' absurd than silicon chips, electrical polarities no less 'obviously' irrelevant than clanking metal. Even though the mind-matter roles of sodium-pumps and electrical polarities are scientifically compelling, they are not intuitively intelligible. On the contrary, they are highly counter-intuitive.

As the eliminative materialist points out, our intuitions change as science advances. Future generations may come to see neuroprotein – and perhaps silicon, too – as 'obviously' capable of embodying mind, much as we now see biochemical substances in general as obviously capable of producing other such substances (a fact regarded as intuitively absurd, even by most chemists, before the synthesis of urea in the nineteenth century). As yet, however, our intuitions have nothing useful to say about the material basis of intelligence.

In sum, this argument of Searle's is inconclusive. Computers made of non-biological materials may, conceivably, be incapable of intelligence. But Searle gives us no reason whatever to believe that this is actually so.

Searle's second argument is less quickly dealt with. The gist is that since all the symbols manipulated by a computer program are utterly meaningless to the computer itself, theories modelled on computer programs cannot explain how it is possible to understand meanings.

He argues this claim by introducing the imaginary example of the Chinese Room. He supposes himself locked in a room, in which there are various slips of paper with doodles on them. There is a window through which people can pass further doodle-papers to him, and through which he can pass papers out. And there is a book of rules (in English) telling him how to pair the doodles, which are always identified by their shape. One rule, for example, instructs him that when *squiggle-squiggle* is passed in to him, he should give out *squoggle-squoggle*. The rule-book also provides for more complex sequences of doodle-pairing, where only the first and last steps mention the transfer of paper into or out of the room. Searle spends his time, while inside the room, manipulating the doodles according to the rules.

So far as Searle-in-the-room is concerned, the *squiggles* and *squoggles* are meaningless. In fact, however, they are characters in Chinese writing. The Chinese people outside the room interpret them as such. Moreover, the patterns passed in and out at the window are understood by them as questions and answers respectively: the rules ensure that most of the questions are paired, either directly or indirectly, with what they recognize as a sensible answer. Some of the questions, for example, may concern the egg foo-yong served in a local restaurant. But Searle himself (inside the room) knows nothing of that. He understands not one word of Chinese. Moreover, he could never learn it like this. No matter how long he stays inside the room, shuffling doodles according to the rules, he will not understand Chinese when he is let out.

The point, says Searle, is that Searle-in-the-room is acting as if he were a computer program. He is all syntax and no semantics, for he is performing purely formal manipulations of uninterpreted patterns. It is the shape of *squiggle-squiggle*, not its meaning, which makes him pass a particular piece of paper out of the window. In this sense, his paper-passing is like the performance of a 'question-answering' AI-program. But Searle-in-the-room is not *really* answering: how could he, since he cannot understand the questions?

It follows, according to Searle, that a computational psychology cannot explain how it is possible for human beings to understand meanings. At best, it can explain what we do with meanings, once we understand them. (Complexity does not help, since all it does is add more internal doodle-matchings.)

The functionalist's first response may be to object that Searle has cheated. Of course Searle-in-the-room will never learn Chinese, for he is not causally plugged-in to the world. No-one can really understand what egg foo-yong is without being able to see it, smell it and poke at it with chopsticks. A computer capable of constructing real meanings would need to be more than a VDU-screen attached to a teletype – which is the sort of computer that Searle-in-the-room is mimicking.

Thus far, Searle would agree. But he responds by imagining that the room, with him (and a new rule-book) in it, is placed inside the skull of a giant robot. Now the *squiggle-squiggles* are caused by processes in the robot's camera-eyes, and the *squoggle-squoggles* cause levers in the robot's limbs to move. Accordingly, the egg foo-yong can be picked up, and transferred into the robot's mouth. But, Searle argues, Searle-in-the-robot has no idea what it is to move a chopstick, and does not know an egg foo-yong when the camera records it.

Notice that Searle, in these imaginary situations, must understand the language (English, we are told) of the rule-books. Notice, too, that the rule-books must be at least as detailed as AI-programs are. They must include rules for using language grammatically (no simple matter, as AI-workers have found to their cost), and rules covering vision and motor control. In short, in order to write the rule-books one would need a powerful computational psychology, involving many specialized theoretical concepts. Whether English is sufficiently precise for this task is – to put it mildly – doubtful. What would be needed is something like an AI-programming language. And this language would have to be taught to Searle before his incarceration, for the story depends on his being able to understand it. We shall return to this point, later.

Searle's crucial assumption is that computer programs are semantically empty. That is, they consist of abstract rules for comparing and transforming symbols not in virtue of their meaning, but merely by reference to their shape, or form. The so-called symbols are not really symbols, so far as the computer is concerned. To the computer, they are utterly meaningless – as Chinese writing is to Searle-in-the-room. Human beings may interpret them as concepts of various kinds, but that is another matter.

That programs are empty in this sense is taken for granted by

Searle. (It is taken for granted also by many computationalists, one of whom concludes that computational psychology, *even though it is the only scientific psychology we have got*, cannot explain the origin of understanding (Fodor, 1980).) But programs are 'empty' only if we think of them in a particular way.

One can, for some purposes, think of a computer program as an uninterpreted logical calculus, or abstract mathematical system. This is useful if one wants to know whether it is capable, in principle, of producing certain abstractly-specified results. (For example: could it get stuck in an infinite loop, or could it distinguish grammatical sentences from nonsensical word-strings?)

But one must not forget that a computer program is *a program for a computer*. When a program is run on suitable hardware, the machine *does* something as a result. There is no magic about this. Input-peripherals (teletypes, cameras, sound-analysers) feed into the internal computations, which lead eventually to changes in the output-peripherals (VDU-screens, line-plotters, speech-synthesizers). In between, the program causes a host of things to happen, many symbols to be manipulated, inside the system itself. At the level of the machine code, the effect of the program on the computer is direct, because the machine is engineered so that a given instruction elicits a unique operation. (Instructions in high-level languages must be converted into machine-code instructions before they can be obeyed.)

A programmed instruction, then, is not merely a formal rule. Its essential function (given the relevant hardware) is to make something happen. Computer programs, when they are running on some computer, are not 'all syntax and no semantics'. On the contrary, their inherent causal powers give them a toehold in semantics. If we accept (with Newell and Simon) that meaning and understanding are grounded in causal powers, in *what a creature can do in the world*, then we can see why this 'executive' function of programs is so important.

Because Searle assumes the utter emptiness of programs, he draws the wrong analogy. At base, a functioning program is comparable with Searle-in-the-room's understanding of English, not of Chinese.

A word in a language one understands is a mini-program, which causes certain processes to be run in one's mind. Searle sees Chinese words as meaningless doodles, which cause nothing (beyond appreciation of their shape) to happen in his mind. Likewise, he hears Chinese words as mere noise. But he reacts in a very different way to words from his native language. English words trigger a host of computational procedures in his head: procedures for parsing grammatical structures, for accessing related ideas in memory, for mapping analogies, for using schemas to fill conceptual gaps . . . and so on. And some English words set up computations that cause bodily actions (for example, 'Pass the slip of paper out of the window').

To learn English is to set up the relevant causal connections, not only between words and the world ('cat' and the thing on the mat) but between words and the many non-introspectible processes involved in interpreting them. The same applies, of course, to Chinese (which is why Searle-in-the-room's rule-book must contain rules for parsing, interpreting and constructing sentences in Chinese). Moreover, the same applies to any new (AI-like) language which the people outside the room may teach Searle, in order that he should understand the rule-book. He would have to learn to react to it automatically, as the electronic machine is engineered to do.

No current 'question-answering' program can really understand the natural-language words they deal with. Too many of the relevant causal connections are missing. But some programs have the rudiments of an ability to compare two symbols, for instance. Whether one chooses to call this real 'understanding', albeit of a drastically minimalist sort, is not crucial. Indeed, to ask 'When does a computer understand something?' is misleading, for it implies that there is some clear cut-off point at which understanding begins. In fact, there is not. The important question is not 'Which machines can understand, and which cannot?', but 'What things does a machine – whether biological or not – need to be able to do in order to be able to understand?' (Sloman, 1986)

These things are very many, and very various. They include not only responding to and acting on the environment, but also constructing internal structures of many different kinds, and inter-relating them in many different ways. And the 'machine' here is defined *functionally*. As Newell and Simon would put it, things capable of understanding are information-processing systems, whose embodiment enables them not only to manipulate symbols internally but also to enter into causal (input-output) relations with the external world. Since, in this sense, even today's computer programs have the beginnings of the rudiments of understanding, cognitive science is not – *pace* Searle – in principle incapable of explaining how human understanding comes about.

In humans and other animals, of course, the relevant causal connections came about through evolution. Genetic mutation and natural selection evolved the mechanism whereby when certain cells in a frog's eye are stimulated by the movement of dark spots of a certain size, the frog's sticky tongue automatically shoots out to the place where the 'spot' (or bug) was located. It is because of this behavioural pattern, which clearly serves the frog's biological interests, that someone might say that the visual input 'means' food to the frog.

Mention of evolution reminds us of another type of computer-modelling, which has only recently hit the headlines but whose historical origins lie in McCulloch and Pitts' papers of the 1940s. Work on 'connectionism', or 'neural networks', is broadly inspired by ideas about the brain, and connectionist ideas are being applied to various problems in neuroscience (see chapters 3 and 4, above).

Within the philosophy of mind, connectionism – especially the variety known as PDP, or parallel distributed processing (Rumelhart and McClelland, 1986) – is now attracting much interest. It has fuelled debate about whether parallel-processing offers a better way of modelling the mind, whether it can effectively ground an evolutionary epistemology, and whether connectionist models are truly functionalist, or computational, in character (e.g. Smolensky, 1987, 1988; Dreyfus and Dreyfus, 1988; Clark, 1989; Churchland, 1990; Cussins, 1990). Searle has even up-dated his Chinese Room, now speaking of a Chinese Gym – in which people excite or inhibit their neighbours' activity much as connectionist units are supposed to do (Searle, 1990).

Searle claims that there is nothing fundamentally different, from a philosophical point of view, between a formalist-AI model and a connectionist one. But many philosophers disagree – some, vociferously. The triumphalism of certain voices is exemplified in a recent collection of papers, whose innocent title *The AI Debate* is followed by the tendentious sub-title *False Starts, Real*

Foundations (Graubard, 1988). This sub-title is not only ungenerous, but unjustified (Boden, 1991).

It is true that PDP-models can do things 'naturally' which are very difficult, even in practice impossible, to achieve by traditional AI methods. Examples include pattern-matching, content-addressable memory, the recognition of family-resemblances, graceful degradation, sensitivity to context and learning by example. It follows that a satisfactory simulation of much, perhaps even most, human thought would probably include some type of connectionist processing, at some level. It is true also that 'sub-symbolic' models (in which the basic units do not code familiar or easily verbalizable concepts) can help us to understand how true concepts can arise, on the basis of causal commerce with the environment and the construction of increasingly objective representations (Cussins, 1990). It is true that future connectionist models may be significantly similar to certain aspects of the brain. And it is true that more attention (of a fairly superficial kind) has been paid to the evolutionary basis of our thought in connectionist writings than in classical AI.

Many other relevant truths, however, are often forgotten – or are perhaps unknown, to philosophers unfamiliar with the field.

For instance, both the formalist and the connectionist research-programmes were originated by the same paper (McCulloch and Pitts, 1943). Most current connectionist models are implemented on von Neumann machines, which is to say that they are simulated by formalist AI-programs. PDP-systems work by differential equations, which are not obviously more 'human' than are strings of programmed instructions: PDP is not essentially tender-minded. Not all connectionist models are PDP-networks. Not all PDP-networks are sub-symbolic. Not all AI-programs take familiar concepts for granted: many (including some of the earliest) are sub-symbolic in the sense defined above. Many connectionist systems use theoretical principles discovered by classical AI. Formalist programs can achieve some things, such as logical reasoning, which current neural networks cannot. Some leading connectionists believe that a neural network will have to simulate a von Neumann machine in order to do logic, and that the human brain embodies a formalist 'virtual machine' when the human mind does logic. Today's connectionist systems are unlike real neural networks in many important ways. Tomorrow's will differ from each other almost as much as they differ from the brain: the space of possible connectionist (or, more generally, computational) systems is almost wholly unexplored. Even a network's designer may not know just how it managed what it did achieve, and may have to discover this by empirical methods *post hoc*. Finally, the few computer-modellers who take evolution semi-seriously include not only connectionists but (for instance) AI-roboticists too (e.g. Brooks, 1991, in press).

In light of these facts, one cannot conclude that connectionism is the one road to the truth, and that classical AI and cognitive science are fraudulent. Better arguments will be needed to show – if indeed it is the case – that functionalism is mistaken, and that the cognitive science based upon it is doomed to failure.

One can conclude, however, that computer simulation has influenced the philosophy of mind in deep and exciting ways. It has revivified the humanist concern with meaning, while also inspiring a newly-plausible physicalism. Surprised though William James might be to hear it, this is an area in which the tough and the tender may be reconciled at last.

References

Block, N. 1978: Troubles with Functionalism. In W. Savage (ed.), *Perception and Cognition: Minnesota Studies in the Philosophy of Science, Vol. IX*, Minneapolis: University of Minnesota Press, pp. 261–325.

Boden, M. A. 1972: *Purposive Explanation in Psychology*. Cambridge, Mass.: Harvard University Press.

Boden, M. A. 1977: *Artificial Intelligence and Natural Man*. New York: Basic Books.

Boden, M. A. 1988: *Computer Models of Mind: Computational Approaches in Theoretical Psychology*. Cambridge: Cambridge University Press.

Boden, M. A. 1990: *The Creative Mind: Myths and Mechanisms*. London: Weidenfeld and Nicolson.

Boden, M. A. 1991: Horses of a Different Colour?. In W. Ramsey, D. E. Rumelhart and S. P. Stich (eds), *The Philosophy of Connectionism*, Hillsdale, N.J.: Erlbaum Press, pp. 3–19.

Brooks, R. 1991: Intelligence Without Representation. *Artificial Intelligence*, 47, 139–60.

Brooks, R. (in press) Computers and Thought Lecture. *Proceedings of International Joint Conference on Artificial Intelligence*, Sydney 1991.

Churchland, P. M. 1981: Eliminative Materialism and the Propositional Attitudes. *Journal of Philosophy*, 78, 67–90.

Churchland, P. M. 1986: Some Reductive Strategies in Cognitive Neurobiology. *Mind*, XCV, 279–309. Reprinted in M. A. Boden (ed.) 1990: *The Philosophy of Artificial Intelligence*, Oxford: Oxford University Press, pp. 334–67.

Churchland, P. M. 1990: *A Neurocomputational Perspective: The Nature of Mind and the Structure of Science*. Cambridge, Mass.: MIT Press.

Clark, A. J. 1989: *Microcognition: Philosophy, Cognitive Science, and Parallel Distributed Processing*. Cambridge, Mass.: MIT Press.

Cussins, A. 1990: The Connectionist Construction of Concepts. In M. A. Boden (ed.), *The Philosophy of Artificial Intelligence*, Oxford: Oxford University Press, pp. 368–440.

Dennett, D. C. 1987: *The Intentional Stance*. Cambridge Mass.: MIT Press.

Dreyfus, H. L. 1979: *What Computers Can't Do: The Limits of Artificial Intelligence*. Revised edn. New York: Harper and Row.

Dreyfus, H. L. and Dreyfus, S. E. 1988: Making a Mind Versus Modelling the Brain: Artificial Intelligence Back at a Branch-Point. *Daedalus: Journal of the American Academy of Arts and Sciences*, 117, no. 1 (Winter 1988), 15–43. Reprinted in M. A. Boden (ed.) 1990: *The Philosophy of Artificial Intelligence*, Oxford: Oxford University Press pp. 309–34.

Fodor, J. A. 1980: 'Methodological Solipsism Considered as a Research Strategy in Cognitive Psychology'. *Behavioral and Brain Sciences*, 3, 63–110.

Graubard, S. R. 1988: *The AI Debate: False Starts, Real Foundations*. Cambridge, Mass.: MIT Press.

Huxley, T. H. 1893: On the Hypothesis That Animals Are Automata, and Its History. In T. H. Huxley, *Method and Results: Essays*, London: Macmillan, pp. 199–250.

James, William. 1907: *Pragmatism: A New Name For Some Old Ways of Thinking*. London: Longman.

Lashley, K. S. 1950: In Search of the Engram. *Symposium of the Society of Experimental Psychology*, no. 4, 454–82. Cambridge: Cambridge University Press.

McCulloch, W. S. 1965: *Embodiments of Mind*. Cambridge, Mass.: MIT Press.

McCulloch, W. S. and Pitts, W. H. 1943: A Logical Calculus of the Ideas Immanent in Nervous Activity. *Bulletin of Mathematical Biophysics*, 5, 115–33. Reprinted in M. A. Boden (ed.) 1990: *The*

Philosophy of Artificial Intelligence, Oxford: Oxford University Press, pp. 22–39.

Nagel, T. 1974: What Is It Like To Be A Bat? *Philosophical Review*, 83, 435–50

Newell, A. 1980: Physical Symbol Systems. *Cognitive Science*, 4, 135–183.

Newell, A. and Simon, H. A. 1961: GPS – A Program that Simulates Human Thought. In H. Billing (ed.), *Lernende Automaten*. Munich: Oldenbourgh, pp. 109–24. Reprinted in E. A. Feigenbaum and J. Feldman (eds) 1963: *Computers and Thought*, New York: McGraw-Hill, pp. 279–96.

Newell, A. and Simon, H. A. 1972: *Human Problem Solving*. Englewood Cliffs, NJ: Prentice-Hall.

Place, U. T. 1956: Is Consciousness a Brain Process?. *British Journal of Psychology*, XLVII, 44–50.

Putnam, H. 1960: Minds and Machines. In S. Hook (ed.), *Dimensions of Mind*, New York: Collier, pp. 148–79.

Putnam, H. 1967: The nature of mental states. Reprinted in H. Putnam 1975: *Mind, Language, and Reality: Philosophical Papers*, Vol. 2, Cambridge: Cambridge University Press, pp. 429–40. (Original publication in W. H. Capitan and D. D. Merrill (eds), *Art, Mind and Religion*, Pittsburgh: University of Pittsburgh Press.

Putnam, H. 1988: *Representation and Reality*. Cambridge, Mass.: MIT Press.

Robinson, Guy. 1972: How to Tell Your Friends From Machines. *Mind*, N.S., 81, 504–18.

Rumelhart, D. E. and McClelland, J. L. (eds) 1986: *Parallel Distributed Processing: Explorations in the Microstructure of Cognition*. (2 Vols.) Cambridge, Mass.: MIT Press.

Ryle, Gilbert. 1949: *The Concept of Mind*. London: Hutchinson.

Searle, J. S. 1980: Minds, Brains, and Programs. *Behavior and Brain Sciences*, 3, 417–24. Reprinted in M. A. Boden (ed.) 1990: *The Philosophy of Artificial Intelligence*, Oxford: Oxford University Press, pp. 67–88.

Searle, J. S. 1990: Is the Brain's Mind a Computer Program? *Scientific American*, 262 (No 1), 20–25.

Smart, J. J. C. 1959: Sensations and Brain Processes. *Philosophical Review*, 68, 141–56.

Simon, H. A. 1979: Motivational and Emotional Controls of Cognition. In H. A. Simon (ed.), *Models of Thought*, New Haven: Yale University Press, pp. 23–38.

Sloman, A. 1986: What Sorts of Machines Can Understand the Symbols They Use? *Proc. Aristotelian Society*, Supp. Vol. 60, 61–80.

Sloman, A. 1987: Motives, Mechanisms, and Emotions. *Cognition and Emotion*, 1, 217–33. Reprinted in M. A. Boden (ed.) 1990: *The Philosophy of Artificial Intelligence*, Oxford: Oxford University Press, pp. 231–47.

Smolensky, P. 1987: Connectionist AI, Symbolic AI, and the Brain. *AI Review*, 1, 95–110.

Smolensky, P. 1988: On the Proper Treatment of Connectionism (with peer-commentary and author's reply). *Behavioral and Brain Sciences*, 11, 1–74.

Stich, S. C. 1983: *From Folk-Psychology to Cognitive Science: The Case Against Belief.* Cambridge, Mass.: MIT Press.

Turing, A. M. 1950: Computing Machinery and Intelligence. *Mind*, LIX, 433–60. Reprinted in M. A. Boden (ed.) 1990: *The Philosophy of Artificial Intelligence*, Oxford: Oxford University Press, pp. 231–47.

Watson, J. B. 1913: Psychology as the Behaviorist Views It. *Psychological Review*, 20, 158–77.

8

Comparison with Human Experiments

Donald Broadbent

This book has gone to the cutting edge of progress, in several aspects of the field. For this final section, I am going to be more general, and in one sense more elementary. I want to link back to the very start of the series, and the first chapter by Roger Penrose. How far does the work described in subsequent chapters relate to his concerns?

The overall debate

Those concerns may have become fogged in the reader's mind, so let me restate them. First, it is known that a machine can arrive at any number that is 'computable'. That is, a number that can be reached by an algorithmic procedure. The reason this is connected with human intelligence is this: suppose we write down a list of possible human actions. Then we could assign each member of the list to one of the computable numbers. For each of those numbers, we know there is some procedure that will work it out; so if we go through that procedure, we shall know which action it is going to be. Then, we know that a machine must exist that could do the same; so, we know that a machine must exist which could arrive at any behaviour that is on the list. It follows that a machine can simulate any human behaviour that we can specify in this way.

When one has such a machine, its actions at any time depend partly on the state of the machine at that time, partly on the contents of a memory store which the machine itself can alter, and partly on input from the environment. One can therefore draw up a kind of table, in which the possible states of the system form the columns, and the possible inputs the rows.

Thus far, Roger Penrose accepts the argument; it is mathematically sound. But sound mathematics do not necessarily apply in the physical world; people used to think that the shortest distance between two points was always a straight line. When they started navigating long distances on the earth's surface, they found that surface is curved in the third dimension. So, one of the axioms of Euclid is false, and therefore the conclusion is false; the quickest way from here to New York is to set off pointing rather North of the bearing of the city, and keep turning gently to the left. So to know if Turing's conclusion is true, rather than merely sound, we have to check whether human behaviour actually matches the prediction from computer model. Penrose argues that it doesn't, that human thinking is not algorithmic, and that therefore computer simulation cannot grasp its full nature. Most, if not all, of the other contributors would probably have disagreed with him; once again, the point is not whether his mathematics are correct, but whether they have been applied correctly to the world that actually exists. Most contributors dealt primarily with contributions in their own areas, and did not take up the general argument. As you will see later, I suspect this was sensible because I do not think it is an argument that can be won or lost. My own role comes back to the beginning, because I want to consider whether people actually do behave as one might expect from the ways that have been found to work well for computers solving similar problems.

The scheme is, first, to remind the reader of some glimpses of the blindingly obvious. You may not be thinking of them at the moment, nor were you when reading the earlier chapters; but I am sure you believe them. Second, I shall try and produce some of the ways in which artificial intelligence has compared successfully with actual observations of human behaviour. Third, I will give some of the things it does not yet consider sufficiently. Fourth, I shall argue that these difficulties are not fundamental and that Penrose's argument seems much less plausible when one remembers the blindingly obvious. Finally, I shall have a go at something that may well underlie the worries that some people have about this approach; I shall think about its relation to one's general attitude to life. I promise that I shall end with one of my favourite quotations, from St Thomas Aquinas, who would (I am sure) be on the side of the angels.

Glimpses of the obvious

Different computers work in different ways

Like many people, I am used to working wih an IBM PC. It often happens that I insert a floppy disc, meaning to work on a particular file, and find that I haven't got that file on the disc. I then take the disc out, go to another machine and copy the file onto it; finally, I come back, insert the disc again, and carry on. The other day I got into a similar situation at home. When I came back to the first machine, it assured me that the new file was still not on the disc. I could not view it on the screen, see its name on the list of files, or copy it to another disc. But according to the second machine, it was there. What had happened?

Each disc contains a list of the files that are on it. But scanning the disc takes time; so when the computer first reads a new disc it is quite a good idea for it to copy the list to its own memory, where it can consult it quickly. PCs do that as well; but my machines at home are of another type, and they go one step further. When you ask the machine to list the files for you, it looks first at the title of the disc to see if it is the same one that was there last time it looked. If it is, and if the computer knows that it has not put anything on or off the disc since it last looked, it gives you the list from its own memory.

Usually, this is a very sensible thing to do, because it saves both of us time. But it is in fact a gamble; it relies on the assumption that I own only one computer. The original model of PC made the opposite assumption and therefore spent time going back to the disc every time it was asked for a list of files. (Nowadays, they get a private signal from the door of the disc drive.)

Neither of these tactics is guaranteed to succeed; each of them is a determinate procedure, but each of them is better in one environment, and worse in another.

Human thinking often gets it wrong

My second glimpse of the obvious is that human thinking frequently gives illogical results. The chapter by Newell, Young and Polk discussed syllogistic reasoning; let me remind the reader of, and amplify, their points.

Suppose one takes the argument:

No member of the Cabinet is a Marxist.
Some Marxists are Stalinists.
Therefore, no member of the Cabinet is a Stalinist.

In a sample of university students studied by Phil Johnson-Laird, a majority would accept arguments of this sort as valid. (See Johnson-Laird, 1983) Of course, most readers are much too sophisticated to do so given time; but in case it went by too quickly, try:

No member of the Cabinet is a woman.
Some women are Conservatives.
Therefore, no member of the Cabinet is a Conservative.

The fallacy becomes more obvious because in this case one knows that the conclusion is false from everyday life; but that is not the whole story. People are much less inclined to accept the fallacy if the order of the words in the sentences is changed; not:

No A are B.
Some B are C.

but:

No A are B.
Some C are B.

That begins to give away the source of the difficulty. What many people do, with a problem of this kind, is to construct a model or picture of the world, built up from the information as it arrives. The trouble with my first example is that it makes you form a picture of two separate groups of people, some respectable Cabinet

Ministers standing in one place wearing grey flannel suits, and another group of Marxists standing somewhere else, who have little red badges in their button holes. When the next sentence arrives, one already has a group of Marxists, so one divides that group into two; one lot with boots and a moustache, and the other lot looking like Gorbachev. It never occurs to you that there are other pictures you might have imagined; so when you are asked if Mr Major might perhaps have appointed some Stalinists, you answer on the basis of your picture, not the logic.

If the second sentence arrives in a different order, one has to add a third group of people before one thinks about its overlap with the first two. One is therefore more likely to spot that group three may have members in common with group one as well as group two.

Johnson-Laird, who originated this analysis, has looked at success with various arguments, given in various orders; and the results are steadily worse the more different 'mental models' are consistent with the sentences that describe the problem. People do not think in the way that, say, a computer language like PROLOG normally operates. PROLOG can draw automatic logical inferences from whatever facts you give it; and most people cannot do that. (The exceptions are those who have learned to build special mental pictures, using symbols other than people in suits with badges and beards; some readers are probably like that, but it did not come naturally!) Remember however that different computers work differently; and it is perfectly possible to write a program that functions according to Johnson-Laird's principles. He has done it; and of course such a program makes mistakes of the same kind as human beings do.

Different people think differently

My third glimpse of the obvious is that one person's mind is different from that of another. Everybody pays lip service to this fact, and very few take it seriously. Let me give just one example, from an experiment here in Oxford (Broadbent and Broadbent, 1978).

We gave people a kind of mail-order catalogue, which they could look through. We told them that subsequently they would be given short descriptions of people and asked to remember a suitable Christmas present for each person. Because there would be too many presents in the catalogue to remember them all, they were asked to name each present using whatever words they wished, so that they could later say those same words to retrieve the present.

What interested us was the structure of the classification system they used. To take one extreme, one person used a system I found very intelligible and congenial. Some presents she simply described as 'Nasty'; she would never wish to give them to anybody, so no other words at all were attached to them. If a present was a possibility, it was then either for an 'Adult' or for a 'Child'; using one word implied the absence of the other. If an 'Adult', some presents were for a 'Man' and some for a 'Woman'; and again one word excluded the other. If on the other hand, the present was for a 'Child', there were three age bands. The whole structure formed a kind of branching tree, in which each twig was separate from other twigs, and one could proceed systematically down from the general to the particular. I resonated to this, and I suspect many people with a scientific leaning will do so. The hierarchic way in which a PC keeps its files is just right for this kind of mind.

Another person was quite different. Some presents were 'Female', some 'Household', some 'Luxury'; but there were also 'Female Household', 'Luxury Female', 'Household Luxury', and even 'Female Household Luxury'. Any word seemed independent of any other word; I found this person's mind very hard to understand intuitively, and my first reaction was that it was a mess.

But think of this person in another way. One can think of this mind as arranging all the presents in a three-dimensional space, with dimensions of male/female, luxury/essential, and household/external. In a computer, this is just as valid a way of arranging memory as the branching tree is. It has lots of advantages; it is economical in terms of the number of words you need to find an object, it avoids missing things you want because they've been put in a different branch of the tree, it allows cross-links between things that are very similar on one dimension although they are very different on another. It's ideal if you want to recall the name of the man who plays football for Everton and has red hair.

These advantages are balanced against a need for much more processing both when you put information in and when you take it out. Whether a computer uses hierarchic or cross-classified ways of getting at information depends therefore on the job it is trying to do; for some jobs, one way is better, and for other jobs, other ways. (So *my* computer, unlike a PC, can keep its files in a cross-classified directory structure!) It isn't surprising that different people think in different ways; each kind is better at thinking about certain things.

That applies even in scientific matters; there are those who explore the strange and powerful things that go on in their own minds, manipulating mental models at a much deeper level than images of Cabinet Ministers and Marxists. There are also people whose main interest is in getting and classifying evidence about the outer world. Very crudely, one can call the first kind Platonists and the second kind Aristotelians, because the difference has existed for a very long time. I believe it will always exist; because each approach is highly important and successful for its own purposes. Neither is 'true' and both are useful.

Discussion between the two is very difficult, because all of us tend to assume that other people have the same experience and thoughts that we do ourselves. Penrose (who says that he is a Platonist) describes very interestingly the way in which he and congenial mathematicians like to discuss problems. They don't agree definitions and axioms, and construct an external public argument. Rather they talk around the problem until one of them says 'Ah, I see what you mean!' This method of argument causes Aristotelians to get frustrated and even angry; they may tend like Peter Medawar (1967) to get quite abusive with those who use undefined terms.

That is going too far; one has to recognize the power and virtues of the Platonic approach. There is no way in which psychologists could formulate the Mandelbrot set by measuring the reaction time of 400 experimental subjects. But there is a serious difficulty in stating the problem, as Penrose did in the first chapter, in terms of alternative explanations of conscious processes. All the evidence suggests that the things going on inside one person's head may be very different from the things going on inside somebody else's head. The kind of argument that convinces one person will not convince another kind of person, and vice versa. All each side can do is to understand the kind of problems for which each approach is better.

Strengths of artificial intelligence

Next, therefore, I am going to point out certain facts about human intelligence that are true, but were unknown to psychologists until artificial intelligence drew them to our attention.

Travelling hopefully

Suppose you want to give a stranger an algorithm for finding taxis in Oxford. Suppose also that your experience is that taxis can be found nine times out of ten at the station, but only three times out of ten in St Giles. You therefore instruct the stranger to proceed first to the station, look for a taxi, and if there is none, go next to St Giles. If there is still none, go back to the beginning. In one sense, this is indeed an algorithm; it can certainly be programmed into a computer. But it is not guaranteed to succeed; it might go on for ever, just like the algorithm, quoted by Penrose, that looks for an odd number that is the sum of two odd numbers.

There is in fact a difference between predicting the action of the stranger, and predicting whether a taxi is going to be found. If one gets people to talk aloud while solving problems in symbolic logic, one notices that they mention certain mental operations repeatedly, although those operations do not necessarily solve the problem.

To avoid getting deep into symbolic logic, let us take the game of 'noughts and crosses', where the same thing applies. You all know the game; there is a square containing a three-by-three arrangement of small squares, and one player has to complete a line of three noughts while the other tries to create three crosses, each entering one character in turn. One could create an algorithm to play this game, by tracing out after each move the consequences of every possible sequence of moves and picking the best one to start. But this would take far too long, even for a computer; at the start there are in fact 352,880 different possible games to explore. So human beings don't do that. What do they do?

One common trick of good players is this; if the centre square is blank, they tend to fill it. They do not know what the opponent is going to do, so they may still fail to win; but their chances of winning go up considerably, because there are more of the 352,880 games in which the winner holds the centre than ones in which they do not. There is another trick that good players have, which is very counter-intuitive; when their opponent is in one corner, they go in the opposite corner rather than a corner on the same side. That seems strange, because it seems to leave the opponent two lines leading from the corner already occupied. It is however very wise; because if one goes in the opposite corner there are ways in which the opponent might make a mistake and allow a fork to be created. If one goes in the adjacent corners the opponent has no chance to make those mistakes, so the best one can hope for is a draw. A computer program based on these principles will do as well as the best human player (Newell and Simon, 1972)

In a restricted game like noughts and crosses, one could in principle work out the consequences of every possible action; though such a strategy doesn't appear in the accounts people give of their own mental processes. They simply act on an input, as a machine might, and the action they produce is one that is *likely* to help them win, although it is not guaranteed to do so. The same principle applies in other cases, where it would certainly not be possible to work out the odds in one's own head.

Suppose somebody is listening to speech over a noisy telephone. If we measure the probability of hearing a word correctly, it is much higher for words that are common in the language than it is for rare ones. A word like 'soil', for instance, occurs more than 100 times in every million words; and at the right signal-noise ratio it may be three times as intelligible as a word like 'soup', which occurs only about 30 per million. There are occasional wrong perceptions, and this means that the listener must be getting only imperfect information from the ear; when there is insufficient evidence, the brain generates a word that was not actually there but is consistent with the message the ear received. Rare words are less likely to occur as misperceptions; from statistical decision theory, we can work out that the difference in correct perceptions is entirely accounted for by this difference in the errors (Broadbent, 1967). If the brain generates a probable word, probably it will be right. The procedure is not guaranteed to be successful but it increases the chances.

Thought needs a language

What I have been discussing is the field of 'heuristics', the use of procedures that do not guarantee success but do make it more likely. This field was mentioned by Penrose; but the point I want to make is that it is not merely a technique used in artificial intelligence. From experiment we know it to be an important part of human thinking. It came into psychology because the very first programs in artificial intelligence made use of it, but there is no doubt that people make use of it.

It leads on to a second point. Consider the game of number scrabble. A pool of counters is placed on the table, each counter carrying one of the digits 1 to 9. Each person in turn draws a digit from the pool, and each knows what the other draws. The idea is to get three counters in your hand, that add up to 15. The first person to do so is the winner. What are the heuristics and how should one play?

If you do not know, that makes my point, because you have just been told. The nine digits can be arranged in a 'magic square', in which every row, column, and diagonal adds up to 15. To win, you should pick the centre digit if possible; and you should go in the corner opposite the opponent if possible (Newell and Simon, 1972). It is the form of the representation, in numbers rather than geometry, that makes it harder to see this; and even to apply it in a new case even though you know the rules from the case you have already met. A number of problems like this exist, where the underlying mathematics is the same, but where it can be presented in various ways. The way the problem is presented to the person undoubtedly affects the chances of their success; and of their being able to transfer their success to a new problem (Kotovsky, Hayes and Simon, 1985).

But this importance of the 'representation' and of the 'definition of the problem space' arises also in artificial intelligence, and in recent psychology it has been laboratories working in that area that have found out most about it. A computer *can* store information in an English sentence; but it is much more likely to be able to answer later questions if the sentence has been translated into predicate calculus. The programming languages such as FORTRAN or BASIC, that may be appropriate for working out sums, are extremely cumbrous for solving logical problems. So for artificial intelligence, new ways of representing information had to be devised, such as LISP. They need to consider problems such as those of 'intensionality' (which were raised in some of the discussions); if we know that the next Prime Minister will have an office in Downing Street, do we know whether John Major will? LISP has ways in which such problems can be handled; briefly, it distinguishes between having two names for the memory stored in one location, and having two names for two identical memories stored in different locations. (See Charniak and McDermott, 1985, p. 60.)

Never stick to routine

The third point that AI has emphasized for psychology is that fixed routines are disaster. The earliest programs used them, tackling symbolic logic; a sequence of heuristics could be tried and success would in the end be achieved, the choice of a good heuristic altering the time rather than the ultimate chance of winning. That was like the tactic I suggested for visitors to Oxford, of going to the station and then to St Giles. But that is a fairly elementary strategy; one would hardly advise the taxi-seeker to keep going towards the station ignoring a large and empty taxi standing by the road-side waiting for custom. So one needs to seize the chance of an unexpected success. And equally if one's action runs into unexpected difficulties, if one takes the wrong turning on the way to the station, one may have to do something out of routine in order to get to the destination. What one needs in fact is not a fixed routine, but a set of rules that say 'If you see a taxi, grab it', 'If you aren't at the station in five minutes, stop and ask', and instead of following a rigid routine you should keep looking at the situation to try and match it to these rules.

Noughts and crosses will illustrate the principle. Clearly a fixed sequence of actions will not do, because one does not know what the opponent is going to do. And I explained earlier that there are over three hundred thousand possible games, so one cannot calculate the right action by following them through. But one can draw up a short list of actions, each of which should be carried out in particular situations. These 'condition-action' rules can be arranged in an order of priority. For instance, one should make a winning move if one can, but if not one should avoid the other person winning; or if not, one should go in the centre square.

A human achievement

Let me put together what this means in terms of human thinking. During 1931 and 1932, Hans Krebs discovered the mechanism by which urea is synthesized. The process is not a reaction of a traditional type, like the rusting of iron; it involves a cycle, in which one key substance is transformed into another, and then the second into a third, ammonia being taken up at each stage. The third compound then gives rise both to urea, and also to the original substance, ornithine. So the ornithine is essential, but is never consumed; it does not act like a fuel, as oxygen does in the rusting of iron. How could anybody ever discover such a thing? There are many organic compounds, many processes transforming one into another, and one would not have the normal hint that substance A disappears when substance B appears.

It is therefore possible to write a computer program, give it the knowledge that Krebs had about the world when he started, and then see whether the sequence of experiments that it traverses agrees with the sequence that Krebs actually performed. If a computer were faced with this problem, it would not be enough to feed the machine with everything that was known about the topic in 1931, and tell it to do experiments to find out the rest. There are far too many experiments it might do. And the program cannot work on a routine set up in advance; there is no algorithm to guarantee success. What one can do is to provide the program with a large number of condition-action rules, so that it reacts differently depending on what each experiment finds. These rules in turn are not guaranteed to succeed; they are heuristics that guide the whole search in ways that are likely to be profitable.

In fact, an actual program containing 63 rules of this type will, first of all, start from the state of chemical knowledge that Krebs had, decide to examine the urea problem by the method of tissue slices, consider various amino acids and ammonia in isolation, get nowhere, and then try them in combination. In doing this, it finds that ornithine gives a large effect (Kulkarni and Simon, 1988).

Now, the laboratory note-books of Krebs were kept, and also he was interviewed many years later; so we know fairly exactly the sequence of experiments that he carried out. Between July 1931 and November 1931, he followed the sequence of experiments I have just described. The program, when it gets to this point, examines a number of other amino acids, showing that they do not act like ornithine, and begins to concentrate on that particular amino acid. It then looks quantitatively at the process and finds that only small quantities of ornithine are needed. Looking at the nitrogen, the program shows that the amounts in the urea correspond to the amount in the ammonia, not in the amino acid. Finally, it identifies citrulline as the intermediary in the process. Krebs went through these various steps between November 1931 and the early summer of the next year, at which point he was sufficiently confident to publish.

Imitating the actions of Krebs depends on having the right rules (heuristics) in the program. Experimentalists may be interested in what they are. They include rules such as picking a measurable process to study rather than one that can be observed but not measured, choosing the faster process rather than the slower, choosing the more reliable rather than the less reliable experimental method, looking first at the substances that are cheap and easily available, and so on. I hope my own graduate students will recognize some of these. People from the humanities in particular may be surprised at the pressure on speed, availability, and so on; they look like careerism or profit-seeking, but they aren't. The point is that experimentalists have a duty to 'sell their lives as dearly as they can'. Some problems will be slow and arduous; but there will never be enough resources, so we must knock out the quicker ones first. If you put those heuristics in, the program does what Krebs did.

The reason why Krebs solved this problem, then, was that he possessed a set of condition-action rules that would form an effective strategy in a world too complicated to predict in detail. It was not done by a process laid down from the beginning, but a computer operating in a similar way can follow the same path. With simpler problems, one can test large numbers of people, say, students solving problems on equivalent triangles. There is no single best way to solve such problems; it depends on the information that is provided. One can show that the choice of a method by the students is at first random, but later comes to depend on what they see in the problem (see Lewis and Anderson, 1985). As Penrose says in his book, the key to solving a mathematical problem is the choice of the correct algorithm; that is what the condition-action rules do.

Growing points for the future

Of course, existing programs are a long way from being perfect simulations of human thinking. Three limitations particularly interest me: the handling of working or temporary memory, the emphasis on what people say about their thinking, and the tendency to assume that the entire system works in a single fashion (symbolic on the one hand, or connectionist on the other).

Working memory

In simulation programs, temporary or short-term memory is essential; they need to know results of previous calculations, to remember what they have just tried, and so on. Tomorrow they can forget such things, but today the contents of short-term memory are key conditions that help decide on the next action. The point that worries me is, that a human being can only recall a short series of symbols, the usual figure quoted being seven. Simulation programs cannot possibly confine themselves to such a small amount; the handling of natural language needs some trace of many words that have been present earlier in the conversation, the solving of logical or similar problems needs more than seven items to be held, and in general it's very rare for any modern system to have a temporary memory as small as our own memory span.

Now of course we do have some trace of more than seven recent experiences; if I say the word 'algorithm' at this moment, you are much more likely to hear that word correctly than you would be if somebody said it to you during your weekly shopping in the supermarket. There are numerous experiments showing such 'priming' after-effects of the past, usually not reportable by the experimental subject but showing in the behaviour we measure. Yet we certainly also have this more restricted set of items that we can reproduce when asked; the telephone number we are trying to keep in mind, or the exact words of a question.

Computer simulations do not usually have a separate form of working memory, that might correspond to this human function. They have concentrated on the much larger work-space needed by their programs; I would prefer to follow the usage of calling that 'virtual memory' (as Ballard did). There is however a rather different memory that recalls a telephone number or the wording of a question. The term 'working memory' is more usefully kept for this second kind of function. But we need to know the computational function of this 'true working memory', and why human beings have it. There are various suggestions in the literature; some likely and some not. In many ways this is a key next step in constructing simulations (Baddeley, 1986).

Knowing more than we can say

The second point is that the classic approach through symbols, the programs that play chess, solve syllogisms or parse sentences, relies too much on imitating what people themselves say about their thinking. We know that is only half the story; for sixty or seventy years psychologists have been collecting evidence that people are greatly helped in solving problems by experiences that they do not themselves know about. In most cases of course human beings do what they say, and say what they do. But one can have special experimental conditions where the opposite is true. Dianne Berry has shown repeatedly that practice on a task may improve the ability to perform that task without any effect on the ability to answer questions about it. She has also found that giving verbal instructions may improve the ability to answer questions without improving the ability to perform the task. As I usually put it, if you want to get on better with other people, don't just go to lectures on psychology (Berry and Broadbent 1984, 1988).

The need for hybrid models

By emphasizing the things people have in their minds, rather than what people do, classic AI has learned a lot about the symbolic level of processing; the internal models that people can talk about and manipulate inside themselves to work out what to do. But in computers there can also be important systems that do not work symbolically, that store the information about the world in a network of connections, without necessarily having any single symbol that represents the result of past experience. During the 1980s, these two approaches have been almost enemies; each tries as far as it can to explain everything. But from an engineering point of view each has advantages for some problems, and disadvantages for others. If one is building a device, the choice of the better system is heuristic; for some things one should prefer one, for other things the other. Increasingly therefore real devices are likely to use 'hybrid models', that have both kinds of system available and use whichever is best for the particular function. The psychological experiments of Dianne Berry and of many others strongly suggest that real human beings do the same. The things we report from our own minds are important, but so also are the unreportable associations, the links that make a student use one algorithm rather than another in solving geometric problems, or the smell that made Proust remember episodes from his childhood. Hybrid models are the wave of the future.

Conclusion

If we go back to Penrose's problem, where have these chapters got us? Remember the nature of the debate; the mathematics are agreed, but their application to human affairs is not. Any computable number can be calculated by a machine, but equally any particular machine cannot establish the validity of all its own calculations. If therefore you want an algorithm that will guarantee success at all problems, there is no way in which a computer can ever do that.

But how should we map the mathematics on to the human situation? When we want to find the shortest way to New York, on the one hand we have to examine Euclid, and on the other we need to equate the earth's surface with the surface of a sphere. If we assume that the earth is flat, we shall get the wrong answer. In the present case, we could get an unambiguous conclusion by equating human mathematicians with systems that can guarantee success on any problem; in that case, they certainly could not be simulated by computers. But that would be a very strong claim, and if we were to make it, we might well be mistaken.

A more modest claim for our own minds would be that in some situations mathematicians can be certain that their solution is correct; this may apply for instance when they describe themselves as 'understanding' the problem. An example occurs in Penrose's simple expository illustration, of finding an odd number that is the sum of two odd numbers. But for such simple examples computers also can come to the correct conclusion. Many real problem-solving programs start by using an algorithmic procedure to check the internal consistency of the 'goal-state', before they start searching for an instance that satisfies it. They have to do this, to know when to stop the search. If the task is to look for a married bachelor, or a true lie, they would never begin; because they would find it impossible to set up the conditions to stop.

In the same way, the problem with odd numbers is that their definition implies that any pair of them will always be even. So a computer could in principle succeed in rejecting such a task. All it is doing, of course, is checking whether this instance is consistent with the rules it takes as basic assumptions; in this case, those of addition. It cannot prove that the rules themselves are right. But, are mathematicians doing more than that?

You can now see why there is still room for debate, about the implications of the mathematics. The debate depends on what, exactly, you think human beings can do. What I have been describing in this last lecture are attempts to imitate some of the behaviour they certainly show. To achieve that, we have to build machines that gamble on probabilities, that are triggered by the conditions they meet and do not use fixed routines, and that take care to represent the world in an appropriate language. In other words, they seem to show the same curious, and apparently irrational, quirks as people. By writing the programs, we have learned that the quirks are not in fact irrational; they arise from the nature of problem solving itself. So there is no doubt that computer simulation has already shed light on our own minds, and I am not yet clear that any defined function has emerged, that cannot be simulated in this way.

I suspect, though, that Penrose's worries stand for something that concerns a lot of humane people about the whole venture of cognitive science. If we explain the workings of our digestions or our arms, that does not affect our image of ourselves. We still choose what we would like to do, even if our muscles will not obey us. When we simulate our brains on a computer, some people feel that this attempt suggests that our choices are not our own, that some strange puppet-master is pulling our strings; we are not even a bus but a tram.

To believe that is contrary to a lot of human experience, and it would also be very unhealthy, because lack of belief in one's own autonomy is known to predict poor mental health, and is suspect politically. A lot of people therefore would like to think that human action is not determined by the physical state of their brain, but by something else. So they are suspicious of simulation that uses determinate physical systems. Yet one can view human autonomy in a different way.

Any action is influenced by a number of factors, partly by the last external event, and partly by the state of the person, including the state of memory. It may also include a random component, unpredictable from the past. Some people want to include their essential selves at that point, not among their lasting features. But if you really believe that you yourself are a random factor, if you think your actions do not depend on your nature, your goals, beliefs, rules of action, and the choices you have made in the past, then a lot of very odd consequences follow for morality and responsibility. Of course Krebs did not succeed because of a random component, but because of the heuristics that he carried inside himself and applied to the synthesis of urea. Of course the actions of saints and political heroes depend upon the internal state of those persons. There is certainly randomness, but that is not the identity or the persistent nature of the person. In this partly determinate, partly random, system, the place to think of yourself is among the lasting factors, that can influence your actions so as to overcome bad luck from the environment, or from internal random factors.

Now, as I said at the beginning, computers also produce outputs that are a function of input, and of internal state including memory. They may also include random factors, unpredictable from the past, as may the weather. (In fact, to have really successful heuristics they must, just as evolution must, but that is another story.) But the thing that makes computers interesting is the fact that their internal states may control the way they respond to their surroundings. If we could determine what the lasting factors are in you, then we could model them in a computer.

Let us be clear what I am saying. There is no assumption that we understand everything about the brain or about physics. It may indeed be (although I do not myself think it likely) that the events we report in our minds take place outside space and time. As long as they cause physical actions and are influenced by physical factors, we can still simulate them in machines. To say anything else is to take away responsibility from Krebs, or Lincoln or St Francis of Assisi.

Let me end with the quotation I promised at the beginning, from St Thomas Aquinas. He is using the same argument, from the reciprocal causation of mind and body; he was of course an Aristotelian.

> Therefore, since this is the case, since bodily disposition affects the passions in this way, it is clear that such affections are forms existing in matter . . . But everything into which corporeal substance or matter enters, is in the province of the natural philosopher. But further it is his task, whose function is to study the attributes, to consider their subject as well. And hence it is the duty of the physicist to study the soul.

So said St Thomas, so say I, and the chapters of this book show that this great enterprise is well under way.

References

Aquinas, T. 1939: Commentary on Aristotle's De Anima. In M. C. D'Arcy (ed.), *Thomas Aquinas: Selected Writings*, London: J. M. Dent, pp. 55–75.

Baddeley, A. D. 1986: *Working Memory*. Oxford: Oxford University Press.

Berry, D. C. and Broadbent, D. E. 1984: On the relationship between task performance and associated verbalizable knowledge. *Quarterly Journal of Experimental Psychology*, 36A, 209–31.

Berry, D. and Broadbent, D. E. 1988: Interactive tasks and the implicit-explicit distinction. *Quarterly Journal of Experimental Psychology*, 36A, 209–31.

Broadbent, D. E. 1967: Word-frequency effect and response bias. *Psychological Review*, 74, 1–15.

Broadbent, D. E. and Broadbent, M. H. P. 1978: The allocation of descriptor terms by individuals in a simulated retrieval system. *Ergonomics*, 21(5), 343–54.

Charniak, E. and McDermott, D. 1985: *Introduction to Artificial Intelligence*. Reading, Mass.: Addison-Wesley.

Johnson-Laird, P. N. 1983: *Mental Models*. Cambridge, England: Cambridge University Press.

Kotovsky, K., Hayes, J. R. and Simon, H. A. 1985: Why are some problems hard? *Cognitive Psychology*, 17, 248–94.

Kulkarni, D. and Simon, H. A. 1988: The processes of scientific discovery: The strategy of experimentation. *Cognitive Science*, 12, 139–76.

Lewis, M. W. and Anderson, J. R. 1985: Discrimination of operator schemata in problem solving: Learning from examples. *Cognitive Psychology*, 17, 26–65.

Medawar, P. B. 1967: *The Art of the Soluble*. London: Methuen.

Newell, A. and Simon, H. A. 1972: *Human Problem Solving*. Englewood Cliffs, NJ: Prentice-Hall.

Contributors

1 Professor Roger Penrose, FRS
  Rouse Ball Professor of Mathematics, University of Oxford

2 Professor Allen Newell*, Dr Richard Young+, Mr Thad Polk*
  *School of Computer Science, Carnegie-Melon University
  +MRC Applied Psychology Unit, Cambridge

3 Professor Dana Ballard
  Department of Computing Science, University of Rochester

4 Dr Edmund Rolls
  Department of Experimental Psychology, University of
  Oxford

5 Professor Michael Brady
  Professor of Information Engineering, University of Oxford

6 Professor Gerald Gazdar, FBA
  Professor of Computational Linguistics, University of Sussex

7 Professor Margaret Boden, FBA
  Professor of Philosophy and Psychology, University of
  Sussex

8 Dr Donald Broadbent, FRS
  MRC External Staff, Department of Experimental Psychology, Oxford

Index

Printed and bound by CPI Group (UK) Ltd, Croydon, CR0 4YY

27/10/2024

14580385-0003